The Measure of My Days

*Published in association with the
Mennonite Church USA Historical Committee*

The Measure of My Days

Engaging the Life and Thought of John L. Ruth

Edited by
Reuben Z. Miller and Joseph S. Miller

Foreword by **Richard A. Kauffman**
Introduction by **John E. Sharp**

Publishing House
the new name of Pandora Press U.S.
Telford, Pennsylvania

copublished with
Herald Press
Scottdale, Pennsylvania

Cascadia Publishing House orders, information, reprint permissions:
contact@CascadiaPublishingHouse.com
1-215-723-9125
126 Klingerman Road, Telford PA 18969
www.CascadiaPublishingHouse.com

The Measure of My Days
Copyright © 2004 by Cascadia Publishing House,
Telford, PA 18969
All rights reserved.
Copublished with Herald Press, Scottdale, PA
Library of Congress Catalog Number: 2004015496
ISBN: 1-931038-25-2
Book design by Cascadia Publishing House
Cover design by Gwen M. Stamm

The paper used in this publication is recycled and meets the minimum requirements of American National Standard for Information Sciences—Permanence of Paper for Printed Library Materials, ANSI Z39.48-1984. All Bible quotations are used by permission, all rights reserved and unless otherwise noted are from *The New Revised Standard Version of the Bible*, copyright 1989, by the Division of Christian Education of the National Council of the Churches of Christ in the USA.

Library of Congress Cataloguing-in-Publication Data
The measure of my days : engaging the life and thought of John L. Ruth / foreword by Richard A. Kauffman.-- 1st ed.
    p. cm.
  ISBN 1-931038-25-2 (trade pbk. : alk. paper)
  1. Ruth, John L. 2. Mennonites--Biography. 3. Mennonites--History. I. Ruth, John L. II. Miller, Reuben Z., 1976- III. Miller, Joseph S., 1952- IV. Title.

BX8143.R88M43 2004
289.7'092--dc22

2004015496

12 11 10 09 08 07 06 05   10 9 8 7 6 5

*To Roma Jacobs Ruth,
John's partner in knowing and living
the measure of his days.*

*"Lord, make me to know mine end,
and the measure of my days. . . ."*
—Psalm 39:4

*And thanks to Alice Parker, who suggested the title
of this book,* The Measure of My Days. *We invited her to
consider John Ruth's life and their shared passion for early
American hymnody, then to recommend a title for this volume. Alice directed us to the wonderful hymn by a son of
England, Isaac Watts (1674-1748), "Teach Me the
Measure of My Days." It was a perfect choice.
The hymn draws on Psalm 39
and is a spiritual gem.*

Contents

Foreword by Richard A. Kauffman 9
Editors' Preface by Reuben Z. Miller and Joseph S. Miller 15
Introduction: A Charge to Keep, by John E. Sharp 17

1 Dreams of the Written Character
   Julia Kasdorf • 29

2 The Germ of Travel With a Purpose
   Jan Gleysteen • 38

3 United With the Song: Conversations with Alice Parker
   Elmer S. Miller • 55

4 If the Earth Is the Lord's, Do We Have to Hate the World?
   Musings on Mennonite People, Places, and Complexes
   Jeff Gundy • 69

5 Perspectives of an Outsider Looking In
   Tony Campolo • 85

6 Peace is in the Details: No Story is too Small
   Elizabeth Morgan • 96

7 The Meaning of "Mennonite"
   Eloise Hiebert Meneses • 108

8 A Meditation on the Necessity of Leaving Community
   Joseph S. Miller • 122

9 A Preacher's Calling: For John Ruth, it Meant a Lot
   Ervin Stutzman • 137

10 Communion as a Gathered Body Or,
    The Body of Christ, Mystical and Sacramental
    John D. Rempel • 151

11 Feed the Hungry and Run for Relief:
    Mennonite Relief Sale as Folk Festival
    Ervin Beck • 164

12 Husk and Kernel: Anabaptist-Mennonite Essence Revisited
    Leonard Gross • 184

13 The Peculiar Beauty of *Gelassenheit*:
    An Interview With Amos B. Hoover
    Joseph S. Miller • 201

14 Dancing on the Bridge:
    Creating Virtual Community Through Mennonite Literature
    Ann Hostetler • 228

15 For Conscience' Sake? Examining a Commonplace
    John Richard Burkholder • 240

16 An Instinct for Community
    Reta Halteman Finger • 258

17 Genius and the Verbal Dance: A Conversation
    about Language, Writing, and Community with John Ruth
    Julia Kasdorf • 273

18 To Make One Story Out of Many Stories: The Local and the
    Global in Church History
    John A. Lapp • 290

The Contributors   303
The Editors   308

Foreword

Why is it that we start out life with the prospect of living a thousand different lives, but we end up living only one? mused Clifford Geertz, the famous cultural anthropologist. Indeed, why is it that we have lived this particular life, the one peculiar to our own development and identity? In some mysterious way, Christians would say, Providence has something to do with the shape and direction of our lives. But still it is worth pondering how different our lives might have been if, at any juncture along the way, they would have taken a different turn.

Geertz's conundrum came to mind while I was pondering the life and work of John Ruth—and his significant influence on me . How different would my life have been had I not attended Eastern Baptist Theological Seminary in Philadelphia, after four years of schooling in Mennonite colleges? How different would my life have been had I not then become involved in Franconia Mennonite Conference, and there met this plain-coated, worldly wise man named John L. Ruth, educated at, of all places, Harvard University?

My original intention was to spend a year at Eastern, then transfer back to Associated Mennonite Biblical Seminaries (now Seminary). But life sometimes intrudes in our plans, and for a variety of reasons I stayed all three years at Eastern. And while there, my wife Suzanne and I participated in the life of several Franconia congregations—and eventually I was employed by Franconia Conference as a staff person.

Franconia Conference became my "AMBS"; it was there that my Anabaptist identity was formed, my theology of church matured, and my earliest thoughts about ministry and leadership developed. It was in this conference that I discovered a different way of being Mennonite. Different, certainly, from my Mennonite upbringing in Lancaster

County where I was more influenced by fundamentalism and evangelicalism than, certainly, Anabaptism. It was different still from the Mennonitism of the Midwest where I went to college.

Franconia, more than either of these other locales, seemed to me then to have kept the vision vitally alive of a nonconformed Christianity, committed to virtues of peacemaking and community accountability. Certainly there were pressures then in Franconia to assimilate into a generic, American evangelicalism. And the wealth of many of these Mennonites in southeastern Pennsylvania can entice conformity with the American mainstream. No doubt those pressures to acculturate have only increased in the years since I moved away. But it was in no small measure due to the influence of key Franconia leaders that this vision was kept alive before and for the people of Franconia. Among such leaders have been Bishop John E. Lapp, Richard C. Detweiler (both a bishop and moderator of the conference and later president of Eastern Mennonite College—now University—and Seminary)—and John L. Ruth, preacher, college professor of literature, peoples' historian, and storyteller.

I had known of John Ruth before, since my uncle Bob Byler was a classmate of John's at Lancaster Mennonite High School in the 1940s. But I came to know John personally when in the late 1960s Suzanne and I attended the small, family oriented King of Prussia Mennonite Fellowship, which met in John and Roma Ruth's home. Sunday mornings were always an adventure there, not least John's sermons. I had never heard preaching quite like John's. If all the world was John Wesley's parish, all the world was fair game also for John's preaching. He could range from literary allusions to comments about current events to stories from the history of Franconia Conference to . . . well, yes, sometimes imaginative expositions of Scripture.

It wasn't clear to me that John put much preparation into his sermons. Rather, they seemed to spring forth from what was on his mind and heart at the time, fed by his rich memory and fertilized by his keen imagination. But what an imagination! John also knew a thing or two about hymnody, having written his dissertation on American hymns, and he cared about how hymns were sung. That, too, caught my attention, since I had been a music major in college.

My favorite John Ruth story from that era, strangely, doesn't involve John directly. Some months after we started attending King of Prussia,

John had a sabbatical year, which he, along with his family, took in Europe, to research Anabaptist origins. While the Ruths were out of the country, the J. Lester Graybill family from Orrville, Ohio lived in their house and Lester studied at Eastern Baptist Seminary. But the house church fellowship continued to use the Ruth residence for Sunday worship. One Sunday when we arrived for church, the Graybill family informed us that one part of the roof was leaking. A storm was forecast for the next day, and the Graybills were concerned that significant damage could result if nothing was done. As a fellowship group, we conferred. And it seemed to us that we had a classical case of a neighbor's ox in a ditch, which justified work on the "Sabbath."

But it wasn't our neighbor in distress—it was our pastor and his family, thousands of miles away, blissfully ignorant of this situation. And it wasn't an ox in a ditch, but a leaky roof on a house. So we disbanded worship, ripped off the deteriorating shingles, and began to reshingle the roof—a task that several of us had completed the next day before the storm arrived.

How different would my life have been had I not had mentors like Richard Detweiler and John Ruth? And how different it would have been for them had they not been shaped by this "strange" group of Franconia Mennonites who still believed that conference mattered, that in that context congregations held each other accountable? This particular constellation of congregations was "in it together," and no congregation should veer too far to the right or the left or change patterns of belief and behavior without conferring together in the body of believers. How different this was from the American congregationalism and individualism that was eroding much of the rest of the Mennonite church.

In a way that I'm not sure John realized at the time, John became a spiritual and theological mentor, showing me that Mennonites offer a "Third Way" which is neither liberal nor conservative but biblical and communal, committed to Jesus' way of discipleship and peacemaking in the world. He also played a critical role in my decision to leave Franconia Conference. When Mennonite Publishing House gave me an invitation to join their editorial staff, I went to John for advice. I had been editing the *Franconia Conference News*, and John served as a consulting editor and proofreader. He knew what potential I had for editorial work, or lack thereof. When I consulted John, he encouraged me to take on this new challenge.

Because of John's formative influence in my life, albeit during a brief but critical time, I was pleased to have been part of the small group of Franconia leaders who first met with John to talking about freeing him from his professorial responsibilities at Eastern Baptist College (now Eastern University) to work fulltime at his story gathering, writing, and film making (on this, see John Sharp's Introduction). And because I owe John much personally, I was also delighted to be asked to write this foreword.

A festschrift is typically a collection of writings by colleagues and former students in honor of a scholar and published upon retirement or some other highwater mark in his or her academic career. This book doesn't quite fit the usual pattern. John appears well and has no intention of retiring anytime soon. And although he has been a teacher all his life, in the best sense of that word, he has not been involved in the academic world since the mid-1970s. Further, the contributors to this volume, for the most part, aren't former scholarly peers or students of John's. Yet in some way they have all been shaped by John and have seen him as either a colleague or a mentor or both.

How different also would the lives of these contributors have been if they had not learned to know John and be influenced by him? To pay him tribute, and to keep the conversation going with John and others, the contributors to this volume offer essays on themes which were and are near to John's heart, such as communal identity and belonging and telling our stories.

Identity and memory are integrally related, John has taught us. If you know who you are and are possessed by what you have to say, you'll find a way to say it. Too often, though, we're not aware of what influences us, both the good and the bad. It is to our great diminishment as a people and individuals to not know our own stories, to fail to see what it is that our own people have to offer, to not appreciate our own heritage. The more intensely you are who you are, he believes, the more others will appreciate it. The great issues of our time have to do with identity and coherence and how you order "your family," about which Mennonites should have something to say.

John hasn't wanted to waste time arguing for the right to engage in the arts in a tradition skeptical about them; life is too short for that, he has said. Just do it, is his advice to other Mennonite artists. Too many of the "persecuted cries" of young artists who feel rejected by their Mennonite people are just a cover-up for poor art. He also doesn't believe we should just put a positive spin on our own or our people's story: That is only propaganda, a model defied by the example of Scripture, disclosing as it so often does the good and the bad about God's people. Creativity, for John, lies in the ability to accept your peoples' scruples and make your point anyhow.

John's gifts with language and storytelling, using a variety of media, are well known. His greater gift, it seems to me, is his keen perception. He has been able to see what other people have not been able to glimpse: in nature, in community life, in the people around him, in history, in literature.

A mundane example: Having attended Lancaster Mennonite High School, John once said he was always impressed with the large hands of Lancaster Mennonite farmers. And he held up his palms as if to imagine his hands might be like that. But his point wasn't about anatomy. With this image he was saying that Lancaster Mennonites' great strength is their practicality, their activism, their dedication to hard work—they get things done, even if they're not always reflective about their activity.

John will point something out to the rest of us that we didn't see on our own, and having had a John Ruth-induced epiphany, we'll nod in recognition: "Of course, it was there all the time. Why didn't I see that?" Well, perhaps we weren't looking, or perhaps we weren't attentive enough. More likely, we lack the depth perception John has, and we couldn't see it even if we were looking straight at what John is seeing.

John's other great gift is his passion for life and for his convictions and calling. One Saturday he came to a ministers' breakfast meeting in Souderton all excited because he had just gotten a new video camera he had wanted for quite some time. He told us of plans to use it to capture on film the stories of a ninety-something man in the conference who had a razor-sharp memory of his childhood and younger years. But another minister at that breakfast meeting had to break the bad news to John: This old man had just died. And John put his head down on the table and wept for what never was going to happen, for what was lost forever, except in his memory.

I heard recently about a youth group asked by their adult leader to share their perceptions of the adults they know. After some reflection and discussion, the youth concluded that adults don't have many friends, are bored with life, and lack passion! How telling of so many adults! But none of this is true for John. This volume suggests he has many friends. He certainly isn't bored with life. And his passion for life and faith and telling the stories of his peoples' faithfulness and unfaithfulness has, indeed, been an inspiration to us all.

How different would our lives have been had this man who grew up along the Branch Creek not accepted the call to be a "preacher" and a storyteller and a peoples' historian? How different would we all be if John had not impressed upon us the need to know and tell our own story? Thank you, John, for responding to the call, and for your encouragement to us to hear God's personal call upon our lives, too.

—*Richard A. Kauffman*
  Senior Editor/Book Review Editor, The Christian Century

Editors' Preface

This volume is a labor that grows out of admiration and love by the writers and editors for the life and ministry of John L. Ruth. In autumn 2000, Salford Mennonite Church gathered together several hundred friends and family of John and Roma Ruth to celebrate fifty years of ministry and service to the Mennonite church. During that wonderful weekend there were many tributes of heart felt appreciation to Roma and John.

Several people gathered together and discussed the possibility of producing a Festschrift to honor John by writing about one of the greatest loves of his life, the church community. We invited writers to reflect on Mennonite community and creative arts—sometimes in tension, sometimes in harmony. The church community and artistic expression have been parallel themes in John's life and ministry. All of us who have known John have marveled at his genuine ability to connect authentically and respectfully with the farmer and the theologian, with the homespun and the deeply complex.

What began as just a germ of an idea has, after nearly two years, become this volume entitled *The Measure of My Days*. As the editors of this Festschrift we are indebted to all the writers for their very generous contributions, gladly offered gratis. The editorial committee consisted of John E. Sharp, Julia Kasdorf, Julie Musselman, Jan Gleysteen, Joan K. King, Joseph S. Miller and Reuben Z. Miller.

We are especially grateful for the exceptional advice and counsel of John E. Sharp, the Director of the Mennonite Historical Committee. His counsel was always encouraging and helpful. Special thanks also to Leonard Gross, the past Director of the Mennonite Historical Committee, Julia Kasdorf, and Jan Gleysteen.

We offer this book not from any one group of writers or editors but from a grateful church community that finds itself international in scope. This is a community's expression of thanks to John L. Ruth: pastor, writer, historian, filmmaker, professor, and Christian friend.

—*Reuben Z. Miller*
  Bammental, Germany and
  Joseph S. Miller
  Lancaster, Pennsylvania

Introduction:
A Charge to Keep

John E. Sharp

The essays in this volume are a tribute to John Ruth, pastor, professor, historian, storyteller, filmmaker, and videographer. Each profession has been a calling, with the charge given at his ordination, to do the work of an evangelist, ever before him. He has exercised these vocations within the spiritual family called Mennonite, whose roots lie in the European soil of the Anabaptist movement. Eloquently and persuasively, John has told this family's story as a reflection of the master narrative—the story of God's reconciling love in Christ.

John Landis Ruth was born January 8, 1930 (the day John Fretz Funk, a prominent Mennonite leader born in John's father's congregation, died at 94). The later John was born to Henry and Susan Landis Ruth on his ancestral farm along the Northeast Branch of the Perkiomen Creek, commonly called "the Branch." The homestead was just a stone's throw from the Salford Mennonite meetinghouse, the center of the spiritual community he later served as minister. The original house had been built in 1808 for Abraham and Susan Shoemaker Alderfer. John's parents moved the family into the farm's "dowddyhaus," just down the lane from his grandparents. Within the radius of one mile lived all of his twenty-two Landis cousins. This was the environment that shaped John's cultural and spiritual community, which has become a persistent theme in his preaching, writing, and storytelling.

Cutting through this tiny community is the Branch Creek, which began and ended far beyond the land of Alderfers and Ruths. It serves, perhaps, as a metaphor for John's intellectual quest, which would take him to Eastern Mennonite College, Eastern Baptist College, and eventually Harvard University. The Branch, with its eternal flow, prompted John to wonder about previous generations who had walked its banks and had cut blocks of ice from its frozen surface. And there were other clues—flint arrowheads and pottery shards—that appeared in the plow's furrow that indicated the presence of the Original People, the Lenape, who had populated this watershed for thousands of years before European immigrants arrived.

John was the firstborn of the Ruth household, followed by four sisters, Lois (Kennel), Eunice (Mast), Martyne (Wetzel), and Carolyn. In 1936 at the age of six, John started school at the Lower Salford Consolidated School. A precocious student, John could be counted on to supply the right answers in class, and his essays were commonly read by the teacher to demonstrate how good papers were to be written.

Attuned early to his conscience and the call of God through the church, John was baptized in 1938 at the age of eight at the Finland Mennonite Mission. Three times a week the family trekked the nine miles up the Ridge to "help with the work" at the mission station founded by Franconia Mennonite Conference members. At a series of revival meetings, John was stirred by the altar call of evangelist Nevin Bender, accompanied by the soulful melody and cataclysmic text of the gospel song, "O, sinner where will you be when the stars begin to fall?" At home, when he expressed an emotional reaction to the song, his mother concluded John was under conviction, and consulted "Pop." They enrolled John in the "instruction class" already in session at Finland. At the conclusion of this instruction, Bishops John E. Lapp and Arthur Ruth baptized John. This was the first of a series of calls of God through the church, which John obediently followed.

In 1944, John's parents sent him to Lancaster Mennonite High School, some fifty miles from home. His parents hoped John would be nurtured spiritually as well as academically at this conservative school. Sometimes, spiritual nurture took the form of revival meetings, during which John repeatedly questioned the authenticity of his conversion, saying he was "an unsuccessful teenager." He was, however, a sufficiently successful student, graduating in the class of 1948. He never imagined that the school's sponsoring body, Lancaster Mennonite Conference, would one day commission him to write its history, a magnum opus of nearly 1400 pages. But he did publish his first article in the school paper, *The Millstream,* at age fourteen. He was moved by four-part musical harmony, and added his bass voice to various ensembles, including a men's quartet.

His high school scholarship was merely moderate, and he once made a comment that was less than exemplary. As yearbook editor, it fell to John to break the news to the intimidating, no-nonsense teacher and dean, Noah Good, that the yearbook would be dedicated to him. When Good, with characteristic humility, responded, "Well, I want to be modest about this," John's inept retort was, "Why, you have nothing to be modest *about*!" Forty years later, John remembered this conversation with a twinge of humiliation.

In 1949 John began his college career at Eastern Mennonite College, Harrisonburg, Virginia. If he did not become intellectualy serious on the campus, he did find another freshman, the vivacious Roma Jacobs from Hollsopple, Pennsylvania. Knowing Roma had other suitors, John quickly made his claim and the two began a rather turbulent courtship.

Nineteen-fifty was a dramatic year. John found himself a candidate for ordination to the pastoral ministry, after his freshman year. The Franconia Conference was calling a minister to serve the mission in Conshohocken, seventeen miles south of his home. At twenty, John was the youngest of three candidates. What could he do, but respond as he would do many times—submit to the will of the church. On the afternoon of August 6, when Bishops Amos Kolk and the recently ordained bishop, Paul Lederach (assistant to Amos, the senior bishop) examined the books of the three candidates, he found the lot in John's book. The young John Ruth was ordained by Lederach with the charge to "do the work of an evangelist," a charge he would take seriously. That night he preached his first sermon at Line Lexington, his father's home congregation. Then, as usual for newly ordained ministers, he "preached around the conference" for the next six months. The week after the ordination, John proposed to Roma, who had been too frightened to attend the ordination service. On May 26, 1951, they were married in Roma's home by John's childhood pastor, Claude M. Shisler. Roma's brother, not yet famous in Mennonite circles as Don Jacobs, sang a solo.

Roma knew by then that John's propensity toward preoccupation would be a factor in their marriage. On their wedding day, John left his wallet on a gas pump in Schwenksville and remembered it only when he needed to pay his toll at the Bedford exit of the Pennsylvania Turnpike. Roma's father, Paul Jacobs, came to the rescue.

John and Roma set up their first home in Conshohocken, where John served the congregation as its pastor and worked at Rittenhouse's farmers' market in Chester. Easter Dawn was born on April 14, 1952. J. Allan followed on January 18, 1954. After three years at the mission, and at the urging of brother-in-law, Don Jacobs, John enrolled at Eastern Baptist College, St. Davids, Pennsylvania. He planned to study history, but a literature teacher, James Wesley Ingles (1905-1984), caught John's attention. The professor, whom John once described as "wonderful," changed his course of study to literature.

After graduating May 1956 with a B.A. in English, John went to work in Philadelphia, editing Sunday school material for the American Baptist Publication Society. In 1957, a graduate fellowship opened the door for him to study English at Harvard University. Mindful of his ordination vows, he approached his bishop, Elmer Kolb, to ask Kolb's blessing on what he dearly hoped to do. After consulting with fellow bishop John E. Lapp, Kolb blessed the educational pursuits of this unusual minister, now also a Danforth scholar about to enter Harvard. At age twenty-seven, with three children—Philip had been born April 7—John and Roma moved to Belmont, Massachusetts, next to Cambridge.

Harvard was the greatest adventure of his life. John relished the challenge of the prestigious academic community but also felt the pressure of making it in the "big leagues." He was free to explore the world of ideas, to engage in debate, and to lose himself in the books of the Harry Elkins Widener Memorial Library. He enjoyed the walk across the famous Harvard Yard—far removed from his eastern Pennsylvania community.

But even here, the scholar could not escape his community of origin. Year laster he learned, to his surprise, that a Mennonite contractor from Philadelphia, Joseph Bechtel (1856-1928), had built the Widener Library. And while browsing its stacks, he made another discovery that linked him to his own past, and helped to shape his future. In what he once described as an "almost mystical experience," he pulled a small volume from a library shelf. It was a history of the Perkiomen Valley, which included mention of a large crowd, Mennonites among them, gathered to hear the famous eighteenth-century evangelist, George Whitefield. In striking contrast to the eloquent preacher, who impressed even Benjamin Franklin, German speaking Mennonites were depicted as practically mute, lacking voice, language, and skill to express themselves.

In the suspension between two worlds, Harvard-trained poet, T. S. Eliot spoke to John:

> With the drawing of this Love and the voice of this Calling
> We shall not cease from exploration
> And the end of all our exploring
> Will be to arrive where we started
> And know the place for the first time. (Little Gidding, V)

"With the drawing of this Love and the voice of this Calling," John would arrive where he had started—the Perkiomen Valley, the place of his people—and he would know it for the first time. He would give voice to those previous generations who had none. And the words of his choosing would be cast in phrases and sentences that are "right" and "where every word is at home." His words, poetic and prose, would be a "complete consort dancing together." All this to reflect a people "not known, because not looked for," which he would call his own, aware that "A people without history / Is not redeemed from time, for history is a pattern / Of timeless moments" (Eliot).

This new calling would find expression in due time, but the task at hand was literature, and in particular, American hymnody. John passed his oral examination in 1960, during a self-described "emotional dip." About the same time, members of a struggling Quaker congregation in southern Massachussetts invited him to supply their pulpit. It was a "beautiful experience" that restored his spirit. He wrote his dissertation on English hymn-writing in America, 1640-1800. In 1968, six years after leaving Cambridge, the evidence of his rigorous academic work, a prestigious Ph.D. diploma from Harvard, arrived in the mail.

When his course work was completed, and at a time when unsolicited invitations to teach came from two dozen colleges, he considered an invitation to teach at Eastern Baptist College (now Eastern University), his alma mater. But how does a Harvard Ph.D. return home, a world apart, T. S. Eliot notwithstanding? His internal struggle was perhaps most dramatically portrayed in a dream: A Franconia conservative had him by the neck and was examining his orthodoxy. Struggling against the stranglehold, John challenged his inquisitor, "Do you know

Greek?" When the man admitted he didn't, John leveled the playing field with a quip, "I don't either, so neither of us knows what we're talking about!"

Professor John L Ruth taught literature at Eastern Baptist College from 1962 to 1976. Pastor John Ruth resumed a spiritual leadership role for the Conshohocken Mennonite Mission. At Roma's insistence, it now became a house church named the King of Prussia Mennonite Fellowship, with a membership of nineteen. The meetinghouse was the Ruth home at 520 Weadley Road. After six years of teaching, John was granted a sabbatical leave for the 1968-1969 academic year. The family packed up and moved to Hamburg, Germany, where at the University of Hamburg, John lectured on, as he once put it, "everything from the American Puritans to Wallace Stevens." Stevens was a Pulitzer Prize winner whose poems have been described as "closest to pure poetry." The following summer the Ruth family, along with Jan Gleysteen, trekked the European countryside, searching for and photographing historic sites that would help tell the Anabaptist story.

Back in King of Prussia, a family crisis of "deepest grief" caused John to resign abruptly as pastor, without as much as consulting Roma. The crisis was precipitated by the choices his teenage children were making, which led to a strong sense of alienation from parents and the church. John felt the need of a stronger Mennonite community to embrace and nurture the children. Goshen College and Eastern Mennonite College had earlier invited John to teach, but at the moment, neither had a vacancy. Instead, in 1971, the Ruth family moved back to the heartland of the Franconia Conference to a house in Vernfield, just two miles from John's ancestral home and from the Salford meetinghouse. The Salford congregation embraced the family, offering them a spiritual home. Willis Miller invited John "into the pulpit right away," and in a few months John joined "the bench" of ministers, while continuing to teach at Eastern Baptist College.

From Salford's pulpit, John the preacher explained his hermeneutic: "Personally, I must admit I take more of my cues from the Gospels than from the epistles. When I look at my Bible, the blackest part at the edges of the pages are the Gospels; and then around Romans 12; then there's one at the Psalms, and one at Isaiah, and one at Deuteronomy."

While Conshohocken had been the place of John's first call to ministry, the Harley Kitchen Restaurant on Sumneytown Pike became the place of a second calling in 1974. Recognizing John's rare gift for communicating the church's story, Franconia Conference leaders, Richard C. Detweiler, Richard A. Kauffman, and Clayton Swartzendruber, invited John to leave the classroom for another teaching assignment: writing books and making films on themes of Mennonite heritage. John had written a play entitled "Twilight Auction" in 1966, a project that gave him a special bond with his Franconia people. He felt he had crossed a threshold, and had at age thirty-six "finally reached adulthood."

Also 1966, John had collaborated with Alice Parker to write "The Christopher Dock Cantata." This was followed by "The Quiet in the Land" movie, and "The Martyr's Mirror Oratorio," both in 1971. By the time of the Harley Kitchen meeting, Franconia patriarch John E. Lapp had already knelt with John in his King of Prussia home to ask God's blessing on this emerging call—which John considered a "second ordination." An informal reference group, the "Heritage Council," with the colorful Walton Hackman as chair, provided practical and emotional support. The council's practical support included evaluating proposed projects, assuring realistic charges (John was generous to a fault), some fund raising, attending to schedules and deadlines.

Schedules and deadlines were not John's forte. There were the occasional "Ruthian lapses," when John was oblivious to clock and calendar. It has been said that John wakes in the morning not with a schedule for the day but with a theme. Clearly calendars and clocks were subservient to themes when John preached a sermon, wrote a book, or guided a group of children on a tour along the Branch Creek. Perhaps this is not surprising for one who spent significant time in other centuries. It was not unusual on a Monday morning, when Salford's pastors met for breakfast at the Energy Station in Vernfield, that a glance at his date book—which he had not consulted recently—would produce a pained expression on John's face. He had missed yet another event.

John typically refused to let a deadline, "artificially imposed," dictate the completion of a project. It is far more important to take the time necessary to research and produce a book that will be accurate, artfully crafted, and useful to future generations. *The Earth is the Lord's* is perhaps the best example: it was two decades in the making and a dozen years past the initial deadline, but is a masterpiece.

Not everyone understood John's new calling. Able-bodied residents of the Souderton Mennonite Homes gathered outside to witness the phenomenon of John and son Jay aloft in a helicopter, shooting footage for a video on retirement homes. It was a bona fide project, commissioned by three Franconia Conference retirement communities. One elderly observer, with a lifetime of manual labor behind him wondered, "Did John Ruth ever work?" When chaplain Curtis Godshall gleefully reported this to him, John "saw his life pass before him in an instant, including such scenes as selling chickens and butter at market, and agonizing over *Maintaining the Right Fellowship* at 3:00 a.m."

In the season of his "second calling," John was astonishingly fruitful, producing a bountiful harvest of books, films and videos. In addition, John gave innumerable lectures, sermons, and guided tours, richly seasoned with stories. He wrote texts for dramas, a cantata, and an oratorio.

Roma always helped put bread on the table for the family. In King of Prussia she did a lot of babysitting and sewing, often making dresses for other faculty wives. In 1981 she began nursing as a licensed practical nurse, having graduated with honors from Montgomery County Junior College. In the early 1970s, Roma became interested in fraktur art. She began creating fraktur wedding certificates for her children, and birth certificates for her grandchildren. Without advertising, people began requesting Roma's frakturs. She has now produced hundreds of pieces—awards, diplomas, family records, and even a hockey stick.

John reached another point of "deepest grief" when his ancestral farm of 110 acres was sold for development in 1987. Ironically, when the extended family offered no hope for salvaging a piece of the land, developers Hiram and Mary Jane Hershey offered John and Roma a part of the property, including its two houses. The Salford congregation encouraged the transaction, and its members helped remodel the old house where John's grandparents—and the generations before them—had lived. Touched by the generosity of his spiritual community, John said, "I got saved all over again."

From his farmhouse basement office overlooking the Branch Creek, John has collaborated with sons Jay and Phil on numerous publishing and production projects. Upstairs Roma continues to create Fraktur art, much in demand. A basement office contains John's computer, books, and files. Given the volume of work John's pen and camera have produced, one might think he could "retire." But John's ordinational charge is still operational—*to do the work of an evangelist*. He reflects, "I've never forgotten that; it still strikes a chord. The work is still ahead. This story—that may reach only a few—is yet to be written." John is referring to the stories contained in his extensive chronological card file, collected over the decades. Practically everything he has written was commissioned; "but, this unofficial thing is my calling; it's an inner call to chronicle the life of the Branch Valley, where nothing happened in three centuries; to take that desert of meaning—Harleysville to Salfordville—and make something of it." Then John will quote, "God chose what is low and despised in the world, to reduce to nothing things that are. . ." (1 Cor. 1:28-29).

For John, the spiritual community, rooted as it is in a specific time and place, also has cosmic dimensions. Preaching on Ephesians 1:1-14 in a 1988 sermon at Salford, John said, "I see our congregation converging from all directions—Sellersville, Lansdale, Souderton, and Harleysville. I think of that convergence and I see a little picture of the cosmos. . . . I feel a premonitory feeling, and I say, this is a paradigm of reality."

This Festschrift is offered in appreciation for John's masterful telling of the story—the story both local and cosmic.

—*John E. Sharp, Director*
Mennonite Church USA Historical Committee
Goshen, Indiana

The Measure of My Days

Chapter 1

Dreams of the Written Character

Julia Kasdorf

It is in our idleness, in our dreams, that the submerged truth sometimes comes to the top. –Virginia Woolf

I don't recall where I found the old Chinese proverb, but as a sophomore in college, I chose it for the epigraph to a small collection of poems about my Study Service Trimester in China published through Pinchpenny Press at Goshen College: "The invention of the written character made the gods and devils wail." The maxim intrigued me and expressed something I had guessed more than known from experience: that writing can be transgressive. I knew that books can change things—books had already changed me—but beyond that, this old proverb suggested that writing itself can destroy or destabilize the old order, especially when it erupts in places where it had not existed before. For the Chinese, it seems, the great metaphor for human ambition and hubris was not eating the fruit of the knowledge of good and evil or stealing fire or building a tower to the heavens, but writing.

At first, writing must have been mimetic, meant to represent the world, because Chinese characters began as pictures. Over time the characters were codified and became artful and abstract, so distorted that most are now unrecognizable as representations, although they still contain traces of ancient images. For instance, a human figure—the shape of the author—can still be seen embedded within the character that signifies "man" or "person" in the simplified system that was imposed by Chairman Mao to expedite printing and promote literacy for the masses. That fact pleases me for its metaphorical possibilities: writers are characters who are also written by others, the contours of their lives traced again and again over time. This notion lingers in the margins of this brief meditation on tradition and becoming a writer.

Book, 1992

The summer of 1992 at Yaddo, the artists' colony made from a robber baron's estate at Saratoga Springs, New York, I woke in a tiny, second-floor bedroom. Without thinking much, I rose from my bed and, still in my night shirt, wandered out into the dark, richly paneled corridor, down a huge staircase, past long stained-glass windows, and out into the Great Hall with its massive neo-Gothic thrones carved of dark wood, through the dim corridor that snakes past the always-off-limits kitchen, into a breezeway where mail and lunch boxes appear each morning for the pampered residents. On the table lay a stack of papers which I recognized to be the unpublished manuscript by my first serious poetry teacher. I stopped, considered the page proofs I had been reading that day, and instantly understood that by publishing my own book of poems, I had surpassed and betrayed a beloved mentor. (There are so many ways publication can unsettle things.)

Shot through with anxiety and confusion, I rushed out into the darkness. Running and stumbling through the woods, I began to hear faint strains of singing in the distance, coming from somewhere beyond the tennis courts. Calmed and drawn toward the tune of a familiar a capella hymn, I walked deeper into the forest until I came upon an old Mennonite meeting house. It was the kind of church my parents joined as young people, the kind I visited with my Conservative Conference relatives in Pennsylvania, before it was razed in the 1970s. On bare, light wood benches, women sat on one side of the center aisle and men on the other; there was a low table in front of a simple pulpit, and behind it several benches beneath a clock. I took it in all at once—the back wall cut away from the meeting house—then slipped into a back bench on the women's side. There I let out a deep breath, safe at last, until it dawned on me that there were no songbooks in the bench racks, and I couldn't remember the words to the hymn. The people were singing from memory, perhaps something from *Life Songs, No. 2*. Furthermore, I was not dressed like the other women who wore traditional cape dresses and white prayer caps. All at once terrified again, I gingerly slid from the bench, slipped out of the church and began running through the woods, weaving between pines, barely avoiding fallen branches and exposed roots, panting, until at last I fell into the arms of my father and older brother, who were just standing there in the forest, each with a hand on the other's shoulder and a hand extended, waiting to catch me.

At that moment, I woke in my narrow bed, sweating, tearful, shaken yet relieved, unable to return to sleep until I could somehow take the harm out of the dream by discerning its meaning, how those fallen branches and exposed roots related to my family tree. Since my arrival at Yaddo two days prior, I had heard stories about the ghosts and nightmares that stir in the old stone mansion, the place's name long ago taken from a child's mispronunciation of the word "shadow." For some artists, a sojourn in the densely shaded estate is profitable; but each summer for a few others, personal shadows or the oppressive shade of the old pines becomes so unbearable, they must leave before their residency is finished.

That day I had spent hours poring over page proofs for *Sleeping Preacher*, and I had also read the 1978 Herald Press booklet *Mennonite Identity and Literary Art* for the first time. Written as a series of lectures that were given at Bethel College in Kansas before there was much serious Mennonite literature published in English, this manifesto charged young writers to create a literary tradition for their people. Throughout the essay, John Ruth, author, clergyman, and former English professor, traced the numerous Mennonite cultural resistances or "scruples" that have stifled imaginative writing in the Swiss Mennonite community that he knew best: the loss of the Pennsylvania German language and a rich oral literature that accompanied it, the legacy of a suspicion of artistic images that had roots in Zwingli's iconoclasm and the Radical Reformation, a distrust of education and high culture, the suppression of individual voices within the communitarian religious ethos, an emphasis on truth-telling and plain speech, and the folk culture's penchant for practicality and thrift. (I must say that I have since found these "scruples" to be shared by many non-Mennonites who come from Protestant farm and working class homes in rural Pennsylvania.)

Despite the many and persistent resistances in the Mennonite community, Ruth urged young Mennonite writers to serve as scribes and interrogators of their cultural and religious traditions, rather than following literary styles in the American mainstream. Like the Hebrew exiles in Babylon, he wrote passionately, we must sing the songs of our people in this strange land (North America)—but from within the context of the covenant community.

Ruth has since told me that he would not write the lectures that became *Mennonite Identity* in quite the same way now, and that he is just thankful for any good literature that represents Mennonite experience at all. I now understand that he is also a writer whose life was written for him in some ways, not least by ordination through lot after his freshman year of college. But the dream came before I knew Ruth as a person, and his sectarian poetic haunted me like a ghost—probably because it articulated my fears so incisively. He had identified and named "scruples" that I, as an emerging writer, had previously known only as an internalized sense of taboo.

Such a clear statement of the sources of my anxiety, along with Ruth's strong and seemingly contradictory imperative to write from *within* the community, shocked my consciousness so that only in the place of dreams could I begin to converse with that slim booklet. Many of the poems in my *Sleeping Preacher* came from stories told by my mother and her aunts, sifted through the sieve of my own memory, and after reading Ruth, I feared I had stolen from or muddied a precious stream of oral tradition. Unconsciously attuned to the "scruples," I feared that I would be cast out of the community. On the contrary, the opposite occurred, and in recent decades, literary artists have been celebrated more than censured in much of the mainstream Mennonite community—but I had no reason to expect this then.

In the nightmare I fled from the artists sleeping in their chambers at Yaddo, ashamed of publishing a book before my high school writing teacher had published hers. Accomplishment is inevitably isolating, and I knew few female peers or precursors at that time. I felt like an imposter, unqualified to take a room in that artists retreat, yet I had fled from my space on the bench of the Mennonite meeting house for the same reason; neither place felt like a safe haven. Why my brother and father caught me in a soothing embrace is still a puzzle. Did my self of the dream need protection and validation from these older men closest to me? Could they assure me that I still belonged somewhere, if only in the immediate family? Maybe the women in the meeting house were stronger enforcers of the traditional norms than the men in my family, so I fled into their arms to escape the scripted domestic life. And yet, their embrace was also a snare.

Growing up, I had wanted to follow my father to a job outside the home and take business trips on airplanes. Like my other brother, I wanted to build model rockets with parachutes made of Saran Wrap and thread stuffed inside, to blast them from a launch pad on the driveway, and blow them up in glorious blazes. As a young girl, the possibilities for such glamorous departures and destructions seemed as available to me as they were to my two brothers, but as I grew older, I became less certain of limitless possibilities, less sure of my desire for flight.

Baby, 1992

A night or two later, I woke again in that strange, narrow bed, my heart racing. This time I had been running around desperately pleading with strangers in some public place, trying to persuade anyone who would listen that I had not killed my baby on purpose. It had died—an abstract, nameless, sexless white bundle—and I had neglected it, but I hadn't meant to kill anyone. I'd just forgotten about it somehow.

I lay awake, trembling, smoothed the sheets and breathed deeply, scrambling to construct an interpretation to stop the adrenaline from rushing through my limbs. Although there was the book in production, I had not written poems for some time, and I suddenly found myself in a place where others cooked my meals and washed my bedding, where uninterrupted afternoons seemed to stretch forever, and where I was expected to write and write very well. Maybe I was afraid I wouldn't start again, that I had killed my small talent—my small self—through neglect and the necessary distractions of earning a living and maintaining a household.

Scanning the walls of my bedroom in that eerie, pre-dawn light, I studied the photographs of Yaddo at the turn of the century: Katrina Trask, railroad magnate's wife in a white gown, her hair gathered up in a puffy bun, surrounded by the stylish artists she had invited up from New York City to vacation or work at the estate during the summer. The ghosts of Yaddo are supposed to be Katrina's four dead children. After her doctor mistakenly judged that Katrina's childbirth fever was no longer contagious and granted the three older children permission to enter their mother's room, all of them contracted the fatal illness, including the newborn. The mansion is still decorated with great, sentimental Victorian portraits of the children, and the Italian rose garden faces a pine grove sheltering the statue of Christalon—an androgynous character named with a composite of the dead children's names. Christalon became the hero of the verse Katrina wrote after their deaths, in her studio atop the mansion's tower, decorated as a white, neo-Gothic prayer chapel with a kneeler set before a marble bust of the Blessed Mother. As chance would have it, I was assigned that tower as my studio, and I knew I wouldn't have been there—nor Anne Sexton, nor any of the other writers who'd worked in that space, probably including Katrina herself—if her children had grown up to inherit Yaddo.

Does this dream mean that a woman must lose her children to make way for her work, that she must choose between two kinds of creativity: art or domestic life? I hope not. In the dream, I had not fulfilled the maternal script that has been written for women, whether they come from traditional, religious communities or mansions full of servants, and certainly, many women in the past have not been free to write, whatever their class. Yet, it strikes me that the source of distress in the dream was not so much caused by the loss of the child as my shame and inability to make excuses for my failure to love and care for the baby. The primary feeling was my frantic rush to apologize to others for what I had done and what I had left undone. What except writing could have distracted me from such a compelling duty?

Maybe the dream is not so much about maternity as anxiety of authorship, a continuation of the nightmare from a few days before. The anguish in both dreams is related to the inevitable choices to run from the good mothers singing without books in the meeting house, breaking with gendered roles in search of new ways of living and writing. What an explosion, what an escape; no wonder the gods and devils wailed.

Book and Baby, 2001

Sitting with my husband in the living room of our house in Bellefonte, Pennsylvania, I glanced up to see Joseph W. Yoder in a dark suit and pinched felt fedora, white silk handkerchief tucked in his coat pocket like the suave star of an old film noir, striding toward me, his hand extended and eyes set on mine.

"But, Joe," I sputtered rudely, offering my hand, "Aren't you dead?"

"Oh that," he laughed, "we just faked the funeral back at Maple Grove so I could get away from Emily and Lily [forgotten name], another woman who was chasing me at the time."

If he hadn't died in 1956, Joseph W. Yoder, Amish-born writer and musician, would be about 130 years old. In 1995 I began research for a doctoral dissertation in hopes of discovering how this man became an artist and public figure, yet maintained ties to his Amish and Mennonite birth community in Mifflin County, Pennsylvania. In 2001, I spent the summer rewriting that study of his life and work in a house that had been built during the year of his birth, in a town that was less than fifty miles from Belleville, where he grew up, and Lock Haven where he taught as a young man, and Huntingdon, where he eventually settled and later retired—though I'd long since given up hope that his choices could be models for writing my own life. That summer, it had been difficult enough to follow his travels through certain decades that he skipped in his memoirs and erased from his collected correspondence, so how would I ever be able to trace him through another fifty years after a phony death? How many more chapters would I need to write? And as he turned toward the door, he seemed about to elude me once again.

"But wait, Joe. Where are you going?" I demanded, "What about my book? What about your books?"

"The books? My memoirs have helped to hide me, you see? Yes, and now your book will help the hoax along, too."

And then he winked, drew his index finger to his nose like St. Nick in "The Night Before Christmas," cocked his head impishly, and ducked through the doors, "Now I'm off to run some singing schools and sell some books in Chiliwack."

Considering the name of that Mennonite Brethren town in the Fraser Valley of western British Columbia, near where my mother-in-law grew up, I woke alone in a creaky metal bed in a room under the eves of a Victorian house at the Chautauqua Institute. I'd been working steadily to finish the Yoder biography, some days stymied by a plague of migraines that came with the first trimester of pregnancy, but I'd agreed to teach a week of workshops at the old center for arts and religion in western New York state because I wanted to see where Joseph and Emily Yoder liked to vacation during the 1940s. That July Sunday evening, I'd unloaded my things and wandered along the lakefront and through cramped streets of ornate summer homes, climbed three flights of exterior metal steps to my attic apartment, then fell asleep, exhausted. On Thursday of that week, I'd mailed off my revision of the Yoder biography. On Friday, the five-month sonogram showed that our baby daughter was developing well, according to the technician's reading of the gray shape sucking a skeletal fist in the murky ethers of my womb. Rid of the book and thankful for a healthy baby at my age, I was doubly relieved as I headed off for a week at Chautauqua, repeating, "Let the dead bury the dead."

So naturally Yoder should appear in a dream so vivid that I woke clutching the pillow in terror of massive rewrites. Then I laughed out loud. No matter how hard we work, the books we write cannot match the mysteries of life. Maybe, as Yoder suggested, the books even obscure their subjects. History or biography will always remain fragmentary and partial—lovely but as vague as a sonogram image. In the dream, Yoder, a longtime bachelor, was fleeing from his wife and that other woman, "chasing him," who may well have been trying to write his life story. Books, letters, and even the defining narratives composed for funeral services always fail to capture the shape and meaning of a life, the dream seemed to warn. At the same time, writing and reading keep the dead from resting in peace, because each time a story is told, it becomes new and different, resurrected in the mind of the reader or listener. Yoder, the progressive, embodies the will toward movement and change, the written character who can never be fixed into one shape. And as his writer, I am a conservationist, trotting on behind, trying to catch and frame the meanings of his life.

Maybe the most generative tension is the wavering space between conservation and change—a book and baby both in the making! Tradition is only the culmination of many changes, some so minute as to be indiscernible, others violent ruptures. What I did not understand when I first read those lectures by Ruth is that cultural traditions are not fragile, brittle things that can be easily destroyed. The tradition that is static, repeating itself over and over again, is terminal. To encourage it to continue—as Ruth did in his essay—is to encourage it to change, and the strongest writers are not those who seek to control the story's meaning, but those who influence its continuity. Now I am only thankful for Ruth's provocations and for the many bits of J. W. Yoder lore he has passed my way.

Those who seek control will be betrayed and disappointed over time, but those who support continuity lean toward the future and keep dreaming. "The traditional gesture is not wearing your mother's dress," I read somewhere, immediately picturing the cape dresses and caps on the old ladies from my childhood, "but raising a daughter."

Chapter 2

In the Beginning: The Germ of Travel with a Purpose

Jan Gleysteen

Founded in 1943, Laurelville Mennonite Camp, located in the hills of Southwestern Pennsylvania, was the pioneer church-owned camp of the Mennonite Church in North America. Before that date Mennonites used rented facilities to host their Children's Bible Camps and Young Peoples Institutes for about a decade.

During the mid-1960s Laurelville Mennonite Camp was transformed from a summer camp primarily serving children and youth, or families, into a year-round, partly winterized, facility offering a wide range of retreats, seminars, and conferences. With it came a name change: it would now be called Laurelville Mennonite Church Center (LMCC).

It should come as no surprise, with Mennonites being known for their love of singing, that Music Week, first offered in 1948, became an all-time favorite with families. Music Week continues to this day as the longest running feature on Laurelville's repertoire. Attended year after year by a core of regulars who brought friends and family, Music Week became the site and the occasion where three-generation photos could be taken.

In the early years Hiram Hershey, organizer and director of the Franconia and Lancaster Choral Singers frequently served as the leader of Music Week. It was Hiram who first introduced Massachusetts native and New York City resident Alice Parker, composer/arranger with the Robert Shaw Chorale, to the Mennonites at Laurelville.

Music Week's popularity as a family tradition created one small drawback: not every member of every family was musically inclined! To remedy this minor problem Laurelville simply added two side dishes to the week's menu: Creative Writing, along with the reading of poetry and short stories, as well as an Arts and Crafts Workshop.

John L. Ruth, pastor, playwright, and professor, polishing his thesis on American Hymnody, 1640-1800 toward his Ph.D. from Harvard in 1968, served as the input person for the group studying creative writing. As a member of the text committee for the soon-to-be-published *Mennonite Hymnal* (Herald Press/Faith and Life Press, 1969), John was just the right person to breach the space between word and music, to share from his rich repertoire of tales behind the tunes.

As staff artist with the Mennonite Publishing House (MPH), I was drafted from nearby Scottdale to conduct the arts and crafts sessions. We had lectures on composition, Rembrandt and the Mennonites, and exercises in calligraphy. The campers made collages, and prints from natural materials found on campus.

Each Music Week traditionally ended with a talent show by and for the participants on Thursday night and, usually well-attended, public performance of music on Friday evening. Also, each year, toward the end of the week, the resource persons plus a small group of loyal perennials (who supplied the late-night pizza) would meet in the director's cabin. There they would evaluate the week and make plans for next year's program.

It was during one such session, in mid-August 1968, that comments were made about the questionable theology, or the lack of real significance behind the lyrics of some catchy tunes favored by several of the participants. It was noted that this was so despite the wealth of Anabaptist-Mennonite materials gathered in the church archives at Goshen, Indiana and Newton, Kansas. Most were also aware of the fine scholarly work done by H. S. Bender, Melvin Gingerich, Guy F. Hershberger, and others, the fresh interpretations of John Howard Yoder, yet the majority of Mennonites—ministerial leadership included—were unaware of who we were as a people. Our people were drifting off in all directions and many, under the guise of being "more evangelical," were all too eager to trade our theology of costly discipleship, the *Nachfolge Christi*, for a mess of warm, fuzzy, feel-good "churchianity."

A New Telling of Our Faith Story

So, that night the idea was born to translate anew our Anabaptist-Mennonite faith story, this time in the languages of music, literature, and the visual arts. The potential range of products we envisioned included an oratorio to be written by John for which Alice promised to compose the music; a biography of Conrad Grebel, likewise by John; a series of slide lectures on "Our Mennonite Legacy" to be shown in our schools and congregations; study tours to the places of our church's beginnings in Europe; the building up of an archive of prints and photos, to be made available to publications and for display in Mennonite and Amish visitor information centers.

We should not produce a Mennonite "Fiddler on the Roof," John Ruth emphasized, so that we at the same time could laugh at, and feel good about ourselves. Neither should we see it as our task to idealize and to idolize Conrad Grebel, Michael Sattler, Menno Simons, or Christopher Dock, to mention just a few. Rather we should portray brothers and sisters of the past warts and all, narrating their triumphs and their shortcomings, their courage as well as their lapses, not ignoring the intense struggles in their lives.

Could we revive, for our generation, our ancestors' concept of *Nachfolge Christi* (costly discipleship) with its components of community, mutual aid, peace and nonresistance, separation of church and state, the concepts of religious freedom and of toleration? Could we present better options to our people than to see them blindly accept the latest fads and trends in popular religiosity, from being tempted by "isms" either to the right or to the left?

It was agreed that night that our work should initially be based on that rich lode of material found in the 1685 edition of Thieleman van Braght's *Martyrs Mirror*. Indeed, once before, during the mid-1700's, when "the flames of war were appearing on the horizon" the leaders of our communities in southeastern Pennsylvania saw to it that the *Martyrs Mirror* would be translated from the Dutch into German. Printed on the old wooden hand-press at the Ephrata Cloister between 1745 and 1748 this *Martyrs Mirror* turned out to be the largest book ever printed

Jan Gleysteen and John Ruth, at one of the Anabaptist Heritage Seminars at Laurelville Mennonite Church Center during the 1970s

Grateful acknowledgment is made to Jan Gleysteen for all photos pp. 26, 41-43.

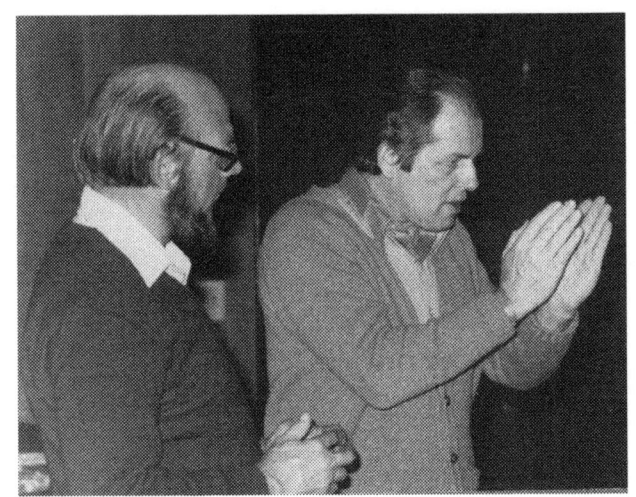

(left) John and Roma Ruth participate in congregational singing in the mid-seventies.

(below left) John, with J. Winfield Fretz, at the opening of The Meetingplace at St. Jacobs, Ontario, 1979.

(below right) John, on the Fish Market Bridge in Zurich, reflecting on the drowning of Feliz Manz on January 5, 1527.

(above left) John, in his home in Vernfield, Pa., in 1970.

(above right) John presents his ideas to the 1971 Christopher Dock Bicentennial Committee.

(left) John, giving the keynote address at the eightieth-birthday celebration of Mennonite theologian and historian J. C. Wenger, in 1990.

Jan Gleysteen, John and Roma Ruth, with their VW Microbus, during their 1969 European research trip.

(above left) John, relaxing in Austria.

(above right) John, on the Lindenhof in Zurich, giving an overview regarding the founding days of Anabaptism in the city, in the 1520s.

(right) John and Roma, near the Krimmler Waterfalls (Europe's highest) in Austria.

Roma and John (r.), with two members of a tour group, singing in the Mennonite meetinghouse of Witmarsum, Friesland, the birthplace of Menno Simons.

in colonial America. More important to us: it reintroduced the tradition of being "Defenseless Mennonites" to a new generation.

Work on our ambitious undertaking, now code-named "*Martyrs Mirror* Project," started immediately. Within days after Music Week 1968 John and Roma Ruth, their children Dawn, John Allan and Philip were on their way to Germany where John had accepted a guest-professorship at the University of Hamburg. For a year the Ruth family would live only a forty-five minute drive from where Menno Simons had spent the last years of his life.

Back home in Scottdale, I tackled my portion of the work by reading, re-reading, then reading once again the *Martyrs Mirror*'s fascinating record of our spiritual ancestors. With each reading I added to and corrected my indices of persons, their testimonies and convictions, the method of their executions, as well as fascinating details about their families, their professions, their social status and the places where they lived and died.

The latter index, the geographical, so indispensable for eventually working up a realistic itinerary and schedule for our research trip, proved to be more complicated than I had anticipated. Four hundred years of nearly continuous destructive wars, shifting loyalties and alliances between kings and emperors, along with a few natural disasters had drastically changed the map of Europe since van Braght chronicled our story.

Rijssel, once a city in the southern Netherlands, was now a city in northern France named Lille. Klausen, a town in South Tirol ruled by the Austrian Habsburgs at the time Georg Blaurock lost his life there by being burned at the stake on September 6, 1529, had only recently become Chiusa, province of Alto Adige, Italy.

Actually, these kinds of changes were the easiest to trace. Shifting boundaries between language groups, disappearing dialects, had also erased the names of towns as written three and a half centuries ago. Moreover, the devastating Thirty Years War (1618-1648), occurring simultaneously with the last three decades of the Low Countries' Eighty Years War of Liberation from Spain, left some 1,200 to 1,400 villages and towns in central Europe so utterly destroyed they cannot be accurately located today.

The towns that eventually replaced them were not always built on the same site, nor did they always emerge under the old name. Many places were never rebuilt at all. The old Langendorf on the Rhine rose from its ashes with a new name: Neuwied. Only one small chapel, now surrounded by an apple orchard, is all that remains of the former Zweikirchen, hometown of Peter Müller, translator of the Ephrata *Martyrs Mirror*. On most German maps it is no longer shown.

Corresponding with the historical and geographical societies of the various regions to be visited was very helpful, but even to this day a small residue of unanswered queries remains. Most likely, growing municipalities have engulfed and absorbed these places, and the previous names of the old neighborhoods have long since been forgotten.

My father, Jan Gleijsteen, Sr., then going on seventy-five years of age, bookseller in Amsterdam, Holland, and lifelong collector of Mennonitica and peace literature, became enthusiastically involved in our project and later proved to be a great help to us on location.

Our fledgling *Martyrs Mirror* Project drew the immediate attention and enthusiastic support of such persons as the elder church statesman and editor of the *Gospel Herald*, Paul Erb; Howard Zehr, then executive secretary of Mennonite General Conference (OM); and bishop John E. Lapp of the Franconia Mennonite Conference.

Paul Erb promoted our work and reported on its progress from time to time in the pages of *Gospel Herald* and in *Allegheny Conference News* of which he also was editor. Howard Zehr worked hard to solicit grants for the undertaking from the Schowalter Foundation, Mennonite Mutual Aid, the Mennonite Christian Leadership Foundation, and other sources.

Additional funds toward the purchase of movie equipment came from Franconia Conference. The newly appointed executive director of Laurelville, Arnold Cressman, pledged office space in the soon-to-be-built meetinghouse on campus, as well as secretarial services.

One year and many hours of preparation and consultation later, I boarded one of Icelandic Airlines' old reliable turbo-props for the long flight to Luxembourg in the heart of western Europe. In my bags, along with a good supply of film and equipment and marked-up topographical maps, was my well-worn, marked-up copy of *Martyrs Mirror*.

Arriving the next day at the Lux-Findel airport, John and Roma Ruth and their children, Dawn, John Allen, and Philip were there to greet me. "I have gone over your plans," said John, "and I took them to the MCC Center in Frankfurt this morning. I used their adding machine to add up the mileage [pause]. We have a lot of territory to cover, a lot of work to do. So [another pause], let's get going!"

Roma moved into the driver's seat and expertly wheeled the VW microbus toward Brussels, Belgium. She would do most of the driving for us that summer, while John and I recorded the scenes just taken, and prepared ourselves for the next stop on our itinerary by reading the accounts of the martyrs there.

During our first days on the road we covered much of Flanders, today divided into a French, Belgian, and Dutch Flanders. When Anabaptism appeared in the Low Countries, about five years after the beginnings of our movement in Switzerland, small groups of believers met in secret in nearly every Flemish town. They and all other non-Catholics caught the full blast of the Spanish fury. Within sixty years the last surviving remnants of these groups all had fled to the more tolerant northern Netherlands, where they contributed greatly to Holland's seventeenth-century Golden Age.

The Martyrs Mirror is full of stories about our Flemish ancestors, their arrests, torture, and executions, forty-seven separate accounts for the city of Ghent alone. We climbed the long stone stairways of Ghent's massive Gravensteen castle and peered down into its deep dark dungeons. Our visit in 1969 was still years before smooth floors and paths, adequate lighting, and informative multi-lingual signs for tourists that diminished some of the ancient fortress' forbidding atmosphere. We found the castle's elderly gray-smocked custodians eager to show us—yes, even to let us put our hands on—the very instruments of torture shown in Jan Luyken's *Martyrs Mirror* engravings.

Other stops in Flanders proved to be less profitable. Arriving in the heart of towns we instantly sensed that each and every building, even when reproduced in traditional style, was post-1918. The historic scene and most of its contents were lost forever during four brutal World War I years of death and destruction about which Erich Marie Remarque would later write his *All Quiet on the Western Front*.

We usually worked till we ran out of daylight, which in northern Europe in mid-summer comes rather late in the day. Often these last moments of low light would provide us with dramatic effects, highlighting the tower of the Great Church of Dordrecht, still standing exactly like it was when Jan Luyken chose to use it as background for his illustration of the execution of Jan Woutersz van Kuyk in 1572.

One night the six of us were given a hearty welcome in a small town in the Dutch province of Zeeland. After a good night's rest and a bounteous breakfast we were about to pay the bill and say our good-byes. There would be, they said, no charge. Our lodging was given to us in appreciation for what North American Mennonites had done for them. Right after the war the Mennonite Relief and Service Commission had brought one of their reconstruction units to their region, to help rebuild their ravaged farms and homes.

We continued our journey through the rest of Holland and into northern Germany. Along the way we filmed the old hidden churches, visited the sites of secret meetings, looked at the few public shame-posts still standing in villages to which the hapless prisoners were once tied up for public ridicule and abuse. We visited one former meetinghouse turned into an auction hall.

In the archives of the Mennonite Church, at that time still located in Amsterdam's historic Singelkerk, we were reverently shown a brittle and dusty little object. It was a pear, the last gift Maeyken Boozers was able to give her little son as she was being led away to be burned at the stake on the market square on the eighteenth of September, 1564. The boy never ate it, but kept it in memory of his mother.

And so we proceeded through Friesland, Groningen, and north Germany, all the while adding to our hoard of film footage and rolls of exposed slide and print film, with which we would later be able to share our faith story in visual forms.

One day we had labored a bit too long past the far end of daylight—yes, even in northern Europe!—and ran out of luck finding lodging. However, it took only one phone call to the pastor of a nearby Mennonite congregation, and soon we adults were welcomed in homes on short notice. The Ruth children chose to sleep in the VW parked next to the church and parsonage. This gift of hospitality led to lifelong relationships between this Frisian congregation, a succession of their pastors, and the Ruths and Gleysteens.

A few days later again, on July 20, 1969, in the village of Godorf on the Rhine, we found room in the inn. But this time John chose to stay in the VW bus, turning on the radio from time to time, waiting to hear the words: "The eagle has landed," as an earthling first set foot on the moon.

The next morning we found that the innkeeper had rolled a black-and-white TV set, and an upright piano into the doorway leading to the breakfast nook. After first dismissing our suggestion that he turn on the TV, he relented and started to play the "Star Spangled Banner" with great gusto, then shook hands with each one of us, congratulating us for the achievements of the astronauts Neil Armstrong and Buzz Aldrin.

We explored the Palatinate where several generations of our Swiss-German Amish/Mennonite ancestors resided before their migrations to William Penn's Woods and points west. In one village, with ties to our story, we admired a picturesque red sandstone fountain, dating back to 1581. This one had three troughs, each one lower and larger: the first one for drinking water and the washing of vegetables, the second one to water the livestock, and the third one for doing laundry. Conservation and recycling practiced for centuries!

We were about to aim our cameras when a farmer came by and said: "Hold it! I think I can improve your picture." He hurried home and returned with two large, well-groomed Belgian draft horses to drink from the middle trough.

Yet, less than an hour later our trip came to a sudden halt.

We were driving the remaining ten kilometers between Bad Bergzabern, Germany and Wissembourg, France. Normally, crossing the border at this point had been a cinch, as the friendly *douaniers* simply waved travelers on to their destination. Not so this evening.

One tall lanky *douanier*, broad red stripes running down his sky-blue pantaloons, stopped us, and peered intently inside our microbus. There, in plain sight, was all our equipment, including the movie camera, the gift from Franconia Mennonites to John's project.

We were denied entrance into France, and advised to come back the next morning at 10:00 to fill out the necessary papers and to purchase permits to "conduct our profession in France."

"No problem," I said to John and Roma. We backed the car around and returned to Bad Bergzabern. There we switched drivers and reshuffled our belongings, being careful this time to cover up the cameras. Shortly thereafter, we rolled into France via secondary roads. We never saw a single customs officer on either side of the line, and soon we were seated before an authentic French mid-evening meal. My time around that part of France in Mennonite Voluntary Service in the 1950s paid off.

This story could go on: Trudging uphill to the Cave of the Anabaptists in the mountains southeast of Zürich before there were any trail markings. Exploring Grebel's ancestral castle inGrüningen. Standing in the rain, crowding under one large black umbrella with the village priest of Gufidaun (now Gudon, Italy) and his friend the schoolmaster, translating for them the story of Georg Blaurock from my beat-up copy of the *Martyrs Mirror* which was now getting soggy as well.

We descended into the deep, dark dungeons of the Oberhaus castle high above the city of Passau, where the songs of the *Ausbund* originated, still being sung by the Amish today, almost 500 years later. We probed the corners of Schleitheim where, at this time, only a few older lifelong residents could still tell us about the *Täuferwegli* (Path of the Anabaptists), a name and a story no longer recognized by most of the town's current residents.

We all returned to the States on August 5, just in time to get ourselves ready for Music Week 1969, which started four days later. Much of that week was spent sharing our fresh impressions with some 150 eager listeners. For the leaders, Music Week ended, true to tradition, with a pizza party in Alice Parker's room, while we discussed the next steps of our project.

Alice, John, and I got together again two months later at King of Prussia, Pennsylvania. Now we had ample prints of the film footage, finished slides and photos, a beginning collection of components to work with. For several days the three of us, enjoying bright autumn weather, explored the sites of southeastern Pennsylvania, Philadelphia, and Germantown, in particular. We met with the combined Mennonite Historical and Research Committee and Germantown Mennonite Church Corporation officers. We discussed our work with J. C. Wenger, John A. Hostetler, Cornelius Krahn, and Andrew Shelly.

While Alice was still with us, we also toured the Ephrata Cloister. There we saw the print shop where the 1748 North American edition of the *Martyrs Mirror* was printed. We visited with Ira Landis, director of the Lancaster Mennonite Historical Society. Later John, his daughter Dawn, and I would spend days in the Rare Book Room of the Philadelphia Free Public Library, examining eighteenth-century Mennonite *Fraktur*.

On Sunday evening, November 9, 1969, John and I made our first public presentation to the combined Vincent and Pottstown Mennonite churches, and a large number of visitors. One of the pastors was visibly moved by the story. "This is tremendous," he said, over and over again. "We have known some of these stories, but with these images the story really comes to life."

Right after Easter 1970, Howard Zehr, executive secretary of Mennonite Church's General Conference (OM) and I traveled to Lansdale, Pa., to meet with John Ruth, with the Christopher Dock Bicentennial Committee, and various other support groups. We discussed the fall 1971 release of John's film, *The Quiet in the Land*, the official premiere of the "*Martyrs Mirror* Oratorio," my illustrated lectures in churches and schools, and the first TourMagination study tour about to take off just weeks later.

Music Week 1970 became the locale to test the the "*Martyrs Mirror* Oratorio" in its embryonic form. Because the oratorio required a massive cast, just about everyone who came close to the stage was drafted, if only as an "extra." And, on Friday night there were almost more singers on the stage than viewers in the audience. This performance with an amateur cast provided John and Alice with ideas on how to perfect it for the professional premiere one year later.

The week's rigorous schedule of rehearsals could not keep a small group of enthusiasts from using their leftover energy to sing, around the clock, every single verse of each of the 653 songs in the new *Mennonite Hymnal*, just off the press. Someone then reported how many days, hours and minutes it took to do it.

That fall, alone or together, John and I were able to add many components to our collections. We experienced the invaluable assistance given to us by historians, librarians, and local experts such as Melvin Gingerich and Nelson Springer at the Mennonite Church Archives and Mennonite Historical Library, respectively, at Goshen, Indiana; Cornelius Krahn at the Mennonite Library and Archives in North Newton, Kansas; and Grace Showalter at the Menno Simons Library in Harrisonburg, Virginia. Lorna Bergey led us to many historical sites, and brought many artifacts for us to record in Waterloo County, Ontario. Walter Klaassen, at Conrad Grebel College, showed a great interest in our work.

Wholehearted and Enthusiastic Moral Support

In October 1970, we met over several days with the Mennonite Historical and Research Committee, chaired by J. C. Wenger at Germantown, Pennsylvania. We reported on our work thus far and showed them about 300 slides. The committee then passed a motion, unanimously, of "wholehearted and enthusiastic moral support for the *Martyrs Mirror* Project, and a willingness to serve as a channel for funds."

January 1971 found us, for one whole week, in and around carefully chosen old farmsteads with lots of character, and at sites significant to our story in southeastern Pennsylvania. Here we would film the winter scenes for the film about Christopher Dock, "The Quiet in the Land."

It was frightfully cold all week. We had fresh and sparkling, pure white snow and deep blue skies above. We carted with us a veritable antique show of props: a two-hundred-year-old wooden tub, a collection of historic butcher tools, and the costumes of course. And with us came the actors scheduled for the day's filming.

One morning we arrived at a perfect little springhouse next to a farm near Chester Springs. Unfortunately the snow in the lane leading to the springhouse showed the distinct imprints of the morning milk truck's tires, not exactly in harmony with our mid-1700s tableau. Before any filming could be undertaken, all of us spent time tossing shovels-full of snow from a nearby field across the offending marks.

Cameras in place now . . . all moves rehearsed . . . everything set. Act III, scene 28, take 1, sound 114; . . . everybody quiet now . . . cameras rolling . . . "Oh, no!" Right then a nice yellow school bus rounded yonder hill, picking up children along the way. "Cut, cut!" Christopher Dock, in his wildest dreams, couldn't have imagined this sort of conveyance for his pupils!

From time to time planes, taking off from Philadelphia, would etch sharp white contrails across the deep blue skies, intruding on our shooting time till they dissipated at long last on this nearly windless day.

The Christopher Dock Bicentennial, was observed at Lansdale, Pennsylvania, from Saturday, October 9 through Sunday, October 17, 1971. It was the occasion to present to our Mennonite world two of John Ruth's completed works, as well as a number of one-of-a-kind exhibits and publications, such as a display of early American (and primarily Franconia Mennonite) *Fraktur*.

John's film, "The Quiet in the Land," depicting the life of Christopher Dock (1698?–1771) drew 5,650 viewers in eight showings while 1,450 people enjoyed "The Christopher Dock Cantata," performed twice that week. The "*Martyrs Mirror* Oratorio," with text by John Ruth, set to music by Alice Parker, drew 2,900 persons in three performances. Also available that week was a handsomely produced program book containing, among other things, a proclamation by Milton Shapp, governor of Pennsylvania, the complete texts of both the Oratorio and the Cantata, and a detailed map plus an illustrated itinerary for a self-guided historical pilgrimage to the sites associated with the first presence of Mennonites in the New World.

With the Dock Bicentennial behind us, John and I had many occasions to cooperate, but never again with the same intensity and duration. We appeared together at a number of Anabaptist Heritage Seminars. In the mid-1970s we were invited to St. Jacobs, Ontario, to help create a Mennonite visitor and information center, later called "The Meetingplace." For this we were able to provide most of the visuals, and John wrote script for captions and recorded narrations. He also produced the center's introductory film about the Mennonites in Ontario.

John's biography of *Conrad Grebel, Son of Zurich* (Herald Press, 1975) written on assignment from Conrad Grebel College, Waterloo, Ontario, appeared in 1975.

The success of The Meetingplace in St. Jacobs, Ontario, in turn inspired the Amish and Mennonite community around Shipshewana, Indiana, to think of setting up their own visitor center. John Ruth, Milo Shantz (principal backer of the Meetingplace), and I were invited to meet with the Indiana folks, to discuss whether some of the components of The Meetingplace could be adapted to meet their needs. Many see the resulting Menno-Hof as the flagship of Mennonite information centers.

Not long after the Dock Bicentennial, John, encouraged and financially supported by a group named Mennonite Heritage Council, gave up teaching to devote all his time to writing and filmmaking.

From my sabbatical under the Laurelville administration I returned to my desk and drawing board at Mennonite Publishing House in December 1971. But as the demand for Anabaptist heritage slide presentations continued to grow, I was transferred from the art office to the Congregational Literature Division. Later, an outside group similar to John's *Heritage Council* was formed to review my work, to help set goals and priorities. This creative circle of scholars and business people was dubbed The Dogwood Group, named after the cabin in Michigan in which most of the meetings were held.

Thirty-five years have passed since the Laurelville Music Weeks of the mid-sixties. During this half of his lifetime, John has contributed to our church a bevy of documentary films, half a dozen books, and numerous videos. His award-winning films, "The Amish, a People of Preservation, "and "The Hutterites: To Care and Not to Care," co-produced with Burton Buller, are often featured on public TV. His latest book, *The Earth Is the Lord's: A Narrative History of Lancaster Conference* (Herald Press, 2001), is definitely his *Magnum Opus*. At 1,388 pages, it is 230 pages longer than *Martyrs Mirror*!

Alice Parker has become a welcome guest in many of our music-loving Mennonite communities where she is often affectionately introduced as a "Congregationalist Mennonite." Our current Mennonite and Church of the Brethren *Hymnal: A Worship Book* (Brethren Press/Herald Press/Faith and Life), includes no less than thirteen compositions and harmonizations listed under her name. This number of entrees is shared by two others, and exceeded only by a greater number listed under "Anonymous," and "Folk Melody."

The 1970s and the eighties turned out to be fruitful years for the recovery of the Anabaptist Vision on the popular level. The Kauffman Museum in North Newton, Kansas transformed itself from a "warehouse of things once owned by Mennonites," into a first-rate visitor center telling our faith story from a Great Plains perspective, featuring the elements of worship, stewardship of the land, education, peace, and service.

The Hans Herr House in Lancaster County, Pennsylvania, and the Brubacher House in Waterloo County, Ontario, were saved, restored, and opened to the public. Steinbach, Manitoba's Mennonite Village; Grantsville, Maryland's Spruce Forest Artisan Village; Menno-Hof in Indiana; the Mennonite Adobe House Museum at Hillsboro, Kansas—to mention just a few—attract tens of thousands of visitors a year.

Walter Klaassen's *Anabaptism: Neither Catholic nor Protestant* (Conrad Press) came out in 1973, followed by Paul Lederach's *A Third Way* (Herald Press) in 1980. The nine-session study guide, *Affirming Our Faith in Word and Deed* (Mennonite Publishing House, 1978) is still relevant today. TourMagination expanded its program from one to three or four Mennonite history tours a year, often in conjunction with our Mennonite colleges and with the Mennonite Board of Missions.

Merle and Phyllis Good have treated us to a steady stream of books, pamphlets, plays, and a film, "Hazel's People." Some of it is perhaps a bit "provincial" (Lancaster) or "folkloristic" (quilts, cookbooks), but as a whole, their work is honestly rooted in our faith community. Laurelville

Mennonite Church Center commissioned Mennonite artist Oliver Wendell Schenk to create the three allegorical portraits of Grebel, Manz, and Blaurock. Peter Dyck, known as "Mr. MCC" to many, avoided retirement by keeping his audiences spellbound with twentieth century tales of our people's pilgrimage.

Michael Hostetler and his associates produced an excellent film on the life of Michael Sattler, "The Radicals," and Canadian filmmaker David Dueck created his intensely moving documentary, "And When They Shall Ask," about the plight of our Russian brothers and sisters during the Stalin era. Unfortunately, both films remain as one-time efforts by these artists. And of course *Mennonite Weekly Review,* an inter-Mennonite paper, having the advantage of not being "owned" by the institutions, continues to tell our faith story through good reporting and well-written, timely editorials.

The Mennonite Brethren historian/educator Paul Toews, Fresno, California, once commented on the important role of the storytellers in our midst. He felt strongly that our Anabaptist-Mennonite faith story be featured at least once every four years in every school and congregation, to be reflected upon once again by those who heard it before, and introduced to the new generations. Historian Leonard Gross, at Goshen, Indiana, suggests once every three years.

Unfortunately, we have entered the twenty-first century with a season of drought, a hiatus in the ongoing telling of the story. For instance, nothing has taken the place of the former Foundation Series and Jubilee educational materials, both firmly rooted in the Anabaptist tradition. We are currently spending most of our resources on the organization, the "scaffolding" of our new denominational structure, failing to encourage, use, or provide channels of communication for the creative community in our midst. It takes the Paul Erbs and the Howard Zehrs, the John Ruths and the Alice Parkers, working together, to serve our people.

Chapter 3

United with the Song: Conversations with Alice Parker

Elmer S. Miller

There is no reason for music unless it communicates, and it should communicate to our minds, hearts and spirits. Sound is one of the most compelling ways to help us drop our defenses, share in our common humanity, rejoice together, mourn together, share each other's quiet and shouting, prayer and praise. Our music schools overemphasize the mental response; our public schools, the visual; our churches the emotional or 'mood' side. We rightly crave the whole: to be moved to transcendence, to be united with the song and each other and all God's creation. —Alice Parker in Melodious Accord: Good Singing in Church *(Chicago: Liturgy Training Publications, 1991, 56-57)*

When Joe Miller called to ask if I would interview Alice Parker for this book my first reaction was surprise at being asked, but quickly found myself excited at the prospect. In my freshman year at Lancaster Mennonite High School John Ruth roomed next door. During the early 1990s, Lois Frey organized a group of Mennonite professionals to discuss the role Mennonite identity may have contributed to the creative processes at work in our various productions. John Ruth was a focal contributor to those sessions. He certainly obliged me to reevaluate my relationship with the church community in which I was raised and nurtured.

After a brief phone conversation with Alice my interest rose even more. We had never met, but I was present when she conducted music during an October 2002 celebration with John and Roma Ruth at Christopher Dock Mennonite High School. It was a transforming experience. My own dance with music has deep roots. While an early teen I became a congregational song leader. I sang in both male and mixed quartets from teenage years through college and seminary years. That included participation in the Mennonite Hour Quartet, together with Nevin Miller, Joe's father. A key part of our missionary work with the Elkhart mission board, Mennonite Board of Missions, among Toba aborigines of Argentina involved singing. Music is also central to our congregational life at Germantown Mennonite Church.

The following conversations took place by phone, email, and personal encounter over lunch at Alice's favorite Szechuan Restaurant in New York City. Alice also made available written materials, some of it cited here, and videos that served as stimulus for many of our exchanges. This text is a product of mutual participation; it would not read in its present form without our joint contributions from beginning to end.

Alice Parker needs no introduction to Mennonites. Her active participation in Family Music Week at the retreat center in Laurelville, Pennsylvania in the 1960s is legend, reinforced by the music compositions that emerged from that experience and by the workshops in congregational singing she continues to direct at Mennonite schools and colleges throughout North America. Her writings, musical productions, the videos produced by John Ruth, all provide rich resources. Clearly Alice's interactions with Mennonites have been, and are, mutually stimulating and beneficial, as the following conversations illustrate.

A New Vision of Congregational Singing

Alice: "My own idea of what a congregation might be asked to do changed radically after I heard Mennonite singing in 1961. One voice began a familiar hymn. On the second note, the entire room joined in the most beautiful four-part hymn singing I had ever heard. It gave me a vision of what hymn singing must have been in days past and could be again in days to come" (*Melodious Accord* 5).

Elmer: How did your initial encounter with Mennonites come about? Did you find them or they you?

Alice: Hiram Hershey asked me to come to Laurelville Mennonite Camp in western Pennsylvania as the music resource person for Music Week, an association that lasted from 1961 to 1970, and included for me some wonderfully encouraging experiences in my own musical development.

I love to remember that first arrival—it was just suppertime, and families were already standing around their tables. I heard someone say "Brother—, will you lead us in prayer" and of course I expected words. Instead, a rich voice started singing (with no announcement), and on the second note the whole group joined in. That sound lingers in my ears, and has much to do with my long enjoyment of my Mennonite friends. (That, and the cooking!)

At this point in my life, I had been working with Robert Shaw for more than a dozen years, and was quite convinced that great choral singing was the result of meticulous rehearsal. This conviction was blown away in that instant—a salutary balance to over-intellectualism and a living proof that when the chain of singing is unbroken from parents to children, the musical result can be—is—superb.

Elmer: Is that where you became acquainted with John Ruth?

Alice: I met John Ruth first (I think) in the summer session of 1962. He came as worship leader in those summers, and I always enjoyed his thoughtful, questioning, rather ironic take on the biblical stories we studied. The summers came to be organized around great choral works: Haydn's *Creation*, Mendelssohn's *Elijah*, Bach's *St. John Passion*, and so forth. The texts were studied in the worship gatherings, the music in rehearsals; then we lived and acted out the stories in our daily life.

Elijah happened amid the 1960s drought, and our cries for rain were answered, just before the performance, with a tiny shower. . . My husband, Tom Pyle, would sing the baritone solos; John's wife, Roma, would take the soprano solos, and we trusted to divine Providence to supply the other needs—and they were always, somehow, met. We'd rehearse and study all week (with a break for the daily baseball game and family times for swimming and visiting). Then on Friday afternoon we'd decide which portions we were ready to perform (in the Lodge, for a small local audience), and John would invoke the whole evening as a service, reading the texts of whatever portions we left out. I've since thought that that must be the best way possible to come to know one of these huge works. The combination of twice daily close study of the texts, and twice daily musical rehearsals, culminated in performances (with piano) which were sung with whole-hearted intelligence and commitment and vocal beauty by people who had come to love it.

Elmer: Are there other specific memories you have of John during those summer sessions?

Alice: One, in the *Elijah* summer, of everyone gathered after lunch for the baseball game, and John was unaccountably missing. Just when the men were about to begin without him, Roma drove down the road to the camp, and out onto the middle of the baseball field. Without looking or speaking to us, she walked around the car, unlocked and opened the trunk—and out stepped John, wrapped in a worn rug—the prophet in the wilderness.

St. John Passion summer (oh, do I remember those discussions about power), we were at supper, when in strode John and a couple of other men with stern expressions. They walked over to Bernard Martin, seated with his wife and three small children, and indicated that he was to come with them. Right now. He protested, but they were implacable—the kid's faces were studies in developing fear. Finally he stood and left with them. . . No words were spoken—none needed to be. (John is a great actor.) This drama demonstrated to a peace-loving people the nature of unprovoked violence experienced by societies living under absolute power in a manner discussions alone did not.

I remember also, in the middle of a 'sermon,' John had us divide into groups of two, with one person standing on a chair and the other kneeling below, then changing places. Most of us felt uncomfortable with being 'above'—it was hard to put ourselves into positions of power. It was an amazing physical experience.

The Influence of *Martyrs Mirror*

Elmer: Are there other experiences at Music Camp that left an impression?

Alice: A subtext during those summers was my education in Mennonite history and thinking—John and Jan Gleysteen took this very seriously, presenting me with a copy of *Martyrs Mirror*, saying "Read it." I did. We had a wonderful day exploring historical sites in eastern Pennsylvania, including the Ephrata Cloister, talking about the whole concept of martyrdom (foreign to my Congregational New England upbringing) and peaceful resistance. At some point the idea of writing an opera was introduced, and grew into the performance that final summer. John wrote the libretto—it was a pleasure to work with, but came very late! I had the first act done around Christmastime, and waited till May, I think, for the second act. I was still writing when camp started, and had to accompany some of the songs myself, as the piano part was not yet completely written down.

I've left out other Mennonite performances of the 1960s, such as "The Christopher Dock Cantata," for which John wrote the libretto. He loved the early American hymns that I inserted to mark the changing scenes, as he had discovered them in his thesis work at Harvard. Then, Hiram commissioned me to write a work honoring Dr. Martin Luther King Jr. on the day following his death, to be performed in one year.

These three commissions were incredible sparks to my own compositional growth at that time. I felt that Mennonites were the only people who saw me as I wanted to see myself—as a composer. By asking me to write for them, they were supplying me with occasions for enormous growth—and I continue to be grateful for this continuing association.

Elmer: Mutual stimulation for creative productivity is clearly apparent in these reflections. Are there other examples you could share?

Alice: After the *Martyrs Mirror* opera (Hiram always called it an oratorio—perhaps more Mennonite), I wanted to write another, but on a lighter subject. John and I discussed possibilities and settled on a family reunion. I asked him for a libretto, and a general story-outline duly appeared. I tried to set it, but got completely tied up in much too complex a story—John's idea of a family reunion had a cast of hundreds, a master of ceremonies, and all kinds of formal remembrances, and so forth.

I wrote a whole series of hymn arrangements for the singing-scene, and these turned into the "Melodious Accord Cantata," all based on tunes from the *Harmonia Sacra*. I asked three or four other people for librettos, and found in each case that people wrote out of their own experience, and these did not suit my musical purpose. (One had a reunion with only a man and his sister!) So finally I wrote it myself, spreading out on the floor all the American folk music I wanted to use, and figuring out the easiest way to connect them within a simple story—a family reunion in which nothing goes wrong! (And people would tell me that it was *just* the way it was!)

This was followed by another commission from Hiram, based on the life of Joseph Funk, *Harmonia Sacra* songbook compiler. I was indoctrinated into the lives of Harrisonburg, Virginia Mennonites—primary research in the library at Eastern Mennonite University reading Funk's actual letters, and collecting different early editions of the *Harmonia Sacra*. So the Laurelville experience continued to bear fruit.

Our families kept in contact through the 1970s and 1980s, though much less intensely. I did visit his school once (St. David's?) for a music workshop, and I somehow remember drinking root beer and eating ice-cream on the porch of their home in Vernfield! The celebration of John and Roma's life at Christopher Dock School occasioned new performances of "The Christopher Dock Cantata" and "*Martyrs Mirror*," and it was gratifying to see how well they lasted. I had had the impression I was working with trustworthy material in the collaboration with John, and that proved to be the case.

Elmer: Were there additional collaborations with John?

Alice: In the 1990s we worked together again on what turned out to be a series of four videotapes of my work. John was a dream to work with as a producer (and behind-the-scenes director)—I have a wonderful memory of him at Elkhart, having been invisible behind the camera for two days, suddenly breaking out and entering into the discussion we were having—a truly theatrical, Pirandello moment! His editing was meticulous—here I remember Roma saying that if she had to listen one more moment to my voice coming up from John's downstairs studio, she would scream! Somehow she survived—and even remade the face of my favorite childhood doll in the process.

Elmer: Somewhere I read that you composed and expressed an interest in becoming a composer at an early age.

Alice: When I had written down my first piano piece at about eight years of age I told my dad I wanted to be a composer. His response was, "Fine! Now you'll have to find a way to support yourself"!

Elmer: Did one or both of your parents play a role in your early musical development?

Alice: My father was New England Congregational; my mother had grown up Scottish Presbyterian. While neither one was a musician, both were church-centered people who loved singing of all kinds. My mother had wanted to play piano but did not have the opportunity to study till after her marriage. All of us five children started lessons at age five.

Elmer: Was your early church life a factor in attracting you to music?

Alice: It was certainly part of it. We sang hymns and children's songs and all kinds of "home songs" at home and in the car. We went to Pops Concerts in Boston and bought a recording of our favorite piece on the way home. There was music at school—choruses and orchestra—and also in local groups. I was attracted to it wherever I found it.

Elmer: How did you come to major in organ and composition at Smith College?

Alice: I had decided early to be a composer and enrolled with that goal in mind. I was fine until my junior year when required to write 'on demand' following the instructions of my teacher. This was extremely difficult—I didn't like to have to curb what had always been an intuitive experience. It was hard to have to make "corrections" and finish pieces on time. I realize now that Professor Josten was trying to make me think rationally about what I was writing, but somehow it didn't take. By the time I graduated I had decided I couldn't go on in a field which made me so uncomfortable. So I had to choose another area for graduate study.

Elmer: Why did you switch to choral conducting at Juilliard? Was Robert Shaw a factor or did you learn to know him after making the choice?

Alice: I decided choral conducting was a career I could live with—I loved all kinds of singing. I sang under Robert Shaw that summer of 1947 at Tanglewood, and enrolled at Juilliard in the fall.

Elmer: It would be of interest to learn something about your career in music, how it developed, its ups and downs.

Alice: I'm reminded of Emily Dickinson's "My life closed twice before its close"—mine not deathly partings, but rather career blocks. The first was at the end of my college years when it became clear to me that continuing in composition studies was simply going to be a frustration. I had an interview at Eastman for graduate work where the head of the theory department told me after 15 minutes that I'd learned nothing at Smith, that if I wanted to come to Eastman I'd have to come as a freshman but he would not advise it. I realized if I tried to work through this, I'd be miserable—I'd not been able to access my early joy in writing at college, and this would be even worse. Since that door seemed closed (was I born in the wrong century?) I decided on choral conducting as a remote second choice.

The irony is, not only did I learn much about music from Shaw and Julius Herford, my "guru" of piano and score study, but the arranging work with Shaw put me in touch with fundamental compositional techniques I'd never learned at school. Shaw had no theoretical training—just an acute ear, a love for language, and a compulsion to have each piece just right for his singers. Somehow, over those twenty years he got me to think before I wrote, to become more and more attuned to the live sound of singing voices, and to be more and more responsible toward the basic melody I was working with.

Elmer: Conducting does appear to have been something of a second choice in terms of what proved most significant in your graduate work.

Alice: After Julliard, I couldn't get a job as a choral conductor (door number two closing); the only one I could find was as a general music teacher at a private day school in Illinois. I had no training in teaching whatsoever, and ended up in the principal's office in tears at least once a week. I made all the classic mistakes—but did do some good performing with the kids and learned enough to know I had much to learn, and that I'd better do just that. I stayed two years so no one could accuse me of quitting, and then I went back to New York with some savings to continue my piano lessons with Julius. He put me in touch with a remarkable woman named Helen Chrystal Bender who ran a small music school in Summit, New Jersey—and did she ever teach me to teach! Children who came to her for piano lessons also had to come to class once a week "to learn music"—and I helped her in that for four years. She taught me to plan and follow through, to prepare materials, to be firm but patient, and to reward the children for every achievement. I was still suffering from what I called the "Juilliard syndrome"—we became so intolerant of our own and others' mistakes that we couldn't just enjoy music making any more.

Elmer: How were you able to recognize the 'syndrome' and break from it?

Alice: It took a while to get over that—my best lesson lives in memory. I'd been coaching an adult group of four elderly women playing two-piano eight-hand pieces, and put too much pressure on them. One began crying, saying it wasn't my fault—she was tired that day—and "Don't tell Helen." Her friends bundled her off and I went straight in to Helen to confess. She looked at me as if I'd run over a dog and called to learn if Lucille was really all right. Afterward she turned to me with a very stern look and pointed finger, saying: "It has GOT to be PLEASANT!" I've remembered that ever since, and tried to apply it every day.

Elmer: What a wonderful lesson! It must have been a tough decision to leave that job.

Alice: About this time Tom Pyle and I were married in San Diego where we'd both been assisting Shaw and Herford at a summer concerts/school. Helen (a superb cook) prepared the wedding dinner and refreshments—a whole table full of assorted cakes. When we got back to New York, Tom had to leave on tour with the Chorale and I continued teaching through the production of three children in the next four years. Then Helen moved to Hawaii and closed the school (she wanted me to run it, but I knew I wasn't gifted in that direction).

I began more teaching at home, both piano and classes, learning more from watching my own children develop, and teaching both in Sunday school at Riverside Church and with the boys' Cub Scout troop. Those were definitive experiences in that I learned that tiny kids (ages 2-5) can sing almost anything; and that if one can survive an afternoon with eight eight-year-old boys in a New York apartment, one can survive almost anything! (We sang a lot, and also made bread.)

My fourth child came along amid this. And just when I thought I had life fairly well under control, with a chance to help Julius in his teaching at Westminster Choir College (to be the flowering of my teaching career), along came the fifth to close that door quite firmly.

Elmer: How were you able to exercise and maintain your interest in music production during this intense period of child rearing?

Alice: All through this time the arranging with Shaw had been my one link with professional music making. My attempt to find satisfaction at the level of teaching taught me more—that I loved to teach theory more than performance, that I loved to get any group singing, and that I was a "classic" rather than an "experimental" musical thinker. I began to compose again in the late 1960s and found I could recapture that old delight if I concentrated on the people for whom I was writing, rather than on what new sounds I could make. It was amazing how quickly the flow of ideas resumed, and how quickly it opened out to many different kinds of musical languages: from songs to anthems to cantatas and even that first opera. I realized I had benefited tremendously from each of those closed doors—I'd had to keep questioning my relationship with all three occupations. Since I wasn't able to work full time in any one, they kept cross-fertilizing each other as I came to have a far more unified look at what "music" meant. I was also more able to depend on my own thinking rather than on what others had told me—so I was finally throwing off excess baggage from my own learning days, and seeing and doing what was right for me.

When Shaw moved to Atlanta in 1968 the Robert Shaw Chorale disbanded—both tours and recordings ceased. So Tom was home and I began to accept invitations to conduct workshops for friends around the country. I found I liked doing this (how exhilarating to step on the plane that first time after twelve years at home with small children!) and could do it well, so we exchanged functions. That worked well until Tom died, in 1976.

Elmer: That must have been devastating!

Alice: It felt pretty much as if the world had come to an end but my children, friends, and music sustained me. While I was deep in sorrow and confusion a friend asked, "If you could have any job in the world, what would it be?" It was a wonderful question and it took me a year to realize that I was already doing just what I like—composing, conducting, and teaching. I simply wanted to do it at a higher level. Again, things worked out and I was able to put the kids through college and get a great deal of satisfaction from my own activities.

When the youngest graduated from college in 1984 I started Melodious Accord to enable me to work with professional singers again—I'd missed that since Shaw moved to Atlanta. Setting it up was another learning experience and I realized I had probably found, unwittingly, the only occupation that would cost me more than putting five children through college! But it has been worth it.

A People Set Apart

Elmer: What an inspirational story! Clearly your work with Mennonites, and with John Ruth in particular, has shaped your career in significant ways. In addition to a cappella singing, are there other contributions Mennonites have made to your faith and life?

Alice: I have always been attracted to the Mennonite notion of a people "set apart," not so much like the Hebrews as "chosen," but of a people naturally suspicious of undisciplined human nature: the tendencies toward brutality, or acquisitiveness, or of anything that leads away from the central virtues of simplicity, piety, and connection with the land. In our society this emphasis seems prescient. Here, even music is seen principally as a commodity, to be bought and sold. It is entertainment, diversion, light pleasure, evanescent. Even church music is not immune from this trend: all the forces that urge churches to buy instruments and sound systems, choir robes and anthems for every age group seem to be the realization of the worst fears of the forefathers.

John argued this point often at Laurelville—itself a place set apart. How can we guard our young people from the seductions of this loud, colorful, and heedless society? By turning more and more deeply into the heart of our tradition and continually asking, "What really matters? How should we spend our lives?" We must make a conscious decision to see those diversions for what they are, and arm ourselves against them, following in the path set out for us.

Elmer: Would you say a word about the role of music in the context you describe?

Alice: What is music in this environment? It is a gift of God, of course, to be cherished and nourished. Mennonite singing is what attracted me in the first place, and I confess to being deeply influenced by those summers and years in conversations with John and his friends. I saw in action in the gathered community the power of the song to unite generations and sects and uneasy neighbors. I saw what happened when the chain of song was unbroken: the children learning by joining in with their parents and grandparents in song, which was almost always directed to the Creator—which could on occasion be frivolous but still was part of the gift. I saw people who sang at all the great and small moments of their lives: not only to celebrate births, weddings and funerals, but at all meals and gatherings. Perhaps this active singing unites people at a level below any spoken creed or belief: it is in our bones and breath.

I read an article this winter about scientists who had just discovered that music affects us through the same neural pathways as food and sex. "Those are necessary for survival," the article continued, "but what is music doing there?" Wrong question, I answer! It seems clear that singing may be the only activity that humans engage in that calls on all of our abilities at once. Breath, body, mind, emotion, imagination, spirit—they are all working together to adorn this moment in time and space, this now, this eternity. When we enter gratefully into the song, we are taking our place in the physics of sound and energy; we are balancing our rational and intuitive minds; we are creating architecture in air, imagining a completeness that we can't find elsewhere in this world. We are most human—and most divine. We are within the Great Song.

♣

During our initial phone conversation Alice commented that music constitutes God's gift to humans to counterbalance the rational in us. This thought has remained with me throughout our interactions and continues to exercise my imagination. It is intriguing because it gets to the heart of the bonds that unite us as a people, in contrast to the dogmas that pull us apart—music and community in creative tension.

How does music nurture the bonds that enable community? Alice Parker and John Ruth have provided some responses to this inquiry through the musical pieces they produced and the films documenting Alice's Music Workshops in action. Certainly *Melodious Accord* speaks to the suggestion as well. Consider the following: "When we sing together in common—whether in joy or desolation or everyday hope—we affirm our common humanity and build our community through this shared craft. Good singing is not the result of a good congregation but the forging of it. No other gift connects us in quite this way." Or again, "Through singing and speaking we communicate with other humans and animals and perhaps, as in the old myths, with rocks, trees, and stars. We converse with the entire universe of which we are a part" (11-12). The Toba would say a hearty yea and amen! They taught me to pay attention to the messages communicated through bird songs; one bird in the Chaco has three distinct songs, each with a different message.

Alice's statement concerning Mennonite suspicions of "undisciplined human nature," and commitment to "the central virtues of simplicity, piety and connection to the land" is provocative. In the church conferences in which John Ruth (Franconia) and I (Lancaster) were raised in the 1940s and 1950s, the ostensible markers of identity were plain attire and nonresistance to war. An equally significant non-codified marker, however, was music. Congregational singing was completely a cappella. Some of the most enthusiastic singing by the older folk was the occasional song in German. "Special music" was appreciated at cottage meetings, the "Old People's Home" (no concern about political correctness), or street meetings, but not in worship services.

Folk songs were welcomed in the right context, such as in school, car, or home. Popular tunes were resisted because our singing was primarily intended to glorify God. A significant genre distinction was made between music for worship as opposed to pleasure. The former was good and proper, the latter required supervision and delimitation. Instruments, primarily piano or guitar, were tolerated at home, but their higher purpose was to inspire divine praise and adoration.

During my college and seminary years at Eastern Mennonite College (now University) there was choral and smaller group singing in worship services, but no instrumentation. I remember long, intense discussions with music director J. Mark Stauffer on this subject. I chafed at the bit for an organ or piano, at minimum, to accompany the major musical presentations of the college, but always to no avail. The basic objection centered on the "slippery slope" argument that instruments would eventually undermine congregational singing as we practiced it.

In retrospect, my dismissal of the argument Brother Stauffer (the proper address for teachers in those days) affirmed was too facile. While many examples of good congregational participation along with special group singing and instrumentation abound, they clearly entail persistent efforts on the part of music directors and a commitment to serious congregational singing by members. Far too often responsibility for good music has been relegated to the specialists. This is not a Mennonite problem per se, of course. Alice noted Congregationalists did not permit special singing during worship service in early New England; this was true of other denominations as well.

Her observation regarding the impact of commodification on church music is also worthy of careful consideration. It may well be more pervasive than many church people would wish to acknowledge. Separate music for age groups, different vestments for choirs, all at a price of course. And the highest price may not be in dollars, but in the loss of *each* individual voice in the congregation that must be heard in the same song to produce the music that unites and inspires a people to worship together in a manner that fosters community. This is not to suggest that instruments and varying styles of music have no place in worship, but rather that the communal value of united congregational voices must not be lost in the process. It is more important to encourage every voice to join in, including the monotone, than to depend on highly trained voices to serve as models for congregational singing.

It is encouraging to see church schools and seminaries pay greater attention to music training than had been true in previous decades. In my youth, our church district had a singing school at Elizabethtown Church that included one class for youngsters and another for young adults. There we learned to read music and sing the hymns found in church hymnals. The idea was to teach all of us to sing to the best of our ability in order that we might participate meaningfully and effectively in congregational worship. For the young people today who have no access to similar training in day school, it may be necessary to offer church music classes so the entire congregation can be effectively united with the song.

Chapter 4

If the Earth Is the Lord's, Do We Have to Hate the World? Musings on Mennonite People, Places, and Complexes

Jeff Gundy

One of the more intriguing people I learned to know in my first weeks at Goshen College was a curly-haired young woman from somewhere in Pennsylvania (for years I had only the vaguest sense of the geography of the place, and assumed that Scottdale and Akron and Lancaster were all pretty much next to each other). Dawn seemed shy and giggled a lot, but she also had a hard-to-define air about her—not exactly sophistication, but a seeming ease with the academic world that I envied.

Her father, John Ruth, I soon learned, was a big-name Mennonite. He had a PhD from Harvard, but still wore a plain coat. He was a preacher, but he still wrote books and made movies. When he talked, people listened, and if I hadn't heard of him, it was just one more indication of how far out of things I was.

Now I had grown up among farmers; the most educated people in my home community were preachers and schoolteachers and a few doctors. There were plenty of intelligent people, but few that I would call intellectuals. My own father was a farmer—not especially shy in person, but with a great aversion to public speaking. He wouldn't even get up in church to make an announcement, if there was any way out of it. So when I started to imagine myself as a writer, a professor, an intellectual, John Ruth became an exemplar, if not exactly a mentor (we wouldn't meet in the flesh for another twenty years). He was someone who had managed to live the life of the mind, without leaving the church.

When I began trying to write about Mennonite literature, his short book *Mennonite Identity and Literary Art* (four lectures first delivered at Bethel College and published by Herald Press in 1978) was the fullest and most thoughtful statement on the subject around. When a few American Mennonites, mostly of the generation after John's, finally began to write creatively in earnest, he was there as a kind of father figure, mostly benevolent but a bit daunting in his enigmatic presence, his massive knowledge, his charismatic storytelling, and his insistence that writing ought to serve the community rather than attack it.

While people like me went off to college and didn't return to our home communities, John not only went back but has dedicated his life to uncovering and preserving the history of the Mennonites of eastern Pennsylvania. While I wrote poems, essays, and books I sought to publish in literary journals and university presses, John wrote church and conference histories and documentaries about Amish and Hutterites. While he wondered why no one had made "full-throated song" celebrating and grappling with the enclosed Mennonite enclaves he knew best, I tried to capture something of the less enclosed, less massive, and less colorfully plain communities that my own ancestors had created on the Illinois prairie. Eventually I realized that while we both worried over the conundrums of community, separation, and worldliness, even those terms—like the word "Mennonite"—seemed subtly but significantly different, depending on one's personal history and associations.

We have met in person only a few times, and rarely if ever corresponded. Yet by now, John Ruth has become one of those rich, complicated figures whose work and person dwell more or less permanently in my imagination—as a mentor and example, but also as a distant partner in various more or less one-sided conversations, disquisitions, even (gentle) quarrels. I am grateful to him in many ways; perhaps especially for staking out positions and ideas that at one point or another I found difficult enough to require some kind of response of my own—and for doing all his work in such lucid, humane, faithful, and generous ways. What follows will I hope be read as I mean it, as a meditation on some issues that his latest work raises for me—not a quarrel but an inquiry into some long-running conundrums of Mennonite thinking and practice.

How Much School Does One Need?

The publication of John Ruth's *magnum opus*, *The Earth Is the Lord's: A Narrative History of the Lancaster Mennonite Conference* is an event among Mennonites for several reasons: for its subject matter, for its encyclopedic detail and graceful style, for its long gestation period, for John Ruth's own stature as cultural figure, preacher, impresario, interpreter of plain culture, historian, and so on. At nearly 1,400 pages with back matter—the index is thirty pages long!—it may be the longest book by a single author that I own.

The Earth Is the Lord's provides a fascinating and nearly obsessively detailed look at one of the oldest and strongest Mennonite communities in North America—one with many vital connections to Mennonites elsewhere. It also, incidentally, helps make clear why those of us at other points on the Mennonite map have often found those from eastern Pennsylvania to be something of a breed apart.

Most congregational and conference histories are more or less celebratory, for obvious reasons, but this one seems particularly thick with superlatives regarding numbers—of congregations, congregants, farms, and wealth. To emphasize the strength and influence of Lancaster Conference in the Mennonite world is simply to recognize the facts, of course, and it would not do to accuse Ruth nor the Lancaster Mennonites of anything unbecoming to the long and deep Anabaptist humility tradition, which this book documents in many of its expressions, including some of the quirkier ones. But the community's satisfaction concerning its long history and prosperity is quite evident, as is a certain assumption that this group is not merely significant but *central*—for several centuries an easier assumption for this particular Anabaptist group than for many others.

As Ruth tells it, the Lancaster story is also one of perpetual suspicion of the world and resistance to particular elements of it. Especially of interest are attitudes and practices related to education, intellectual speculation, and imagination. Among Lancaster Mennonites, the broad pattern seems to have been that advances in technology, transportation, and the like—those that aided in making money and getting about—

were adopted with little fuss, while those that might threaten communal control encountered much greater resistance. Thus even conservative Lancaster Mennonites began quite quickly to drive cars and to use tractors, but getting an advanced education remained suspect—at least until the economic advantages of education began to overwhelm the fears of its consequences.

The costs of this suspicion, Ruth suggests repeatedly, were substantial. In the late nineteenth century, he comments, "In Lancaster County itself, no Mennonite mind was trained in the wisdom of the world so that it could speak eloquently in the world's language to share its spiritual heritage... They interpreted their lack of interest in what might be called the life of the mind as a godly humility. But... we also sense an unwelcome result of this attitude: the frustration of an intelligence that might have made better sense of the heritage if its story had been accessible" (Ruth, *The Earth* 631, 633).

Some of Ruth's ambivalence about this suspicion of education is apparent here. A less generous observer might put it this way: For centuries Lancaster Mennonites presented their best minds with a choice: sacrifice whatever intellectual ambitions they might have to the established order, or go into some sort of exile. During the long period when the congregations continued to grow in numbers and influence this policy seems to have been little questioned, at least by those who remained.

Ruth describes and analyzes this syndrome and its eventual effects more thoroughly than anyone has before. Its origins, he believes, can be traced back to Europe: "The centuries-old distrust of *die Gelehrten,* the educated ones, so deeply imbibed when the main culture of Switzerland and South Germany had persecuted the withdrawing Anabaptists, was still playing a powerful role in rural Mennonite pockets of industrializing America. Most of Pennsylvania's Mennonites had never known any other way to do Christianity than to keep themselves 'little and low,' culturally speaking" (Ruth, *The Earth* 806).

Other Mennonites shared this suspicion, of course, but to varying degrees; by the beginning of the last century, many progressive Mennonites further west were thinking quite differently about the world. Historian C. Henry Smith, a key figure in the history of both Goshen College and Bluffton College, visited Lancaster in 1906. Ruth notes his bemused reaction: "With his more liberal orientation, it seemed strange to [C. Henry] Smith that Lancaster would drag its feet so stubbornly regarding education ... the conference was so fearful of the worldly effects of schooling that it would tarry another thirty years before it was able to make an educational move of its own."

It seems clear, as Ruth notes, that the Lancaster communities were formed mainly by immigrants who left Europe with the memory of persecutions and martyrdoms still fresh, and carried the wounds of those events with them even through centuries of general tolerance and prosperity in Pennsylvania. Later immigrants, both Amish and Mennonite, certainly had their own mistrust of the world, but in many cases their conservatism had been tempered by a less brutal European experience and by increased toleration and cooperation with their worldly neighbors. They would mainly settle farther west in the new country, and develop their own ways of sorting the essential from the optional.

One result was that the first Mennonite colleges formed in those more progressive western communities, placing the Lancaster Mennonites in a curious position. Ruth writes of Hesston: "The freer atmosphere in the Kansas community closer to the frontier eventually produced a strange historical relationship: the richer home community in Lancaster would send students and teachers all the way west to Kansas, where at Hesston an old Mennonite school was organized" (Ruth 630). His commentary on Goshen College is equally rueful:

> Thus would arise an ironic situation in which the older, eastern Mennonite communities, having the most potential students, were forced to send them over great distances to study in communities having far more limited economic resources and Mennonite population—if they wanted their youths to attend Mennonite colleges." (Ruth, *The Earth* 631)

These observations, and their emphasis on the material and demographic wealth of Lancaster, imply a certain frustration that its prosperity did not lead to the formation of academic institutions there to nurture leaders—perhaps ones more to the community's liking. I suspect that Ruth has envisioned a quite different history—and as a fan of speculative fiction I love to ask "what if" questions myself, even if they have no clear answers. What if, for example, there had been an early move to found a Mennonite college in Pennsylvania? If Lancaster College was now entering its second century alongside Goshen, Hesston, Eastern Mennonite, Bluffton, and Bethel—or perhaps instead of one of them—

how might the intellectual landscape of American Mennonites be different? Would such an institution resemble today's Goshen, or Eastern Mennonite, or Bluffton—each of them significantly different but all about the same size? Might it be more like Messiah, much larger for having tapped into wider streams of evangelical students and contributors? Might it be the Mennonite equivalent of Wheaton or Calvin, more conservative than any current Mennonite college but at least as academically rigorous? And, if such a college had existed for the last century, what would it have meant for generations of Lancaster Conference Mennonites to have lived with its resources near at hand?

On Tables, Pulpits, and the Death of the Universe

Shortly after *The Earth Is the Lord's* came out, before I had read or even seen it, I had a long conversation with my friend Gerald Biesecker-Mast, who had just read the book. Gerald is often excited about Mennonite topics; this was no exception. He regaled me with anecdotes, including the one about the great Smoketown pulpit/table controversy.

A considerable scandal resulted when two brothers and their sister sneaked into the nearly completed meeting house in 1889, ripped out the just-installed pulpit, and replaced it with a preachers' table they had built themselves. (Strangely, the main suspect in the case was a Martin M. Zimmerman, while the real perpetrator was named Martin W. Zimmerman. But perhaps not so strange for Lancaster County, where a few names seem to repeat over and over—Ruth describes how he became almost mesmerized by the many men named John Landis who kept emerging from his research.)

Over the same semester break I'd been reading several science fiction epics that I'd picked up at a used bookstore. Those books, though not as massive as John's, were bulky enough in their own right to engross me for several evenings each in their hundreds of pages of fine print. They found their scope not by accumulating intensive details about a small group of people in a small corner of Pennsylvania, but by taking the widest and longest of views. Most ranged over billions of miles of interstellar space, at least one over millions of years as well. All assumed that the conditions of human life and even basic physical laws would change radically in the future; one envisioned the extinction of the entire universe that we know, and ended with a plucky band of humans trying to make their way into an alternate universe to survive.

I drove home slowly that night, pondering again my half-guilty, half-grateful, perhaps arrogant sense of distance from the kind of carefully bounded community that John Ruth writes of so lovingly (and not without his own ambivalence, of course). A largely oral, tightly restricted community can maintain itself and even thrive for centuries, as the Lancaster example shows. It can try to resist change, or to control change when it becomes inevitable. It can oppose education beyond a certain level, fearing the effect of too much knowledge among its impressionable young people.

Such communities naturally have little use for novels, whether of the realistic sort that portray all varieties of grim human difficulties or the fantastic type that operate on such vast scales as to make their readers reflect on other matters of scale. I was experiencing this dissonance firsthand as I tried to get my space operas and Gerald's story of the pulpit to cohabit comfortably in my mind. It was impossible not to wonder, I found: Is the God who made the enormous and ancient universe really heavily invested in the problem of whether a few dozen people in a modest building on an obscure planet in the Milky Way should hear their preaching done from behind a table or a pulpit?

This is the point at which, depending on your tradition, the bishop notes rather heavily that some questions are mistaken in their very asking—or the robot begins to flails its arms and whoop, "Danger, danger, alien approaching." If I had not read such wild tales, would I ever have thought to ask such a question? Now that I have, how can I help but ask such questions? Will I ever again be of any use to a community that defines itself in terms of such issues?

Pondering this took me once again into the tangled concerns around those much-abused words "community" and "the world." How much openness and how much control do self-conscious communities need to endure and to thrive? What *kinds* of each? What stances toward the world, what blends of engagement and distance and celebration and criticism, are both right and practicable?

Living in Another World

[E]very living and healthy religion has a marked idiosyncrasy. Its power consists in its special and surprising message and in the bias which that revelation gives to life. The vistas it opens and the mysteries it propounds are another world to live in; and another world to live in—whether we expect ever to pass wholly over into it or not—is what we mean by having a religion. (George Santayana, *Reason in Religion*)

Another world to live in. Lancaster Conference has surely been one of the most successful long-term Anabaptist experiments at creating and preserving a distinct small culture which is at least once removed from the regular world. It seems clear that the origins of Anabaptism contain this impulse to create another world to live in, as Santayana suggests, and seldom has any Anabaptist group better managed to concentrate their energies to create and control even a small corner of the world than in eastern Pennsylvania. The familiar rhetoric of opposition to the world is memorably stated in the Schleitheim Confession of 1527:

> Everything which is not united with our God and Christ cannot be other than an abomination which we should shun and flee from. By this is meant all Catholic and Protestant works and church services, meetings and church attendance, drinking houses, civic affairs, the oaths sworn in unbelief and other things of that kind, which are highly regarded by the world and yet are carried on in flat contradiction to the command of God, in accordance with all the unrighteousness which is in the world. (*The Schleitheim Confession* 2)

One way of thinking about Anabaptist history is as a long and often agonized argument about the terms outlined here. The radical dismissal of "everything which is not united with our God and Christ" has been the basis for much of our thought, if not always our practice. But as even other sections of the Schleitheim Confession acknowledge, large elements of the human world are bound to disagree with this view. Most Protestants and Catholics, not to mentions Jews and Muslims and Buddhists and Hindus and agnostics and atheists, still persist in thinking that they are not entirely abominable, whatever their sins. What is to be done with them? Must we understand them as fundamentally deluded, deprived of the truth revealed only to us? Can the gathered community only relate to "the world" on such rigidly dualistic terms?

By the early twentieth century, Ruth shows, the Lancaster answer was mainly twofold: on the one hand, strengthening visible marks of separation, especially dress codes; on the other, increasingly aggressive mission programs. While the Lancaster Mennonites were strengthening their dress codes, other American Mennonites were approaching the question of how to maintain identity amid assimilation quite differently. Some sought to live in the world without visible markers of separation, to maintain their communities with more porous boundaries.

There is no room here for a detailed historical analysis of all this, but let me offer one suggestive anecdote. Bluffton College was founded in 1899 by representatives of the General Conference Mennonite Church. Early in its history, Bluffton became a "mixed" institution, with a majority of non-Mennonite students and a looser connection to the church hierarchy than the Mennonite Church colleges. When I joined the faculty in 1984, roughly half of the faculty and less than twenty percent of the students were Mennonite, and in some quarters the opinion that Bluffton was not "really" a Mennonite college was commonplace. (I was somewhat reassured when a senior colleague at Hesston, upon learning that I'd accepted the job at Bluffton, assured me that Elmer Neufeld, the president, was "a true Mennonite.")

At my first faculty retreat, Margaret Weaver, a much-beloved Latin teacher at the local high school and the wife of a senior faculty member, was the guest speaker. She described listening to Garrison Keillor's radio show—itself something that at one time would have been forbidden as worldly. (As many readers know, Keillor often sings hymns with his "Hopeful Gospel Quartet" and tells stories about Minnesota Lutherans and a small sect he calls the "Sanctified Brethren," which sounds a good deal like some stray band of Anabaptists.)

Weaver described Keillor musing on the Shakespeare sonnet which begins "That time of year thou may'st in me behold" and ends with the couplet "This thou believ'st, which makes thy love more strong: / To love that well which thou must leave ere long." The phrase she repeated and reflected upon has stuck with me all this time: "Learning to love the world," she said—that's what education is all about. Learning to love the world and its creatures in their beauty, their confusion, their pain and heartache and their kindness and solidarity—each of them, we are told, made in the image of God.

How do we square this idea with that other idea of "the world" as an abomination we must shun and flee? Not easily. I myself believe judging the whole human world outside the tiny Anabaptist enclaves to be some kind of undifferentiated abomination seems absurdly, almost comically arrogant—though I would quickly add that distinguishing what is good from what is evil in the world seems crucial indeed.

Still, after living for almost twenty years in a situation where Mennonites form a significant but not numerically dominant part of a mainly functional community, I have become convinced that among the others, the English, the worldly, whatever we wish to call them, are many in whom the light of the Spirit shines bright, and that it is important to say so. If there were to be another Amish division today, I would stand with those who believe that the truehearted may indeed be saved, whether they keep the Ordnung or not.

Isn't it an easy target anyway, this "world"? I saw this on a billboard recently: "TV, Sports, Movies. The friend of the world is the enemy of God." There was a number to call for a complete explanation, but I didn't have time to write it down, and I suppose that I would just get into an argument if I called, anyway.

There are plenty of things in the world which are worth resisting, including much of what is associated with television, sports, and movies. And I realize that a billboard is hardly the place for nuanced analysis of media culture. But such proclamations seem terribly blunt instruments once one has spent enough time in the open world to find that, along with all the trash and evil, there is much that is beautiful and true and good there.

Many others in this generation of Mennonites have made a similar journey, which is not very accurately described by the standard term "assimilation." Artists and writers, among many others, have gone out into the world to study and learn, perhaps less compelled than earlier peers to make an either-or choice between their home community or complete assimilation. Often, Mennonite artists went off to find (as Di Brandt says) that what they had been told about the world was simply not true. "The rest of the world, for us, was *other*, but as I found out when I got there, it was not at all other in the way we had imagined, in the way we'd been told. Its otherness, I could see immediately, was not the otherness of people lounging indifferently on the road to hell, but consisted rather in a completely different set of terms, a different set of rules to live by" (Brandt 32-33).

With the partial breakdown of the separation between Mennonite communities and the rest of the world it has become easier for some artists to negotiate passage between, or to define their own places to exist. For example, Julia Kasdorf formally joined the Episcopalian church at nearly the same time as her book entitled *The Body and the Book: Writing from a Mennonite Life* appeared. The essays form a sometimes agonized and sometimes appreciative response to Mennonite culture—as one with roots in Big Valley, Pennsylvania, and a family tree full of Spichers and Peacheys, Kasdorf knows well the issues of boundaries and transgression that I have been tracing here.

I suspect, though, that the dualism of Anabaptist or "other" has always been exaggerated, that the choices have often been less simple than they may seem. Consider J. W. Yoder, like Kasdorf a Big Valley native and the author of *Rosanna of the Amish*. He got a good education, traveled widely, led singing schools, worked as a college administrator and recruiter, published both defenses of Amish ways and strong critiques of certain practices. Was he then "inside" or "outside" the Amish community? Both, and neither, surely. John Ruth himself, with his Harvard PhD and his return to the ancestral homestead in Lower Salford Township, with his career in film and video and his many books, has lived both a deeply traditional and a startlingly unconventional life. The same could be said, in one way or another, of Conrad Grebel and Menno Simons—in their efforts to be faithful to their tradition, they broke radically with some aspects of it. Even Jesus, surely, did so, both fulfilling the Law and revolutionizing its meaning for generations and millennia to come.

Many Mennonites today find that in the postmodern world "community" can and must be multiple, spread widely over space, maintained through various means of communication and travel. Since the advent of e-mail I keep in much closer touch with my scattered poet friends and family members than ten years ago—it is convenient and more or less free to hit reply, compose a few lines or whole paragraphs, perhaps throw in a poem or two if there's something new. It's much easier to send photos of the new cousins, as well, as my mother remarked when she forwarded the latest ones.

I have an Amish friend, a poet, whose e-mail address was given me by the editor of a magazine we both had published in. When I contacted him that way, he somewhat sheepishly replied that it was mainly for communicating with editors and that he expected to close the account soon. We are back to writing old-fashioned letters. It's fine. But I keep finding his letter, at the bottom of a stack of things, months after I meant to reply.

Traditionalists can talk at length of the costs of change, and this is no blanket celebration of whatever happens to be new. I would not surrender the community of memory that has sustained my own life, nor relinquish the dream and the charge of remaking the world in the image of God, which is surely our most important work. But I would insist that our current state of transformation is not necessarily cause for despair, and that indeed even to bemoan our departures from "tradition" requires choosing one particular set of traditions from a very diverse and complicated history. From the start there have been different versions of what it meant to be Anabaptist; there has never been a single practice to which everyone conformed. People have been doing it many ways since the beginning, and will continue.

Further Adventures in the World

Recently I found myself driving up Route 23 in my bright blue little car, listening to Van Morrison on my CD player. I was on my way to read my poems at a conference to a bunch of people who may or may not know who Mennonites are. Two of my friends who teach at another Mennonite institution were on their way as well—with not a plain coat or a covering among us.

As I drove north toward Ann Arbor it was like driving under an enormous roof as the clouds lowered and darkened. I watched it coming, then suddenly the big drops began whapping on the windshield and the brake lights came on in front of me as drivers slowed to deal with this sudden loosening of the heavens. And I drove on, past the U-haul trailers, past the yellow buses from Bedford Public Schools plodding slowly in the right lane. To the west the clouds were lighter and higher—this wouldn't last too long—but while it was here there was no escaping it. It was the world.

And we drove on, slower now, trailing behind us skirts of water pulled up by our tires, streamers that hung in the air like the tails of comets, like the clouds of glory that Wordsworth claimed we enter this life trailing. And the gray mini-van and the brown Trans Am and the black SUV and my bright blue Neon all pressed on toward the north, each vehicle bearing its human cargo toward some particular place, though I knew where none were going except myself, and had only instructions on a piece of paper describing my own destination.

I have been talking of "the world" in terms of *people* who are other, English, not Anabaptist. It seems just as important to consider the physical world, and the mistrust and worse with which Mennonites (and other Christians) often treat it. A naturalist told me recently of standing by an Amish farmer's mailbox chatting with the man when the two of them spotted a nest with some baby birds in the hedge nearby. Reaching for the birds, the farmer said something like "Now there's something that doesn't need to be," and crushed them with his bare hand.

I do not mean to slander either Amish or farmers by making too much of this incident. But is this what it means to be in the world but not of it? Who is closer to *Nachfolge*, do you think, that farmer or the speaker of this poem by Todd Davis?

> **Evensong**
> Near the gravel pit just below
> the crest of Norman Hill, two
> fox sprawl, end of day warmth
>
> rising from earth. Across the road,
> hay turned into windrows rings
> William's field, gold against green
>
> against gold. To the west, sun
> lowers itself down the ladder
> of the sky, as heavy clouds break
>
> to reveal burnished red of ash
> leaves, a fox's tail disappearing
> into the undergrowth. At this hour,
>
> what isn't prayer? (86)

I suspect the final question here is not one that many of those John Landises or those other Lancaster people whose names I can't keep straight would have asked. They might have not been surprised by the idea that faith is somehow incarnate in one's life, in the physical world, but they might have been more inclined to connect it with well-painted barns and straight rows of soybeans than with the apprehensions of beauty the poem offers.

The natural world also offers some intriguing analogies for social organization. There is the community of the cornfield—uniform, pragmatic, organized for maximum productivity and immediate yield. It will generate much useful product if the weather is right. But it requires care from the outside to maintain its purity; by itself, the corn can't crowd out all the weeds. It must be plowed, planted, fertilized, cultivated or treated with weed killers. It is unstable on its own—it wouldn't last a month, let alone a year, without attention and manipulation.

There is also the community of the climax forest. It is organized for stability through diversity. It incorporates a wide range of species, plant and animal. It yields many products which sustain its members' lives in both obvious and subtle ways. It changes constantly with the weather, the seasons, the relative success or failure of one species or another. But it is self-regulating, with feedback systems that restore balance and harmony when disruptions occur, and self-sustaining. Both cooperation and competition are part of the daily round of things.

My point here is almost embarrassingly obvious, but I will state it anyway. The climax forest, like most other natural ecosystems, tolerates and indeed requires diversity of many kinds. Unnatural systems like the cornfield simplify and industrialize natural systems for the sake of efficiency and production. They resist diversity and enforce conformity and uniformity. This may or may not be a good strategy for food production, but as a model for social organization its problems need not be labored.

Where Else Will We Live?

Donald Barthelme has it right, I think, when he writes, "Art thinks ever of the world, cannot not think of the world, could not turn its back on the world even if it wished to" (Barthelme 181). Even the most extravagant science fiction and fantasy novels, no matter how strange or distant their settings and characters, cannot not think of the world, just as the most rigorous Anabaptist cannot really live anywhere else, cannot avoid eating and breathing and drinking the stuff of the universe, cannot abandon the body except in death. Going one step further, Robert Bly suggests that making art, far from being a dangerous aberration, is a necessary function for a human being who aspires to a spiritual life: "What did Blake say?—'No person who is not an artist can be a Christian.' He means that a person who refuses to approach his own life actively, using language, music, sculpture, painting, or drawing is a caterpillar dressed in Christian clothes, not a human being" (Bly 43).

What if we have been crippling ourselves and our children all these years, in the name of safety and necessity and *Nachfolge*? What if the activities of art are indeed not only not antithetical to following Jesus, but essential? Those functions will not be denied, of course—if some of their modes are denied they come out in others: singing, quilting, gardening, *Fraktur*, even farming and conversation. But they can certainly be hindered, even crippled, and many who cannot bear to see that happen will flee the community that tries, taking from it their leavening presences.

Imagine if, for three hundred years, we had refused to allow our children to run. Walking is good enough, we told them—you'll get there eventually. Running is dangerous, you'll fall down and hurt yourself. If you can't get there walking, it's just too far away. Anyway, the rest of the world is just like it is around here, only more dangerous.

What happens, after three centuries of no running? Do those muscles atrophy? Does the desire for it disappear, and the knack for it as well? Do a few runners slip away through the fences and find others who run cheerfully and gaily? Where do they go? Will they come back and tell us of their travels? Could it be that, even now, we could follow them out beyond the gates? Could we open the gates and go just a little way down the path we see, faint but distinct? It follows the floor of the valley and then disappears into the trees.

A long time ago I wrote a poem, one of those that I never quite came to understand myself. As I worked on this essay, trying to understand why the dream of another world seems so powerful and so ambiguous, it came back to me.

Dream of the New Room

We have only this large, dull room, like a small-town hall
meant for 4-H clubs and oversized reunions, more space than
we'll ever need but barren, echoing, flat. There is no way outside. Who knows how we got here? Is anyone watching? No
sign.

Yet we plot escapes. We decide to hide a map in our genes. If
we can leave a sign, our children may find what else they
need.

And then, through some magic or will we open a door. Too
excited to breathe, we take our first steps into the new room,

not sure it will hold air, not sure it will even be real. Quiet paces into the darkness. *It seems to be here,* someone says. I walk toward what may be a window, say the word *home* in wonder, so dim I do not know the direction my yearning should take, taking comfort from this new room, that I can walk out into it, that it seems to be here.

I think now that we must seek out these new rooms, whether they appear in dreams or in visions or in the hills and valleys of the earth on which we have been given to live. We must not fear to walk out into them, placing our feet carefully, listening and watching and sniffing the air, talking to each other about what we think we have found. We must not try to keep these new spaces to ourselves, but must welcome all who wish to gather there with us. We must keep telling and retelling the old stories, and inventing new ones as well. We must remember that all of our stories, even the oldest, were once not stories at all—that they are memorials to the acts and dreams and wishes of living, breathing, flawed and contentious human beings who entered the world as did each of us, naked and wet and helpless,to be held and comforted and fed, tended and taught until they could take their own places in the only world we have, the world where we have been told that God is everywhere.

Works Cited

Barthelme, Donald. 2001-2003, Spring. "Not-Knowing." *The Georgia Review* 55.56.1: 170-83.

Bly, Robert. 1988. *A Little Book on the Human Shadow.* San Francisco: Harper & Row.

Brandt, Di. 1996. *Dancing Naked: Narrative Strategies for Writing Across Centuries.* Stratford, Ont.: Mercury Press.

Davis, Todd. 2002. "Evensong." *Ripe: Poems.* Huron, Ohio: Bottom Dog, 86. Used by permission, all rights reserved.

Kasdorf, Julia. 2001. *The Body and the Book: Writing from a Mennonite Life.* Baltimore: Johns Hopkins.

Ruth, John. 2001. *The Earth Is the Lord's: A Narrative History of the Lancaster Mennonite Conference.* Studies in Anabaptist and Mennonite History, vol. 39. Scottdale, Pa.: Herald Press.

———. 1978. *Mennonite Identity and Literary Art.* Scottdale, Pa.: Herald Press.

1527. "The Schleitheim Confession." Pamphlet reprinted from 1973, Yoder, John H., trans. and ed., *The Legacy of Michael Sattler.* Classics of the Radical Reformation, vol. 1. Scottdale, Pa.: Herald Press.

Chapter 5

Perspectives of an Outsider Looking In

Tony Campolo

What John Ruth did for me was to introduce me to the Anabaptist lifestyle and value system. This countercultural way of life, that takes the Sermon on the Mount seriously and sees it as a requisite for the here and now, was very different from the dispensationalist theology with which I was familiar. To me, the kingdom of God was the new heaven and the new earth that would be established following both the rapture and what my Scofield Bible said were the seven years of the tribulation. That is what I had learned from the teachings of John Darby, which the Scofield Bible subtly communicated through its extensive footnotes, and that was the basis for my worldview.

In those days, I viewed the world as a sinking ship and saw the task that lay before me and all other Christians simply to rescue as many of those souls threatened with drowning as possible. The church was the lifeboat which would bear us, the rescued souls, safely to our salvation, while the ship itself went under. Evangelism was the task of declaring to people that their only hope in this world was to make the decision that would prepare them for the next world. This world was *not* my home; I was just passing through. My treasures *were* laid up somewhere beyond the blue.

Social action programs seemed futile to me back then. If the world was doomed in the near future, it seemed to me that there was no point in addressing the socioeconomic problems. Why try to stop wars since it was clear that there would always be wars and rumors of war? Why try to end poverty, since the poor we would have with us always? For someone who thought as I did then, that this world was a sinking ship, all social action programs could be likened to the futility of re-arranging chairs on the decks of the sinking Titanic.

The Preacher from Conshohocken

Then along came John Ruth, this young preacher from a little Mennonite church in Conshohocken, Pennsylvania, who challenged all of that kind of thinking. John contended that something of the kingdom of God could be actualized in history. He dared to propose that the kingdom of God was even now being expressed in Christian community. This community of which he spoke was not by any means perfected, but was composed of people who had not resigned themselves to being less than what God wanted them to be. Its people were committed, not simply to individualistic sanctification, but to becoming a sanctified fellowship that would stand over and against the dominant culture, endeavoring to be God's showcase of what the whole world could become if people endeavored to live out the Sermon on the Mount.

Harvey Cox, in his book *The Secular City*, describes a fictional city called Nova Hutta, established by the Polish communists after World War II. There was to be decent housing for everyone, excellent schools for the children. Parks with trees and fountains were scattered through Nova Hutta. Full employment was provided for its citizens, and crime was nonexistent. Health services existed for everyone, and the elderly were cared for in ways that preserved their dignity. Insofar as it was possible, Nova Hutta was to be a perfect city.

Nova Hutta was created as a demonstration to the rest of Poland of what was in store for them when the nation was transformed according to the plans of the communist party. The city was a foretaste of the future. Far better than any speech or book, Nova Hutta was to declare the character of the world that was to be.

Of course, as we now know, Nova Hutta failed to live up to its proposed destiny, and Poland was not transformed into the utopian community that Nova Hutta was supposed to model. But the idea of Nova Hutta is what is important for our discussion here—the idea that a community set down in the present could reveal what the future holds in store for the rest of the world. Nova Hutta can be used as an analogy for the church in the Anabaptist theology of John Ruth. The purpose of the church is not simply to be a gathering of baptized believers who occasionally get together for worship. Instead, its purpose is to be a community of believers who live and work and play together. It is to be a people bound together in Christian love who are developing a societal system that incarnates what things will be like when the kingdom comes on earth as it already is in heaven. In such a community, people will be able to live out the radical Christianity outlined in the Sermon on the Mount.

In the thinking of the rest of the world, it is unrealistic for people, when hit on one cheek, to turn the other. It doesn't make much sense to go a second mile when you are already forced to go one. Giving your cloak to somebody, who has just stolen your coat, seems ludicrous. Returning good for evil does not appear to those outside the Christian community to be a smart way to live.

Anyone attempting as an individual to live out these directives of Jesus is doomed to failure. They are far too difficult to be followed in the context of a society that is basically governed by a philosophy of Social Darwinism. But in Christian community such seemingly extreme behavior becomes possible. The community reinforces the values and requisites necessary for discipleship. There is, within community, a revitalization of commitment to the radical lifestyle set forth by Jesus.

It would be a mistake to think that the Anabaptist community intends for Christians to write off the rest of the world as hopelessly lost. The Amish may be world-rejecting, but the Mennonite way of life as espoused by John Ruth embraced a world that God loves and which God sent Jesus to save. The purpose of this Christian community is not only to be a living sign of that kingdom of God, which will one day be realized at the *eschaton*, but also to be an instrument through which God declares that kingdom to the rest of the world. The community is a means for carrying out Christ's challenge to evangelize all the peoples of the earth. When the good news is declared that the kingdom of God is at hand, Christians should be able to point to their community and say, "Look! Here is a foretaste of what is to come. See how we care for each other, meet each others needs, enjoy each other, work together and worship together." To the rest of the world, the Christian community should be saying, "Our way of life should give you some idea of what is to come when Christ returns and fulfills his promise to establish 'The Peaceable Kingdom.'"

We do not offer much, if we say to the rest of the world that Christianity is the best hope for this world, but offer only an abstract concept of that hope. The community of faithful Christians, called the church, is supposed to be a concrete expression of what we mean. Church is not simply a gathering within a community; it is the community itself. Church is all that Christians do with each other as they endeavor to realize God's will for their lives.

It must be understood that Anabaptists who are committed to Christian community do not claim that they have attained the perfection that will come when the rule of God in society is fully actualized, but they do claim to be "pressing toward the mark of the high calling of God in Christ Jesus." The community always sees itself in process, and it invites the rest of the world to join in its journey toward the ultimate realization of the kingdom of God. For the salvation is both a present reality (though incomplete) and a future hope—when it will be what it is even now striving to become.

To outsiders, the most notable characteristic of this counter-cultural community is its commitment to nonviolence. The Anabaptists take at face value the words of Scripture that tell us such things as—

"Blessed are the peacemakers, for they shall be called the children of God."

"Those who live by the sword, will die by the sword."

"Love your enemies, be good to those who would harm you."

"If your enemy hungers, feed him. If he is naked, clothe him."

We live at a time when the whole world is desperately in need of the Anabaptist call to nonviolence. Presently, there are those in high places in America's government who have been deceived into thinking that it is possible to end terrorism by killing all the terrorists. They fail to see the obvious reality, that for every terrorist who is killed, more will rise up to take his or her place. The violent repression of terrorists who contend that they are struggling for justice will not succeed. Those who believe in their cause will view the violent repression at the hands of those who are viewed as oppressors, as further evidence of their need to rise up and destroy their enemies.

The Israelis certainly have failed to learn this lesson. As they struggle against their dragon, the Palestinians, as Frederick Nietsczhe might say, they themselves are in danger of becoming a dragon. Their attempts to quash the terrorists who threaten their lives have not only made suicide bombers into heroes in the eyes of their enemies, but have generated more hatred which, in turn, gives rise to more terrorists. The Israelis have lost the moral high ground that they once possessed as the suffering servants of God, and have become terrorists themselves. What is needed is for them to listen to the voice crying in the wilderness that tells them to beat their swords into plowshares and to learn war no more.

Is there a peace brigade that will march into the West Bank, stand between the two warring factions and say, "In the name of God, stop!?" Is there a people who will say, as their Master once did, "Put up the sword!" Are there Christians who will risk their lives to stand between the warring parties and act as a buffer between those who would do violence against one another? If such a peace brigade ever does arise, I believe that there will be Anabaptists among them.

Our own United States of America, the only remaining superpower in the world today, has come to trust in its power instead of in God. We may put "In God We Trust" on our coins, but we trust in our war chariots instead. Not learning from the tragedies of history, we seem hell bent on repeating them. We go on using our power to try to solve our problems with terrorists, even when we know that such policies are not working. We think we can bring down Castro via an embargo, when 40 years of trying to bring down that dictator has only left him more firmly in control of Cuba than when he started. Because of the embargo, children in that country are denied medicine, hospitals lack desperately needed supplies, and the economy of Cuba leaves many in needy straits. And all that has been accomplish is the rising of a growing resentment against America among the Cuban people.

Having learned nothing from the failure of the embargo to bring down Castro, we employed the same strategy to deal with Saddam Hussein. The embargo we put in place to bring down that tyrant only raised his status in Iraq, as well as throughout the Arab world. His ability to defy America gave his shaky regime the flying buttress that he needed to keep it from falling down.

According to special ambassadors from the United Nations assigned to deal with Iraq, the only casualties of the embargo are a half million dead children. Literally, tens of thousands are daily on the verge of starvation and still the beat of threatening war drums goes on.

What would happen if America suddenly declared repentance and followed the biblical admonitions to do good to our enemies, to feed them in their hunger, to clothe them in their nakedness, to minister to them in their sickness? Could returning good for evil actually have brought coals of fire down on Saddam Hussein's head, as the Bible says? Might it have undermined his arrogance and eroded his popularity with a people who, incredibly, were victims of his militaristic power plays? What if we established such good trade relations with Iraq that their well-being was tied up with ours? Could not such Christian action change the political landscape, not only in the Middle East, but throughout the rest of the world? Anabaptists, at their best, would say, "Let's give it try."

In glorifying the Anabaptist community, I do not want to suggest that there is unanimity of opinion among its people. There are many among them who seriously question the principles of nonviolence in dealing with America's enemies. Generally, they are older, wealthier types. It has been said that those who become military oriented conservatives tend to be people who have a lot to conserve. Economic prosperity has a way of changing political ideologies, and a great number of those older, hard working Mennonites have greatly prospered.

What is fascinating is that the Anabaptist nonviolent philosophy seems strongest among the young in the Mennonite community. It is usually the young who abandon the religious traditions of the past, but with the Mennonites, those who have taken the strongest hold of the tradition of nonviolence have been the young. In my own experience, being a part of several Mennonite Youth Conventions has been truly inspiring. To see thousands of young people reaffirm a commitment to the countercultural principles of Christianity, even as many of their parents and grandparents are beginning to question them, excites me.

A Rampant Concern for the Poor

Another theme that runs rampant through the Mennonite community is a concern for the poor. There are over two thousand verses of Scripture that call upon the followers of Jesus to reach out to those who are needy. Yet many believers in the Bible seem to pass over them. I do not know how the rest of us in Christendom have so often failed to see that caring for the poor is a primary emphasis of the Bible.

The God of the Judeo-Christian tradition has always shown a preference for the poor, but somehow many of us have missed it. In Genesis we read how out of all the people on the earth, Yahweh chose an impoverished enslaved people who cried out in their despair, championed their cause, and led them from their poverty into a land flowing with milk and honey. When settled in the Promised Land there emerged some in Israel who became rich and powerful, and exploited the poor and weak. Over and against such exploitation, Yahweh sent prophets to decry injustice and call for repentance.

When the ultimate prophet, Jesus of Nazareth, came to proclaim his kingdom, he announced that his regime would be marked by good news to the poor and healing for the brokenhearted. Despite such a clear mandate to help the poor, too many churches have accumulated great wealth for themselves and shared relatively little of it to alleviate the hunger of the world. We Christians spend billions of dollars to build huge edifices to honor one who said, "I dwell not in temples made with hands."

To the true Anabaptists, the calling has always been to live simply, so that others might simply live. They know that if Jesus had a choice between stained glass windows and feeding hungry children in Haiti, he would choose to feed the hungry children.

The only description that Jesus gives of judgment day is one in which we will be judged in terms of what we did for those whom he called "the least of these." If we fed them, he said, then we fed him; if we clothed them, then we clothed him; and if we ministered to them when they were sick, then we ministered to him.

A sacrificial commitment to the poor fostered an array of social services by Mennonite agencies. The Mennonite Central Committee is a key example of such efforts to reach out to those who suffer privation. Young people regularly volunteer to give years of their lives to work among the poor in Third World countries, in Appalachia and in urban America. Whenever a disaster, like an earthquake or a hurricane brings massive destruction, the Mennonite Disaster Service is able to mobilize its people almost overnight, to respond with immediacy and efficiency.

The emphasis on community can be witnessed in all of Anabaptist mission work. In response to a desperate need to help the poor in Haiti, the poorest country in the Western Hemisphere, a group of Mennonites founded an array of literacy centers on the Isle de la Gonâve. These programs were developed to serve the poorest of the poor, who had little chance of escaping their oppressed condition unless they could learn how to read and write. Such people are generally exploited by government officials, because they cannot read enough to learn of their rights. They are often cheated when they go to market because they do not know how to count. "Worst of all," as one woman said, "I did not feel like I was a human being who was worth anything before I could read or write."

But these literacy centers have become more than just places where people learn the "3 Rs." They are also places where community building is going on. In the process of learning, the students converse with each other, lead discussions, tell their life stories, and share their personal convictions. They get to know each other in depth and develop intensive friendships. In the end sometimes community building becomes even more important than literacy training.

Finally, in the Anabaptist tradition, there is the matter of foot washing. When John Ruth first told me about it, it struck me as strange. The idea that along with the celebration of the Lord's Supper, Mennonites wash one another's feet was even somewhat repulsive to me. I could not figure out the point of it, and I could only think of it as a practice that belonged to another place and another time.

In ancient Israel, when travelers walked dusty dirt roads with their feet clad in sandals, the washing of feet at the end of the journey made some sense, but I didn't see that it had any place in our modern world. John was not offended by my questioning, and went on to explain that foot washing, along with baptism and Holy Communion, was an ordinance given by Jesus. He pointed out from Scripture that, if for no other reason than obedience to Jesus, foot washing was a practice that ought to be observed. That fact alone might have made his case, but John had more to say about foot washing. "It helps to sustain the community," I remember him telling me. "When there are hard feelings between Christian brothers, getting them to wash one another's feet is a way of bringing them together." He went on to tell me how, as a boy, he had seen men who had been angry with each other break down in tears and be reconciled as a result of having gotten down on their knees in front of each other and going through this humbling practice. Foot washing, John explained, broke down the pride and haughtiness that hinders the building of community. He contended that it had a wholesome leveling effect on the body of believers, so that no one would think that he or she was better than the others. On a pragmatic level, John saw foot washing as a major contributor to the building of the church community.

Years later, as I reflect back on my many learning experiences with John Ruth, I see how important community is to the whole Anabaptist lifestyle. Anyone trying to live out the directives that lie at the core of John's Mennonite Christianity will find herself or himself at serious odds with the dominant culture. Only with the support of a Christian community can such a lifestyle of nonviolence, loving one's enemies, sacrificial giving to the poor, and materialistic simplicity be sustained. This is true especially in the context of a society that believes that the powerful control of others, especially one's enemies, is the only basis for security, and that egoistic self aggrandizement via the accumulation of consumer goods is the *raison d'etre* for human labor.

Sociologists Peter L. Berger and Thomas Luckmann, in their book, *The Social Construction of Reality*, write that for anyone to maintain a set of counter-cultural convictions against a society that deems them erroneous, there must be what they call a "plausibility structure." They are referring to a group within the larger societal system wherein the individual can regularly revitalize his or her countercultural convictions and gain assurance that he or she is not crazy. Rather it is the dominant society that has not embraced the believers' practices and values that is crazy.

An individual may leave the countercultural group from time to time, according to Berger and Luckmann, but it is essential that such ventures be followed by renewal experiences that can only be had by returning to the community. An ongoing separation from the group will result in the group's beliefs and folkways becoming increasingly unrealistic and even foolish to the separated individual.

For those who would be Christian, this revitalization via community requires what some theologians have called "the gathered/scattered motif." Simply stated, it means that to live out the radical requisites of Jesus, individual Christians must gather to remind each other of the validity of what they believe and to recommit themselves to their beliefs and to each other. This sharing of kindred minds and hearts can create what one sociologist, Herman Schmollenbach, says is a shared ecstasy in community which he labels "communion." In such ecstatic renewal, individual Christians are prepared once again to go into all the world with their gospel about the kingdom of God.

Christians can be in the world, but not of it, for only so long. As the world around them increasingly exercises its seductive influences, they soon will find that their spiritual survival requires a return to the group. In accord with Scripture, they must "neglect not the assembling of themselves together." Only in the gathered community will there be the kind of plausibility structure that affirms their identities as Christians and gives them new strength for their convictions. Jesus becomes powerfully real in the context of Christian community. In community, there is validation of the words of Jesus who said, "Wherever two or three are gathered together in my name, there am I in the midst of them."

In today's world, many delude themselves into thinking that community is not needed to maintain Christian life and practice. This kind of thinking is not only bad sociology, but it is also bad spirituality. Recently there have been some who have speculated about the creation of the "cyber-church." These people contend that the Internet can enable Christians to link up with messages about God's Word without ever having to go through the trouble of going to a real church, and that fellowship in chat rooms can be a substitute for face-to-face intimacy with a fellowship of like-minded Christians. Those in the Anabaptist tradition could say "no" to such talk, not because they are anti-technological, but because they believe something mystical that comes from God happens in the context of the Christian community.

To pick up the original theme of this chapter, I have come to believe that God is at work in our world, rescuing it from its fallen condition and restoring it to what it was meant to be when it was created. I have come to understand that both the present and the coming kingdom of God promotes a lifestyle and practice that contradict much of what our power-oriented materialistic society is all about. And, I have come to know that this lifestyle and these practices can be sustained and propagated through the medium of Christian community. Therefore, any group of people who seek God's kingdom with all of its justice and well-being had better stand upon what Anabaptists have been trying to be and do since the days of Menno Simons.

Social action programs without community will not bring in the kingdom. For those of us who seek the kingdom of God, it is the community that gives the assurance that the one who has begun in us the good work of building the kingdom, will complete it on the day of his coming.

Within community the conviction of an impending *eschaton* wherein the kingdoms of this world become the kingdom of our God stays alive. The rest of the world may be doomed to cynicism, but the people of God, bound together in Christian love, shout back at those who are cynical, "Maranatha!"

Chapter 6

Peace Is in the Details: No Story Is Too Small

Elizabeth Morgan

When I was a 1960s Eastern College student, John Ruth taught me to love stories and work for peace. So I submit for him, and as a testimony to his gentle suasion, the following address, given May 2002 at the Brandywine Forum and sponsored by the Center for Global Engagement, housed at Eastern University. The conference participants were to look at aspects of peacemaking through the lens of the parable of the Prodigal Son.

Sometimes I feel like the luckiest woman in the world. My field being literary studies, I get paid for reading and talking about stories, every day. So although I am not a theologian or trained peacemaker, I feel at home in a conference that focuses on a highly provocative story told by one of the best storytellers who ever lived.

My students and I talk a great deal about the difference between "statement" and "story," both language acts that can be true or false, past or present. Usually students settle on the idea that a statement is linear, delivering information to an audience that can receive it passively or disinterestedly, while a story is indirect (Emily Dickinson would say "slant") and thus demands the engagement of the audience to discern meaning. The hearer/reader has to play the game the story sets up. And often the game entails entering the negative space of the tale—filling in the gaps strategically left by the storyteller for just that end.

It is interesting that Jesus often told stories at a point when his audience, students of the Law with their yellow legal pads poised for use, was asking for statements. When a young lawyer asks him what he must do to be saved, Jesus tells him that, among other things he is to love his neighbor as himself, eliciting a more exact question, "And who is my neighbor?" Rather than giving a straight definition Jesus tells the all too familiar story of the Good Samaritan. And one can imagine the poor young attorney choking over the answer he is expected to give. To call a Samaritan—a *Samaritan*—good would mean surrendering one of his mostly deeply entrenched racial prejudices. Notice that the young man can only say "The one who showed him kindness," and we imagine him walking away puzzled by what he has just admitted. This would be comparable to telling a group of contemporary Israelis the story of the "good" Palestinian, or Palestinians in the Jenin refugee camp the story of the "good" Israeli. Stories have the power to make us see and engage the world as a richly complicated place, partly because they catch us off guard.

My interest in post-colonial women's novels springs from just that reality. I want to know the detailed and wonderfully complex lives of persons in the developing world, not just statistics, profiles, and strategies for their advancement. Novels let me in; they take me places I could never have found on my own. I'm not alone in this desire for intimacy. In *Poetic Justice: The Literary Imagination and Public Life*, development ethicist Martha Nussbaum relates our need for moral imagination to the reading of novels. While working on "quality of life" assessment at the World Institute for Development Economics Research in Helsinki, she and global economist Amartya Sen used Charles Dicken's *Hard Times* to ground their critique of standard paradigms of assessment—to expose the reductionism of such paradigms and their failure to address human complexity. This "baggy monster" of a novel kept the complicated lives of the poor and causes of poverty front and center for them. Thus Nussbaum is willing to argue that one of the best ways to keep economics from becoming a "dismal science" is for students of economics to seek a "more complicated and philosophically adequate set of foundations" through reading novels (Nussbaum 8)!

She is not suggesting that novels replace political documents or economic analyses, but she is saying that political and economic treatises would be perfectly consistent with their goals if the view of human beings underlying them was that supplied by novels. "Government cannot investigate the life story of every citizen in the way a novel does with its characters; it can, however, know that each citizen has a complex history of this sort" (Nussbaum 44).

The parable of the Prodigal Son is a story that makes richer use of negative space and complex moral engagement than almost any I know. As hearers we cannot *not* play with the details—those present *and those missing*. Where is the mother in all of this? Was there a younger brother, ready to follow the prodigal on his "great adventure" and get away from the sullen older brother? Was there a sister who had her own thoughts about inheritance customs of the time? What was it like at the dinner table in those days *after* the son received his legacy but *before* he left home (the Luke account)? What did the neighbors think when the well-to-do father ran out to great his tattered guest, a job for the servants or women of the household, if anyone? What exactly *did* the prodigal do while away from home? We know the older brother's speculations, but can we trust him? In short, the story must become ours through an active hermeneutical process, one where we enter the messiness of the scenario, dragging all of our own messiness and troubled relationships with us, and work both with what we find and what we imagine, *all* of which is swept up in the father's loving reconciling arms.

I have entitled this narrative "Peace Is in the Details: No Story Is Too Small" because I believe that big actions can only survive when there has been sufficient groundwork, and that groundwork can take place anywhere anytime the spirit of God is allowed to shed light on the struggles, large and small, of our lives, and when we are willing to engage the complications of those struggles. I will begin with a personal story, follow with a set of cultural stories, and end with a modest global imagining.

CAIT'S DEATH

I cannot remember when I was not against the death penalty—for the usual reasons: there are too many mistakes for such a "permanent solution;" there are too many racial, IQ, and class inequities; there is no conclusive evidence that the death penalty deters violent crime and a good bit of evidence that it *is* violent crime, especially in states where the electric chair is still in use. Plus, for me, it seems to contradict the gospel call for forgiveness and truncate the possibility of transformation. I've never been able to forget a story I heard on public radio told by a man named "Race Horse" who, having been evangelized by no one, found himself in the worst conditions of solitary confinement—"the hole"—in a Southern prison. It was dark, they had taken his clothes, he was defenseless. Inexplicably, and quite suddenly, he was caught up in the assurance that God loved him, and his life was never the same.

Well, all of these fine sentiments were royally tested five years ago when my niece, a dear young woman with whom I shared many traits and ideas was brutally murdered, along with two young coworkers, in a Starbucks Coffee shop in the upscale Georgetown community of Washington, D.C. It was the end of a fourth of July weekend; there was an accumulation of money in the safe. Cait was the manager in charge of clean up. An assailant with two firearms entered the coffee shop and killed all three young persons without taking a penny. Obviously something untoward happened in there. Cait died from three gun shot wounds to the head and chest with the keys to the safe clutched in her hand. She was quite capable of refusing to give them up. It is also possible that Emory Evans, a young black man working at Starbucks to raise the money to enter Howard University as a music major, was upstairs when the "robbery" began and, sneaking down, attacked the assailant from behind, setting off a torrent of reactive gunfire.

The Starbucks manual expressly tells employees *not* to use heroic measures in the face of crime; certain young people will ever be brave. To no avail, in this case: All three had "bled out" by morning and were removed in those ubiquitous body bags that make the news with maddening frequency. Because it was Georgetown, because there were three victims, the news clips of the removal played over and over again.

The search for the assailant went on for a year and a half. The FBI became involved because the prime suspect had committed several violent crimes, killing one security guard and wounding a Prince George County police officer, and because he was involved in cross state drug running. D.C. does not have the death penalty; the feds do. Janet Reno called for the death penalty and we had to face facts: We were a divided family. My mother, sister, and I stood firmly against capital punishment; others were less sure. Luckily Carl Cooper, the assailant, took a plea bargain, and confessed to enough crime to get him life in prison without parole. But all of this helped clarify my own thoughts.

What do people *hope* to glean from execution? Closure? Some books cannot be closed. Cait's could not. The arrest brought great relief, but we don't want closure on her life or even her death, for the *way* she died tells us a great deal about the world we live in and the kind of work that needs to be done to make all of our neighborhoods safer places to live.

Justice? What was done to Cait and Emory and Aaron was grossly unjust. Killing Carl Cooper would not take that away. Killing everyone on death row would not take that away. It is an affront that will remain on the record until all injustice is wiped away by divine intervention. There are some injustices that human law cannot reconcile—and ought not to try.

Peace? If we had waited until Carl Cooper's trial and ultimate execution for our peace, we would be troubled people indeed. In such a rending of life and family, peace needs to be immanent, continually sought, recognized in small acts. Peace is in the details. For my niece, Molly, Cait's older sister and a shock and trauma nurse, who well knows what bullet-riddled bodies look like, peace came through an undertaker who cut a small oval out of a sheet and let her look at the side of Cait's face that was at rest, quiet. For my nephew it was being able to give the eulogy for his little sister. For me, it was planning the service, filled with poetry and Scripture that had meant much to me. For all of us it was the memorial service itself when during the final hymn, "Amazing Grace," people spontaneously moved into the aisles so that they could hold one another . . . and hold on. Witnessing Carl Cooper's execution would have been cold comfort, indeed, compared with these details.

In February this year, I received a letter from my sister in which she was reflecting on the memorial service for Cait. She said: "I can only think on it with pleasure: turning destructive hate/venom into love and forgiveness, good memories of this essentially good child. There's no doubt that I think Carl Cooper—having admitted to at least five murders—should be imprisoned. I have no idea how to redeem him, to correct his hurts and terrible passions, nor do I have much hope for that—though I think about it, may try to visit him someday. He's not an idiot." Peace is in the details of a life that refuses to give up on life.

El Salvador: Portraits in a Revolution

On a broader scale, I have found the same persistent, transformative reverence for life to be present in refugees from war-torn El Salvador. In 1984 my church voted to become a Sanctuary Church, granting asylum to political refugees from this beleaguered Central American country at a time when the U.S. government was reluctant to do so. (Subsequent findings by a UN Truth Commission have brought about much warranted apologies from our State Department.) Working with refugees here made us aware of refugees *there*, inside El Salvador and in surrounding countries. Eventually, having heard many stories of peasants chased off of their land in the interest of creating a "free fire" zone, I helped to put together a book of these stories, particularly the wonderful tale of their insistence on being permitted to return to their homes before the war was over *to wage peace.* One group of refugees from a UN refugee camp in Honduras, actually *walked* home to northern El Salvador when the government and UN officials refused them transport (the former because they didn't want farmers in the way of the war, the latter because they feared for their safety).

But it is my opinion that these refugees had been waging peace the entire seven years they lived behind barbed wire in camps—they were waging peace in the details of their lives. When they entered the camp of Colomoncagua their literacy rate was 15 percent. When they left it was 85 percent. Those who had first grade taught those who had no schooling. Those who had second grade taught those with first grade. They knew that building peace would require being able to read documents and newspapers. Courses in accounting and business administration were given by the few folks who had those skills. They engaged in technical training as well, setting up workshops with the help of international assistance in shoemaking, leatherwork, chicken farming, hammock weaving, machine repair and other crafts that could be turned into lucrative mini-factories when they returned home.

Members of communities stayed together in the camps, so that when they returned to El Salvador, the community organizing they had developed would not be lost. They planted cooperative gardens and ate in collective kitchens because there weren't enough kitchen utensils for each family. Every detail of their daily existence was a preparation for times of peace at home. One woman had buried her corn grinding stone under a particular tree in the northern province of Chalatenango, knowing that she could return to that exact spot after repatriation and pick up her daily routine. That hope kept her going for seven long years in exile.

More than all of these practicalities, they wrote songs and kept music alive. They compiled the stories of their exile into song sequences and told stories from the Old and New Testaments, seeking parallels to their own stories. Rufina Amaya, who spent years as a refugee in Honduras, was the sole survivor of the El Mozote Massacre of 1981, where 800 evangelicals were murdered out of a suspicion that they were supporting forces in opposition to the government. There was never any clear evidence of their complicity with the FMLN; in fact, as Protestant evangelicals, they were most likely apolitical in the national struggle. Rufina's whole family was murdered in the massacre, while she hid out of sight under a tree, vowing to stay alive so that someone could tell the story.

And tell the story she did, over and over again for more than ten years, at the Colomoncagua refugee camp and after her return to Morazon Province in El Salvador. She told it with excruciating detail, sparing herself none of the pain of remembering, so that her memory might inspire public recognition. Neither the Salvadoran government nor the U.S. State Department was willing to acknowledge her claims. Finally, after peace accords were signed in 1992, a team of forensic anthropologists went to the scene and validated her account, bringing clarity and restitution. (Mark Danner's work *The Massacre at El Mozote*, published first in the New Yorker, 1993, and later as a book by Vintage, 1994, gives the clearest account of Rufina's steadfast witness.) The last time I saw Rufina, she was living in a small house in the city of Segundo Montes, working the land and functioning as a local church organizer.

She lives in Segundo Montes because a Jesuit priest named Segundo Montes believed in what the peasants from Morazon were doing in the refugee camps in Honduras. He visited them often, talking about their past, present, and future. He told them not to let others do their planning for them but to take charge of their own destinies. He was not a famous man... until he too was murdered by the Salvadoran army along with five of his Jesuit brothers, but even then he remained in people's memories an ordinary man, a man who loved economic theory and who loved peasant people. His fame ultimately was in the details of *their* lives. For on the day of his funeral in November, 1989, they found the courage to walk home to El Salvador to name their repatriated village after him and to begin the search for a sustainable peace.

I was in El Salvador the day in 1992 that the peace accords between the government and the FMLN were signed, with a group of women from Eastern Baptist Theological Seminary interested in the role of women in the Salvadoran church. What a bonus for that delegation, planned months before the hope of a signed treaty! Flags that had been kept under wraps for a decade were on wild display. People stood side by side who had been enemies two days before. At one point, Beethoven's "Ode to Joy" was played over the loud speaker (did you know it had Spanish lyrics?) and all joined hands and sang. A short moment in time, but profound. After the negotiated peace, development projects proliferated. In the Lower Lempa region, several communities, most of them ex-FMLN, met as a group to discuss agricultural plans. One *campesino* from a settlement "across the road" came and introduced himself as an ex-military combatant. "We both have the same problems," he said, "and you've had help getting organized that we didn't have. Can we join?" The answer was a solid "yes"—one word that carried a weight of portent.

One of the most powerful stories of the "return," however, may be much smaller in scope. As recorded by Linda Crockett in *The Other Side Magazine* (May and June, 2002), an old woman trying to avoid entering a refugee camp in the worst years of the war had been taken prisoner by the military government and tortured. A bag of lime dust was placed over her head; she was sexually tormented and humiliated. Eventually she was returned to her community a madwoman: guilty for false confessions given under duress, incoherent, hopelessly angry, spiritually lost. The members of the village healed her; there's no other word to put on what they accomplished as they listened to her, absorbed her anger, held her, rocked her like a baby.

As Crockett explains, "Here was a community of poor peasants who acted on their deep faith in a God of healing to accomplish what highly trained professionals often cannot—healing severely traumatized torture victims." Peace, healing, shalom is indeed in the details, when ordinary people believe in the power of transformation and do extraordinary things.

Can Peace Go Global?

But all of this was in 1992. What of now? With the Middle East in tatters, is there any evidence that peace can still be found "in the details"? If I may be so bold, I think there is far more chance of finding it there than in the official negotiations and global summits of strutting world "leaders," although I continue to believe in such gatherings. One day as I was driving to Eastern College in my pudgy little Toyota Tercel I heard a broadcast featuring two psychiatrists communicating by phone, one from the University of Tel Aviv (obviously Israeli) and the other from a Palestinian study center in the U.S. They were analyzing the psyche of suicide bombers *and regularly finishing each other's sentences.* When the show's host pointed this out to them, they laughed and said how good it had been to "meet" one another. On the sixteenth page of the *New York Times* of April 7, 2002, was a photo of nearly 10,000 Israelis rallying at the offices of the Israeli Defense Minister, to call for a withdrawal of Israeli forces from the West Bank and for *peace* talks. *Ten thousand Israelis?* What is this "minor" news story about?

Amos Oz, a well-known Israeli liberal academic, has been calling regularly for withdrawal of Israeli forces from occupied territories. But what were we to think when the relatively unknown Ishai Menuchin, major in the Israel Defense Forces reserves and chairman of Yesh Gvul, the soldier's movement for selective refusal (tell me you had heard of them!), wrote in the *New York Times* (March 9, 2002), "We can show our fellow citizens that occupation of the territories is not just a political or strategic matter. It is also a moral matter. We can show them an alternative—they can say no to occupation. When we begin to see Israel's situation in that light, perhaps we will be able to let go of our fear enough to find a way forward." Peace is in the words of an unknown resistor, an unknown soldier.

But lest this seem a recipe for Jewish enlightenment, assuming perhaps that the Muslims are beyond light, let me bring to your attention the observations of Marianne Pearl, whose journalist husband Daniel Pearl was brutally murdered by Muslim extremists in March 2002. She continued in Pakistan after the murder to assess the mood of the Muslim community, and received many sympathetic communications, including the following: "May God give you strength. Danny's murderers are not Muslims and must be brought to justice." "I am really saddened by the news and astonished that a Pakistani brother can do this" (*New York Times*, April 19, 2002). We will never know the names and fates of the persons who wrote these letters, but their impact is cumulative.

And let me remind you of the activities of the "Women in Black" a group of Israeli *and Palestinian* women, who for *years*, have stood vigil on Friday afternoons to protest Israeli occupation of the West Bank and

Gaza. This so impressed Catholic and Protestant women of Northern Ireland at a 1991 conference on "Women and International Conflict," organized by the Association for Women in Development (AWID), that they talked about jointly and publicly attending funerals of "all victims of 'random assassination.'" One could argue that these "events" have had little effect on the crises, either in Northern Ireland or the Middle East, but who knows what reconciliation may grow out of these mustard seeds and what these everyday connections have done to transform the lives of individuals living in unlivable situations.

Which brings me to my final, and broadest question—what good can any of this activity, inspiring as it is, do us if the details don't "add up," if no one is "connecting the dots"? Let me give a secular and a theological response, hoping that they do not stay in separate camps.

In a book entitled *Empire* (Harvard University Press, 2000), touted by a number of sources as the next great idea since "deconstruction" (take "great" here to mean big, inclusive), Michael Hardt of the Literature Program at Duke University and Antonio Negri from Rebibbia Prison, Rome, Italy, argue that the antiglobalization forces that have been making such a splash at World Bank, IMF, and WTO gatherings are really pockets of "resistant" globalization. Their argument goes like this: Believing that alternatives to global takeover (whether by Pepsi Cola or a first world military force) are possible, opposition movements become integral parts of a cross-cultural democratic society, and because they have access to the same computer technology that makes it possible for Pepsi Cola to know what is happening in their plants all over the world, they can remain aware of opposition movements of a variety of types in many places. And by "linking up," these localized oppositions can become global resistance to multinational exploitation.

Hardt and Negri are not talking about anarchists here, but about environmental, labor, child advocacy, and other movements asking hard questions about multinational commerce. They call this an "alternative globalization movement," generated by, of all things, the power of love (their word choice).

Their speculation, and they admit it is idealistic, is that by breaking "down the walls that surround the local (and thereby separate the concept from race, religion, ethnicity, nation, and people), one can link it directly to the universal" (Hardt, Negri 362), not in such a way that local difference is obscured, but that it is valued both for its specificity and its connectivity. Case in point: Students in North American universities became aware that their sweatshirts (via Reebok and Nike) were being produced in Mexmode, an assembly factory or *macquiladora*, in Mexico, where the workers not only received low wages and verbal abuse, but were, in some cases, fired for protesting against worms in the food of the company cafeteria. Enraged students and administrators brought international awareness to the case, and Mexmode, through Nike, made changes. Single mothers at the factory, with little education and no prior work experience have received two raises in the last year and been allowed to form a union. Cafeteria food appears to be safe. Child laborers have been removed from assembly lines.

The colleagues in this movement have not seen each other. But they know all about each other, via the same methods of communication that feed any global "trade." And the networking has just begun. As Juarez Nunez, a labor expert at the Autonomous University of Puebla, Mexico, predicts, "Companies are going to be required to do more than abide by weak regional laws. Their codes of conduct must set global standards that treat workers as world citizens, and guarantee them certain levels of dignity and respect" (*New York Times*, October, 8, 2001).

What's a sweatshirt but a college "detail," a little something picked up for a back-home cousin or Saturday mornings in the gym? In this case, however, it became a whole educational process, a *cause celebre*, linking labor with consumer through media access and mutual concern.

What might happen when all of these details collect, when the dots are connected? When a mother in Ireland hears about a mother in Israel? When laborers in Mexico partner with students in Boston? When an FMLN farmer meets an ex-combatant farmer? When two victims' families correspond through "Murder Victims' Families for Reconciliation," an anti-death penalty support group? Hardt and Negri call this dynamic "an accumulation of struggles" (Hardt, Negri 263). As believers, we might say that liberating ideas, like great blooming trees, grow out of faithful mustard seeds.

Jesus knew well that healing—shalom—was in the details. While he could have healed whole soccer fields full of disease-ridden and unhappy persons, making a wonderful splash in the public eye, he instead moved from sweaty sick bed to sweaty sick bed, from suffering individual to suffering individual—one at a time—healing obscure persons with little means to contribute to his cause. And, in some cases, he seemed to want everyone else to know the details as well. When the woman with the eighteen year hemorrhage came to him, hoping to steal a little bit of power and slip out the back of the crowd, he called her forward and asked her to tell her story to the assembly, as humiliating as that story must have been to her. Why? Was this questionable voyeurism, or an acknowledgement that the details of the case matter? She had lived them. Did she need to put them "out there," to make them as much a part of her current story as the miraculous cure?

Hardt and Negri say at one point in their book, "The counter-empire must also be a new global vision, a new way of living in the world" (Hardt, Negri 214). What is this if not an unwitting complement to the kingdom of God where Shalom, not unilateral power, is the goal? If peace is in the details of all of our lives, every moment counts, every action counts, every risky act of reconciliation with one's neighbor and protest against injustice adds up. Every story counts. May all the significant details of our struggles to live peacefully with ourselves, with our families, with our neighbors—even the ones whose naming makes us choke—be caught up in the love of a God who painstakingly made the world and can help us make it anew!

Works Cited

Crockett, Linda. 2002, May and June. "At the Well," *The Other Side Magazine*.

Hardt, Michael, and Antonio Negri. 2002. *Empire*. Cambridge, Mass.: Harvard University Press.

Menuchin, Ishai. 2002, March 9. "Saying No to Israel's Occupation," *The New York Times*.

Nussbaum, Martha Craven. 1995. *Poetic Justice: The Literary Imagination and Public Life*. Boston, Mass.: Beacon Press.

Pearl, Marianne. 2001, April 19. "Why Good Hearts Must Go Public." *The New York Times*.

Thompson, Ginger. 2001, October 8. "Mexican Labor Protest Gets Results." *The New York Times*.

Chapter 7

The Meaning of "Mennonite"

Eloise Hiebert Meneses

I have found myself troubled in recent years by the discussion I hear in Mennonite churches on "identity." The perception is that Mennonite identity is being lost, and that it needs bolstering lest we collectively forget who we are. Various things, from dress to dogma, are discussed as essential elements that distinguish us. And the fear seems to be that without a unique identity we will simply blend into the larger culture and thereby cease to exist.

My discomfort with this discussion comes from the vagueness, even confusion, I hear in the construction of the "others"—the ones from whom we would distinguish ourselves to create and maintain our own identity. Are we Mennonite versus Lutheran or Presbyterian? Are we Mennonite versus American? Or are we Mennonite versus Black, White, or Hispanic? Is this identity problem a matter of theology, culture, or ethnicity? Or have we simply conflated the three of these, and invented a community that finds its identity in the exclusion of others?

Ethnicity

To sort out the question, I will begin with the last of these matters, ethnicity. Then I will consider our relationship to the larger American culture. Finally I will address our status as a denomination of the Christian faith. At best, Mennonites are committed and faithful disciples of Jesus Christ. When that core of our identity remains in place, these other things–theology, culture, and ethnicity--can be valuable *parts* of who we are, creating the community that John Ruth has so well documented. When any one of them becomes the whole, even Jesus may find himself unwelcome in our communities.

As an anthropologist, I find the study of ethnicity to be helpful, even crucial, to understanding identity. Identity means to be the same. People everywhere understand this sameness to be in relation to some group of which one is a member. Of course, we are all members of various groups, from churches, to neighborhoods, to baseball teams. But no group holds sway over us so powerfully as the ethnic group. Barth has noted that ethnicity "classifies a person in terms of his basic, most general identity, presumptively determined by his origin and background" (Barth 13). That is, of all our various identities, ethnicity plays the trump card, pronouncing who we are at the most basic level.

The reason for this is fairly simple. At bottom, ethnicity is a matter of *family* writ large. And family is the strongest organizing principle human beings have. A quick survey of the world's cultures reveals that people everywhere live in families, that these are often organized into larger descent-based groups such as lineages, clans, and tribes, and that at the largest level the symbols of family are used to create ethnic groups.

Like all family based groups, ethnic groups believe they are of common biological origin. They claim common ancestry, often with the use of an origin story. The Jewish people, for instance, are bound together by their common descent from Abraham and Sara. The Hopi people believe that they have a common mother who emerged from a hole in the ground. African-Americans are descended from Africans brought to America under slavery. And certain Dalits of India (untouchables) believe that they are descended from a man who broke the taboo on eating beef and was punished subsequently by being refused entry into temples. Stories such as these combine history with fiction to produce an argument of relatedness based on common descent.

The members of an ethnic group, because they share descent lines, are all "brothers" and "sisters." They have common "blood." Lineages are traced to find the degree of relatedness. Of course, if the relationship is too close, intermarriage is impossible. But on the whole, ethnic groups prefer, and sometimes even mandate, marriage within the group. Exogamy, or marrying out, is seen as traitorous, or even perverse. Again, the reason is quite clear. If marriage is permitted between ethnic groups, the claim to be one family is diluted. To which group would the children belong? Retaining our progeny and maintaining the boundaries of the group require marrying our own "kind." Other people are in other "families," that is, ethnic groups, and can be related to on superficial social or economic levels. But intimacy is for family members only. The deepest relationships must be within the ethnic group.

Since membership in the ethnic group is supposed to be by birth alone, one cannot choose one's ethnicity—or so it is thought—any more than one can choose one's family. The "givenness" of birth makes ethnicity powerful. It persuades us that our ethnicity is who we truly are, like it or not. In fact, there is a logical leap from biology to culture in this argument, causing us to think that our most essential social and personal characteristics are matters of genes. Ultimately the argument results in racist thinking. If our biological group gives us our deepest identity, then all of our most important characteristics must be rooted in it too, including values, skills and abilities, morality, and intelligence. It took anthropologists more than sixty years to recognize that there is no biological root to culture, and to state that for humanity "not one item of his tribal social organization, of his language, of his local religion, is carried in his germ-cell" (Benedict 12). Yet even now, the argument from family causes people everywhere to consciously and subconsciously attribute personal and cultural characteristics to biology.

Study after study in anthropology has shown that ethnicity is largely a socially constructed phenomenon (Barth, 1969; Leach, 1977; Romanucci-Ross and De Vos, 1995). That is, beliefs about birth and family relatedness are exaggerated at best and sometimes entirely fabricated. African-Americans, for instance, are descended from a wide variety of ethnic groups in Africa, and, furthermore, are genetically 25 percent of northern European ancestry due to mixing. In Jerusalem, one can meet Jewish people of all possible shapes, sizes, and colors because of their various ancestries other than that of Abraham and Sara. These other ancestries range from groups in Europe and Russia to ones in the Sudan and south India. In this country, there is a steady flow of members of other groups, including Blacks, Hispanics (or Latinos), and Native Americans, into the "White" category every year which is achieved by residential relocation and subsequent intermarriage (Porter). So, intermarriage, though taboo, occurs frequently, yielding "mixed" blood to all of us.

Furthermore, "passing" or changing one's ethnic group occurs as well. Sometimes this is by adoption, as in the case of the many adoptions of Yao children by Chinese. And sometimes it is a simple shift of ethnic identification in adulthood, as in the case of the traders of Thailand who become Mon because it is better for business (Foster). Some wealthy nineteenth-century Africans actually purchased the right to become "White" legally from the Portuguese. And, a proverb from north India complains of a tumbling fall from one ethnic group to another of lower rank because prices have fallen, making the family poorer and poorer.

Ethnic groups never exist in isolation. They define themselves in distinction to other ethnic groups in a socially and economically competitive arena. "White" is a North American category in distinction to "Black." The pastoral Maasi of Kenya are defined in distinction to their neighbors, the agricultural Kikuyu. Pygmies of central Africa live in distinction to the Bantu. Ainu of Hokkaido are distinguished from Japanese. Hence, anywhere you live, the local social world is divided up into a set of ethnic groups that are defined somewhat artificially in relation to one another and to the whole.

There are two implications of the fact that ethnicity is actually artificially constructed. The first is that all ethnic groups are conglomerates of people of different backgrounds lumped together depending upon the other groups in the system, and the second is that markers are needed to identify membership. Any of the American ethnic groups, White, Black, Hispanic, Native American, or Asian, can easily be seen to be a conglomerate of various peoples. For instance, the term "Hispanic" in the United States includes immigrants from a wide variety of Latin American cultures and presumably from Spain. Ironically, there are no "Hispanics" in Mexico. There one encounters Spanish, Mestisos, and Indios, any one of which become "Hispanic" when they cross the border into the United States. So, the categories are always local in time and space, and shift according to history.

Markers include not only skin color, but language, dress, religion, and other cultural items. Biological markers are preferred because they help make the family argument about ethnicity. So "Blacks" and "Whites" are identified by skin color in the United States, and Europeans are identified by their strange round eyes ("pig eyes") in China. But often biological differences are not adequate to make the distinctions. Many Japanese entertain enormous prejudice against Koreans, but cannot recognize them as physically different. So cultural markers must be adopted, such as the ability to speak a standardized form of the language. Further markers may include living together in certain neighborhoods, having certain types of employment, religious commitments, and preferences for certain names, dress, and foods.

All of this bears upon the necessity of being a member in good standing in one's own community. A third or fourth generation Hispanic in the United States who does not speak Spanish or converts to Protestantism (out of Catholicism) will be chided by older members of the community for having left his or her ethnic identity behind. Members of other groups may "forget" such a person's ethnic identity because the markers are gone. A member in good standing retains the markers to show loyalty to the group. In Sri Lanka, one is not truly Sinhalese unless one adheres to Buddhism (Obeyesekere in Romanucci-Ross 222ff). To convert to Christianity is to identify with foreign whites, and to convert to Hinduism is to identify with Indian Tamils. Only by remaining Buddhist can one be truly Sri Lankan!

In fact, the tendency to attach religion as a marker of ethnic identity is strong worldwide. Consider the Irish Catholics, or Orthodox Serbs, or Muslim Palestinians, or Jewish Israelis. Among tribal peoples, the merger of religion and ethnicity is complete, with a single name, such as Yanomami, or Innuit (Eskimo), or Maasai referring at the same time to the people and to their particular religious beliefs and practices. Indian castes are arguably simultaneously ethnic and religious groups organized into a system that marks out differences hierarchically.

Why should religion so commonly be coopted as a marker of ethnic identity? Because both religion and ethnicity demand the deepest levels of commitment from their members. When they do not coincide, membership in religious groups can compete for the loyalties of people in ethnic groups. The simplest solution is to merge the two, yielding a commitment far stronger because it creates a religiously sanctioned, birth-based community—one that can give its members a *total* definition.

Ethnic groups are valuable, even necessary, because they contain our cultures and because they provide protection for us in the larger arena of competing groups. It is in the context of our ethnic groups that we learn our languages, practice the rules for social interaction, receive our most basic values, and discover our own essential worth. Furthermore, without ethnic groups we would be unable to form political units large enough to obtain necessary resources such as land, jobs, influence in government, and social services. In this country, ethnic groups form voting blocs and are appealed to as such by politicians. Statistics from the census are used to make provision and policy decisions by various levels of government. So, contrary to popular American opinion, there are not two levels of civic structure, individual and state, but three: individual, ethnic group, and state.

But while cultural nurturance and political protection are the plusses of organizing ourselves into ethnic groups, exclusion and conflict are the clear minuses. The twentieth century was the bloodiest in human history, arguably because of the religio-ethnic distinctions used to fight over resources. Sometimes the conflict is overt and violent, as in Bosnia, or Rwanda, or the streets of urban United States. And sometimes it is more subtle, as in the segregation found in America's churches and suburban residential neighborhoods. In either case, identification becomes exclusion, which leads to conflict.

Is "Mennonite" an ethnic group? I have observed many Mennonites functioning fully as if it were one. Do we have to be born into our community, bearing the name of an ancient lineage? Do we become nervous at the prospect of our children marrying "out"—meaning not out of the faith, but out of the "family"? Is the loss of distinctive dress a concern because it is a sign we are becoming worldly, or because we won't be able to readily recognize one another? Have our distinctive cultural values such as timeliness, the work ethic, planning, frugality, simplicity, and service become not values in themselves, but markers, identifying ethnic members in good standing (Meneses)? If so, then we have become an ethnic group, one among many, serving the same purposes that any ethnic group serves and causing the same problems.

From Ethnicity to Culture

Let us move on from ethnicity to culture. Perhaps being Mennonite is primarily a matter of distinguishing ourselves from other Americans. Certainly, that is what most other Americans think we are doing, with the Amish as an easily identifiable case. We are the people who have rejected the American values of materialism and progress, and have refused to assimilate, or join the melting pot. So, we identify ourselves by our cultural separateness.

In the past, many Mennonites expressed this separateness in terms of simple dress and technology. The cultural difference was easy to see. I sometimes hear Mennonites suggesting now that our identity troubles are due to the fact that we no longer have these markers. But I would suggest that our separateness is still present and strong, though in more covert form. In the area where I live, Mennonites associate with one another through networks that create an entirely separate social world. That world is invisible to people not connected with it, but is revealed quickly when they attempt to join our churches and communities. In churches, Mennonites' eyes light up most readily when recognizing old, familiar faces. Newcomers are met pleasantly enough, but with discomfort and embarrassed silences. Many Mennonites just don't know how to make friends with new people!

In Mennonite dominated communities, new businesses, from auto repair to restaurants, can find it difficult to get customers. Again, where I live, certain restaurants, Mennonite owned, are landmarks identifying the physical and social topography for insiders. They are places where you will meet *real* people, the ones you *know*, not strangers. Other restaurants are just part of the backdrop. Furthermore, Mennonites in business tend to do business with one another, sometimes with discounts for insiders not given to others. We see this as an extension of the church community into all of life. But our exchanging services with one another creates a community that is both inclusive and exclusive at the same time.

Of course, the origins of our separateness have to do with a particular form of expression of the Christian faith, a certain conception of what it means to follow Christ. Especially, we heed Jesus' words to be "in the world, but not of it." Our refusal to take on new forms of technology and dress has been a symbol of a commitment to another world, the kingdom of God. And our formation of strong communities is indeed the result of a lived Christian faith. There are real theological reasons for our separateness and our rejection of American culture.

Yet, everyone has a culture. Human beings cannot grow up or live out a life without one. To begin with we must speak a language. To maintain a separate language, such as German or Pennsylvania Dutch, does not free anyone from speaking in a language per se. Then, we must build homes, eat food, wear clothing, and organize our families in some fashion. That fashion will be particular, not general, resulting in a certain culture, not an escape from culture. To refuse to move forward in a culture merely commits one to a previous version of it. Many of our cultural "distinctives," from horses and buggies to quilting to black cars, were not the least distinctive in nineteenth century America—we borrowed them!

I am suggesting that by maintaining separate ways, Mennonites have merely privileged one culture over others as being more religiously pure. This is not entirely without merit. I believe that all cultures are in need of redemption—of transformation by Christ into ways of living that honor God. And certainly some of our distinctives were deliberately invented because they reflect a value on Christian plain vs. worldly, fancy, or vain, living. The meeting house, a cappella singing, and, of course, plain dress are in this category. But to choose a certain hairstyle or set of worship songs or an arrangement of the sanctuary as being the only truly Christian one is certainly to miss the point. It was the Pharisees who tried to resolve the problem of lifestyle by stipulating exact correct procedure to the smallest level.

My concern is that some of the discussion about identity has more to do with a desire to be culturally distinct than a desire to follow Christ's example. We must have a culture. All humans are "embodied," made of flesh and blood, living in particular times and places, and belonging to certain peoples. Furthermore, there is a healthy acceptance, even a pride, we should have in the cultural aspects of our identity (Kasdorf). Yet, clinging to our cultures can actually be dangerous! For one thing, cultures *always* change. Those that fail to do so go extinct! And for another, attempts to hang on to certain forms of a culture can result in cultural idolatry, that is, the elevation of culture to the status of an all-powerful provider, putting our very faith in jeopardy! Is "Mennonite" a culture? I hope not! Because if it is, it will have to eventually die, as all earthly things do.

Denominational Status

Finally, what about our status as a denomination? Are we Mennonite versus Lutheran or Presbyterian or Catholic? This is certainly the most historically accurate meaning of the term. To recite the obvious, our name comes from Menno Simons, the Catholic priest who joined the Anabaptist movement of the Reformation and renounced war.

Those Europeans, and later Americans, who followed Menno's teachings became known as Mennonites. We remember especially the religious persecution that followed, with record of it contained in *Martyrs Mirror*. We are the people who, out of Christian love, refused to fight (though as a conference speaker noted recently, "Sometimes it was close!") and so paid the ultimate price of losing our lives at the hands of the members of other denominations.

A couple of years ago I attended an international meeting of Mennonites. There were speakers from a wide variety of different countries, with simultaneous translation into three languages. On the whole it was a wonderful event, allowing Mennonites from different cultures to celebrate their common experience of the Christian faith. Yet, as I listened to speakers from Africa, Asia, and Latin America, I began to notice a pattern. Many of them seemed to be trying to root what they said in sixteenth century European history, rather than in the early church or the teachings of Jesus himself. Would our sixteenth century religious ancestors have approved of this? Worse, I feared at this conference that it was really the approval of North Americans that was being sought by references to Anabaptist history. I asked myself the question, "If I were Brazilian, or Congolese, or Indian, or Tanzanian, in what sense would I see the violent history of reformation Europe as part of my own story?"

Let us rethink this one. Was the Reformation God's idea? Surely reform was—it is always necessary for the church to examine itself and yield up accumulated rigidities and hidden sins to God for healing and transformation. But was it God's intent that his body, the church of Jesus Christ should be divided into the hundreds of denominations that now exist? (I once read a Catholic pamphlet warning children about Protestantism. A drawing depicted the major reformation leaders up to their necks in water, drowning in a sea of division!) The New Testament is rich with admonitions to unity despite disagreements. At that time, there was *one* church, its members were to love and serve one another, quarrels were to be worked out in the context of church discipline and leadership, and only unrepentant sinful members were to be expelled. The apostle Paul worked especially hard to keep the body from being dismembered. I don't think that separate churches were what God had in mind.

Yet, since the nineteenth century, these European divisions have been spread to the entire world! We forget that the Reformation took place in only the Western branch of the church. The churches in Ethiopia, in Syria, and in India are far older than the European church, and have had their own history. Must an Ethiopian convert take sides in the theological debates of sixteenth century Europe to join a local church in Addis Ababa? Must our church leadership in Tanzania know the history of the debates between Luther and Zwingli to advise their congregations? How much do we Europeans know of others' theological histories? Are we willing to familiarize ourselves with Orlando Costas and Samuel Escobar because our Latin American Mennonite sisters and brothers have been influenced by them?

The river of the Christian faith has been wider than the European branch of it, and does not leap unaltered from the first century apostle Paul to the sixteenth century Menno Simons. Actually we are a minor tributary of that river! This is not to say that we are unimportant. Denominations are of value for the theological gifts they can give to the larger body of Christ because of their separate histories.

Lutherans, for instance, can teach the rest of us much about grace. They have investigated it intellectually and practically well beyond the other denominations. I remember a Lutheran friend of mine commenting on a "backsliding" Christian friend of ours. "Well, God is a fisherman," he said. "He lets us have a little slack in the line, then he slowly reels us in." My friend was completely confident of God's willingness and ability to prevent one of his children from straying. Long years in the Lutheran church had given him not only an intellectual theology but, an experience of the Christian faith that confirmed that theology. He was able to teach me to relax in God's care in a way that Mennonites, with a more performance-oriented theology, were not.

However, Lutherans burned Anabaptists at the stake, drowned them in rivers, threw them down wells, and so forth. There is a Mennonite museum that depicts these martyrdoms in full-sized figures for viewers. It is intended to remind Mennonites of their heritage. Yet, as I went through, I wondered what it would be like to go through that museum as a Lutheran or Presbyterian! Would they say we have failed in 400 years to forgive them? They are, after all, not pagans, but brothers and sisters in Christ! Will we forge an identity for ourselves by carefully remembering the wrongs done to us? More subtly, will we refuse the gifts they might offer us, theological and otherwise, that might balance out our own Christian experience?

Viewing the denominations in terms of giftedness will remind us that we all have something to offer one another—and many good things to receive. Mennonites know about living out the Christian faith through careful attention to Jesus' words in the Sermon on the Mount and a commitment to nonviolence. Our knowledge comes not only from the intellectual theological work that we have done on the matter, but from centuries of lived experience. We can call people to discipleship as well as conversion, and warn them of interpreting grace too "cheaply."

Yet, to make our theology a matter of a distinct *identity* is to cheapen it tremendously! Do we believe only Mennonites should pay attention to the Sermon on the Mount or be nonviolent? Hopefully not! We believe these principles are correct for *all* Christians. We should hope that our theology *does not* distinguish us in the future, because we want other Christians to hear our voice, repent, and begin to live in accordance with Jesus' admonitions to love one's enemies. If we enter into inter-denominational dialog, we should hope *not* that the various denominations will "retain their identities" and "be appreciated for who they are," but that the dialog will result in resolution and agreement! Somehow, paradoxically, God's grace and his judgment of our lives come together. If we engage in dialog with Lutherans over the matter, let us forgive one another for the past, and concentrate on finding the Holy Spirit's word to us all now about how these two truths fit together. Our theology is a gift, and gifts are for giving away.

By now you may think me an iconoclast. But actually, I am, quite simply, an Anabaptist! The original vision for following Christ that Anabaptists held was of a simple faith in Jesus, resulting in a Christian walk that was untrammeled by politics or culture. Perhaps we are in need of the same reform that we once demanded of the Catholic church! Politics and culture are necessities of life on this earth, but they are relative, which is to say they can be different in different times and places and be equally good. For that matter, they can be equally bad, so any cultural form we create will be in need of constant reevaluation, and any theological expression of the one faith that we emphasize will be in need of balancing from others' experiences of God's work in their lives and histories.

What Then of Identity?

What then of the identity question? It certainly is true that we cannot express the Christian faith apart from our particular ethnic, cultural, and theological histories. Once again, they are part of our embodied existence, our earthly, creaturely nature. John Ruth reflects this when he says,

> Let us have respect for that chapter of God's salvation-story, which it has been our lot to inherit. Let us remember that it was in terms of the story of a people that we learned about God's will in the first place. (Ruth 24)

But, as this quote suggests, our people and our inheritance are *vehicles* for God's will. They are not in themselves the sources of our salvation. So, identity is not to be pursued for its own sake. God is! Identity will be a natural result of walking with God, a gift from God, in fact, not an anxious, artificial construct.

In biblical history, the Israelites tried to create a total identity by merging ethnicity, culture, and theology. In the process, they forgot that they were not just chosen ones, but ones chosen for a purpose. That purpose was to give light to the whole world! Isaiah spoke for God saying,

> It is too light a thing that you should be my servant to raise up the tribes of Jacob and to restore the survivors of Israel; I will give you as a light to the nations that my salvation may reach to the end of the earth. (49:6)

Yet, by the time of Jesus, the Israelites had degenerated into an inwardly focused ethnic group, one among many in the Roman Empire. With a strong emphasis on family and community, religion had become a thin veneer over what was really a matter of ethnic identity.

In response to this situation, John the Baptist declared boldly,

> Do not presume to say to yourselves, 'We have Abraham as our ancestor'; for I tell you, God is able from these stones to raise up children to Abraham. Even now the ax is lying at the root of the trees; every tree therefore that does not bear good fruit is cut down and thrown into the fire. (Matt. 3:8-10)

Jesus' words on the subject were far more frightening! When some of his listeners tried to object to his reference to them as "slaves" by claiming freedom based on their biological inheritance from Abraham, Jesus accused them three times of being "children of the devil"! These listeners were disciples "who had believed in him," yet Jesus said of them, "there is no place in you for my word." The encounter ended with an attempt on Jesus' life. (John 8:31-59)

I sincerely wish that as Mennonites we were less worried about our identity, and more concerned about our *witness*. Identity is inwardly focused; witness reaches out. Identity is maintained by exclusion; witness invites inclusion. With my undeniably modern and fancy Bible computer program, I have searched the NRSV version of the Bible for the word "identity." There are no references. The words "witness" or "witnesses" yield 136 references in both Old and New Testaments. The term means to testify to what one has seen or heard, that is, to speak the truth as one knows it. Jesus is "the faithful witness" to God in Revelation 1:5. And Acts is rich with the discovery by the disciples that they are to be witnesses to Jesus "in Jerusalem, in all Judea and Samaria, and to the ends of the earth" (1:8, and there are 13 other references in Acts alone). This is quite in line with our history! The strongest desire of the early Anabaptists was to be witnesses to the story of Jesus in the Bible as they had experienced it (i.e., "seen and heard" it) in their own lives. I am merely suggesting that we follow their example.

What then is the central story, the deepest truth, of our lives, the one that gives us our only permanent identity? It is the story of God's redemption through Christ, of the new Kingdom that he announced, and of the growth of that Kingdom through the ages toward a final climax in his second coming. *We* do not write, or construct, or create this story. We choose to join it, become part of it, enter in to it, because we wish to know its Author. We give up ("relativize") all our other identities to dwell in this one, and thereby receive back from the hand of God the special and particular calling that he has on our lives. Lesslie Newbigin says that

> the Christian life [is] one in which we live in the biblical story as part of the community whose story it is, find in the story the clues to knowing God as his character becomes manifest in the story, and from within that indwelling try to understand and cope with the events of our time and the world about us and so carry the story forward. At the heart of the story, as the key to the whole, is the incarnation of the Word, the life, ministry, death and resurrection of Jesus. In the Fourth Gospel Jesus defines for his disciples what is to be their relation to him. They are to "dwell in" him. He is not to be the object of their observation, but the body of

which they are a part. As they "indwell" him in his body, they will both be led into fuller and fuller apprehension of the truth and also become the means through which God's will is done in the life of the world. (Newbigin 99)

Finally, what is the effect on the rest of the world of our indwelling, or witnessing to, this story? It is important to remember that the true purpose of the kingdom is the glory of God. We are not just saving ourselves. When the whole of creation is singing God's praises, it comes into right relationship with him, and thereby finds its own authentic identity and true joy. So the purpose of our witness is in fact to reorient the whole of creation back toward God. The rest of the world will be redeemed by our witness to the story of the kingdom. And, the identity we seek, like the butterfly of happiness, will come to us naturally when we are not pursuing it directly. It will emerge from its cocoon and spread its wings lightly over us when we fix our eyes on Christ and dwell in him.

WORKS CITED

Barth, Fredrik, editor. 1969. *Ethnic Groups and Boundaries.* Boston, Mass.: Little, Brown & Co.

Benedict, Ruth. 1934. *Patterns of Culture.* Boston, Mass.: Houghton, Mifflin Co.

Foster, Brian. 1982. *Commerce and Ethnic Differences.* Athens, Oh.: Ohio University Press.

Kasdorf, Julia. 2001. The *Body and the Book.* Baltimore: Johns Hopkins University Press.

Leach, E. R. 1977. *Political Systems of Highland Burma.* London: University of London, Athlone Press.

Meneses, Eloise Hiebert. 2001, Oct. 30. In "The Virtues and Vices of the 'Mennonite' Culture," *The Mennonite,* 4-6.

Newbigin, Lesslie. 1989. *The Gospel in a Pluralist Society.* Grand Rapids, Mich: Eerdmans Publishing Co.

Porter, Benita. 1990. *Colorstruck.* New York: B. Q. Press.

Romanucci-Ross, Lola and George De Vos, Eds. 1995. *Ethnic Identity: Creation, Conflict, and Accommodation.* Walnut Creek, Calif: Altamira Press.

Ruth, John L. 1978. *Mennonite Identity and Literary Art.* Scottdale, Pa.: Herald Press.

Chapter 8

On the Necessity of Leaving Community: A Meditation

Joseph S. Miller

It was a land flowing with milk and honey. For a number of years my family and I lived on a breathtakingly beautiful farm thirty miles north of Philadelphia. Our farmhouse was a grand three story stone structure reposing on the southern exposure of a gentle hill. Our mailing address was Indian Creek Road, which was a tribute or perhaps actually a claim of triumph over the native people who had once considered it nothing less than a Promised Land. But others also considered it a Promised Land. It was after all the "American" poet Walt Whitman who from Philadelphia, a colonial day's journey from our farm, had sounded his "primordial yelp"—not back toward Europe, but facing west—ringing out his song of self across the American continent.

Some one thousand feet from our barn was Indian Creek. In fact it was on our farm that Indian Creek emptied itself into the East Branch of Perkiomen Creek. The Perkiomen in turn flowed into the Schuylkill and finally the water entered Delaware River. Long before our family lived on that farm, called by local people "Indian Creek Haven," native people had lived there. The fields of our farm were especially rich in their abundance of Native American artifacts. Arrowheads and stone implements were regularly gleaned from our farmland.

It was John L. Ruth, our pastor, friend, teacher, and neighbor who helped our twentieth century community to remain mindful of the other communities that had lived on the same land we inhabited. I remain grateful for John's genius in remembering and telling, not just the contemporary story, but the stories of generation upon generation. In his telling of all such stories, John contextualized these specific stories within the backdrop of the master story of God's shaping community. For John, it has really always has been one human story in which God calls, sends, and names people as his own.

The Indians of what would become Montgomery County, Pennsylvania, established a series of communities up and down Indian Creek, the Perkiomen, and the Schuylkill. Hundreds of years earlier, where Indian Creek emptied into the Perkiomen, stood the lodges of the Lenni Lenape—on the very spot of our later farmhouse and barn. When working the soil of our garden, I was always deeply aware that on that very ground families of the native people had lived. With the coming of Europeans, these original people were forced into an exile from the land they loved and called their home. Jay Ruth observes of these original people: "They speak of land, river, trees and animals with reverence. And this land, we need to remember, is their home in a way no European parchment can ensure. A mysterious watching figure at wood's edge suggests an ancient lore that has been banished by our stern domestication—and now excavation—of this once sacred setting" (Ruth 2).

Alas, the native people, forced to leave their homeland, entered into a momentous decision to migrate west—called by a voice they would have certainly known as divine. Their call was both exile and exodus. Their exile from what was known and settled to what was new was a sad recognition of their need for a promised land where they could worship and serve their Creator. It is doubtful that the Lenni Lenape had ever heard of Abraham and Sarah, but I believe all exiles are predicated on the master narrative of Sarah and Abraham. Every person who has ever been called by God to pack a bag and has set out for a new land is a child of father Abraham and mother Sarah.

It was from that very farm that my own family felt a call to leave that verdant land along Indian Creek and move to Eastern Europe to serve the church as helpers in a new Christian community in Budapest, Hungary. I don't suggest that my family's moving away from the land along Indian Creek was as hard as the native people's own exodus, but I do feel kinship with them. Moving from that land was one of the most difficult things I have ever done. But there was a call from God to a new land so that we could worship and serve God in that place.

Paradox in Every Promised Land

This is a meditation on exodus and Promised Land. The Old Testament storytellers seem to be preoccupied with the dialectic of exodus and Promised Land. The biblical narrative yearns for all families, peoples, and nations to experience that most basic human need for a place where people can worship and serve God. The ancient narrative knows that there is the germ of paradox in every Promised Land because when there is comfort and "settledness," the ability to serve and worship God becomes increasingly difficult. I am suggesting that every Promised Land over the generations requires at times an exodus to remain true to the greater call that God constantly is making to every individual, every family, every community, and every nation to serve and worship God.

The God of both the Old and New Testaments is continually at work guiding and leading people in this dialectic of a Land of Promise and the need for exodus. The Land of Promise that God provides is always by definition a place where people are safe and settled, not just to be comfortable, but as a base from which they are able to worship and serve God. To worship and serve God is the reason for every Promised Land. But it seems axiomatic that every Promised Land in time becomes a land of bondage. For a multiplicity of reasons, some self-imposed and some externally imposed, worship and service of God can no longer occur.

The biblical story has hardly begun when Adam and Eve are driven into exodus/exile from the garden of Eden because in paradise their ability to worship and serve God was corrupted. It is only in their forced exodus into the wilderness east of Eden that the "primordial couple," as Milton calls them, could worship and serve God.

Genesis 11:30 introduces a new direction in the Old Testament story. Here is the start of a large section of the Bible that tells of a particular family. God's overarching vocation for this chosen family is for them to be a blessing to all the peoples of the earth. This family's great gift to the other families of the world is their own relationship with God—their ability to worship and serve God. God commissions this family to teach other families how they too can serve and worship God. Time and again, the chosen family demonstrates that to serve and worship God, a family and community will need to enter into the exodus/Promised Land paradigm.

This section of the Old Testament begins with the call of Abraham and Sarah and ends at Mount Sinai, when the family becomes a nation under the leadership of Moses. Chapter 12 establishes the major themes of the family's worship and service of God and their exodus and Promised Land.

What was the pillow talk like between Abraham and Sarah as they made their exodus from their homeland and journeyed to a new land to which God directed them? In the eleventh chapter of Hebrews, there is a long list of men and women who showed sincere faith in God. Hebrews presents Abraham as one of the "super heroes" of faith. He becomes an example of devotion to God. Hebrews 11:8 records the installation of Abraham into the biblical Hall of Fame: "By faith Abraham obeyed when he was called to set out for a place that he was to receive as an inheritance: and he set out not knowing where he was going."

Dare we ask the impolite questions? Dare we ask "unfaithful" questions of the Bible? Dare we ask: "Just a minute. You are telling me to believe that this guy Abraham hears a voice (gets this idea—this sense of call) and packs up his whole family and all his belongings and heads off for a place that he doesn't know about?"

The Bible doesn't share with us any conversation or discussion about whether Abraham talked with his wife Sarah or other members of his family about this call to abandon his Promised Land of hearth and kinship. The Bible records that Abraham gets the idea of exodus and a new Promised Land and announces that the family is moving: lock, stock, and barrel. The motivation behind this exodus is that Abraham cannot worship and serve God in his homeland.

So what do you imagine the conversation between Sarah and Abraham was like as they are lying in their tent at night, somewhere between Haran and Canaan—between a worn out Promised Land and a new Land of Promise? "Abe, are you really, really sure that you heard God correctly? Are you absolutely sure that when you think you heard God talking to you it wasn't just an upset stomach from too many falafels?" Maybe Sarah went on: "Some of the others are mumbling about why we can't worship and serve God just as faithfully back in Haran. Why go traipsing south to some God-forsaken land when Haran works perfectly well?" Still on other late nights the tables must have been turned with Abraham sharing deep doubts, and Sarah keeping the faith for the entire family.

If Abraham and Sarah are anything like you and me, there were long hours of lying in their tent at night talking in low voices about the call. Faith in God, and call from God doesn't mean that we do not keep checking and rechecking to make sure we are indeed on the right track. Abraham and Sarah kept monitoring the call from God and responding to that call. They would have had to keep adjusting to God's continual call and direction. I think God doesn't just make one call; God keeps calling and directing us in stages to ever new places so that we can worship and serve God.

Outrageously Honest

Many generations later, Jesus is living on that very Promised Land to which Sarah and Abraham were called. Jesus picked up the Bible's narrative on the dialectic of Promised Land and Exodus. Jesus knew that a Promised Land inevitably becomes a place that requires exodus if people are to remain faithful to God's call to worship and serve God. Once, Jesus was traveling from the Galilee in the north toward Jerusalem in the center of Israel. A large crowd traveled with him. A sizable portion of the crowd was considering making a commitment to following Jesus. They were determined to go with Jesus all the way in their worship and service to God! They committed themselves all the way in their discipleship; all the way in their trust in Jesus; all the way to Jerusalem. But then abruptly Jesus, shocking the people accompanying him, said the most outrageous thing. He demanded their exodus and exile in order for them to really experience fully the community he was establishing.

Just as they were ready to commit to discipleship, Jesus said something that caused hesitation about the high cost of discipleship. He said right out of the blue, "If you want to be my follower—if you want to order your life around what you see in my life—then you will need to hate your father, your mother, your wife, your children, your brothers and your sisters. The fact is, says Jesus, the greatest exodus of all is for you to leave the dependence on this life and even to hate life itself! Jesus says it is only through such an exodus from the primacy of family, home, and one's life that it is possible to gain a place in the ultimate Land of Promise, which is heaven. It sounds shocking! The fact is that Jesus meant to be shocking. Jesus grabbed their attention that day by being outrageously honest.

Deciding to be fully committed followers of Jesus Christ means much more than accepting a set of ideas. Being a fully committed Christian means literally following Jesus in his own exodus from kith and kin and hearth and home. The text says in Luke 14:25 that the large crowd of potential disciples was following Jesus. But, where was Jesus actually leading these people? Several chapters earlier in Luke 9:51, the gospel reports that Jesus is heading for one last time to Jerusalem. Bible scholars identify this as a major transition point in Jesus' life and ministry. Commentators on the gospel of Luke call this "turning his face toward Jerusalem" of Luke 9:51 Jesus' "little exodus."

Jesus heads to Jerusalem and premature death. When Jesus tells those seeking to join him in chapter 14 of Luke that they must hate mother, father, sister, and life itself he is saying: "Are you ready to die with me? Are you ready to join me in an exodus from family, home, and life itself?"

There is an interesting word that comes to mind when I read Jesus' disturbing statement about needing to hate family, homeland, and life itself to be his followers. That word is *hyperbole*. The word is interesting here because it means that a person is exaggerating for effect, but what actually is being said should not be literally understood.

I suspect Jesus is not using hyperbole here. He is serious. That is the scary part! That's the troubling part! It is scary and troubling to me as I consider whether I am really committed to being a follower of Christ. The cost that we must pay to be true followers—to be true Christians—is to lay everything we value on the table. It is only then that we can become fully what Jesus demands of his disciples.

We are all challenged together not to reserve anything that might keep us from being totally and completely committed to Jesus Christ and making Jesus Lord of our lives. The Quakers are insightful when they talk about the *cumbered* life that threatens to hold us back from becoming fully committed Christians.

Preachers often ask people to examine their lives and rid themselves of sins that hold them back from being fully committed Christians. Usually, we think about the wild and woolly stuff: cussing, carousing, gambling, lying, and cheating, all those things of country-and-western songs.

I believe Luke 14 is not about the obviously bad stuff holding us back. I suggest that this text addresses a much more subtle, and maybe even more dangerous temptation that keeps us from being fully committed followers of Jesus. For many of us this Bible passage says that the good and worthy things of God's perfect plan can also keep us from full commitment to Jesus. Sin always is seeking to twist and distort what is good—so family and life itself can be stumbling blocks to being fully committed Christians. The Garden of Eden and all Promised Lands can become places from which we need exodus.

Dietrich Bonhoeffer, the brilliant young theology professor in Germany before and during World War II, wrote *The Cost of Discipleship* (1937). His book talks about cheap grace and costly grace. Because of his open criticism of the Nazis, Bonhoeffer was put to death. He writes that true disciples of Jesus will hate family, profession and even homeland:

> This breach with all our immediate relationships is inescapable. It may take the form of an external breach with family or nation; in that case we shall be called upon to bear visibly the reproach of Christ, the *'odium generis humani'*... In the last resort it makes no difference whether the breach be secret or open. Abraham is an example of both. He had to leave his friends and his father's house because Christ came between him and his own. On this occasion the breach was evident. Abraham became a stranger and a sojourner to gain the Promised Land. Later on he was called by God to offer his own son Isaac as a sacrifice. Christ had come between the father and the child of promise. This time the direct relationship not only of flesh and blood, but also of the spirit, must be broken. Abraham must learn that the promise does not depend on Isaac, but on God alone. (Bonhoeffer 88)

Bonhoeffer reflects on the new thing that was possible for Abraham after he was able to place his most valuable possession on the altar table of Mount Moriah.

> Since he had shown himself ready to obey God literally, he is now allowed to possess Isaac as though he had him not—to possess him through Jesus Christ. No one else knows what has happened. Abraham comes down from the mountain with Isaac just as he went up, but the whole situation has changed. Christ has stepped between father and son. Abraham had left all and followed Christ, and as he follows him he is allowed to go back and live in

the world as he had done before. Outwardly the picture is unchanged, but the old is passed away, and behold all things are new. Everything has passed through Christ. (Bonhoeffer 89)

Many Christians need an exodus away from inappropriate focus on family, profession, and even homeland. Just as Jesus had to leave his hearth and home in Galilee and "turn his face toward Jerusalem" so too we must we leave family and homeland so that we can enter into exodus with Jesus and join him as he goes to the cross. I discovered that discipleship meant packing all my belongings and leaving a most lovely and comfortable place like a farm along Indian Creek for a land never before seen. I discovered that discipleship meant supporting and encouraging our son to take a year off from his college studies to work with displaced persons in war-torn Bosnia.

Jesus intended to shock those who were listening to him in Luke 14. I am sure some of the people were even upset with Jesus. How dare he say we have to hate our families and life itself? But lots of times we need to be shocked. Sometimes a shock is all that can get through our rationalized haze of religiosity.

This tool of shocking his listeners into action or at least reaction reminds me of the time Tony Campolo preached at a chapel service at Lancaster Mennonite High School. If you have ever heard Campolo preach, you know how passionate he feels about the poor and disadvantaged. During the chapel at Lancaster Mennonite High School in the heart of a very wealthy and settled Mennonite community Campolo was preaching to these privileged high school kids about Jesus' demand that Christians do something about people starving around the world.

Campolo said to those students, "People are starving right now! In these minutes that we are in this chapel service 1,000 people—1,000 fellow human beings are going to die from starvation—and the truth is that you don't give a damn about these people! Campolo went on: And the greatest tragedy of all is that you are more offended that I just used that word than you are about the 1,000 people who have died while we have been in this chapel service!"

Shocking? You bet! But what is it that is shocking? What is it that we allow to offend us as Christians? That is Jesus' whole point. Jesus meant to shock his listeners into making a choice—into knowing and counting the cost of being a Christian. Even to the necessary point of hating the Promised Land. Hating family, profession, religion, friends and life itself if these things are more important to us than Jesus. Jesus says that to be a fully committed Christian means putting everything on the table—even the Promised Land!

My parents, grandparents, and great grandparents saw themselves as separated from the society around them. Their self-identity was one that divided the world into two parts: the plain, simple Mennonite Christians and those people whom they called "worldly." The word *worldly* for my relatives was code for all those institutions and people who accommodated to the secular world.

My Mennonite relatives were rather typical of their fellow church members in arranging their lives so that the temptation to be conformed was as limited as possible. They wore special "plain" clothing, drove black cars, and generally tried to be nonconformed to the society around them. Beulah Stauffer Hostetler identifies Mennonites' attempts from 1882 to 1942 to remain separated from the world around them as "defensive structuring." Hostetler explains that this Mennonite desire to remain unconformed to the world resulted in numerous rules that were codified for members of the Mennonite church. These rules were in many ways a modern version of the Jewish *nomism* that faced the early church. The rules within the Mennonite denomination were designed to regulate the appearance of members and specifically to limit contacts with nonmembers. All these rules were designed to guarantee nonconformity to the world (Hostetler 259).

Mennonites had drawn heavily on the apostle Paul's dictum to the first century Christians living in Rome regarding how to live in the world, but not of the world. The key scriptural touchstone used by Mennonites as they created their Promised Land of isolation was Romans 12:2: "Do not be conformed to this world, but be transformed by the renewing of your minds, so that you may discern what is the will of God—what is good and acceptable and perfect."

Paul wrote his letter to the New Testament Christians living in Rome intending to inspire and encouraging them to find ways to live as citizens of Rome and as citizens of God's kingdom. No easy task—this living in "two worlds." The believers in Rome struggled to discern how much to allow "this age" and "the world" around them to shape and mold them.

In 1950, Paul Mininger, a Mennonite church leader and president of Goshen (Ind.) College, penned an amazing article questioning the way Mennonites practiced nonconformity. Mininger wrote in "The Limitations of Nonconformity":

> The result is that we isolate ourselves so completely from [the world] that we are not able to fulfill our social responsibility and we are not in sufficiently close touch with it to reach it effectively with the gospel. We have sometimes sought to get out of the world rather than to live the Christian life and give our Christian witness within the world. We have been too well satisfied to live and let live (or live and let die!), rather than live and make alive. We have built walls to keep the world out and those same walls have kept the gospel in. (Mininger 167)

Mininger concludes his article with this ringing call for Mennonites to become engaged in the issues that confront the world:

> We often hear it said that we "are in the world but not of the world." We too often forget that we are for the world. If we concentrate our energies upon saving ourselves and preserving our traditions, or even upon being nonconformed, the values that we have will certainly vanish in our hands. The only way to really retain true spiritual values is to quicken them with the divine imperative of witnessing to the world. The paradox of Jesus is whoever will lose his life for my sake shall find it. (Mininger 167, 168)

The apostle Paul did not advocate withdrawal into isolated enclaves, seeking to be followers of Christ in desperate isolation. There is no advocacy in the New Testament for the withdrawal from society as was practiced by the Essene community at Qumran. Rather, Paul teaches something even more challenging. The apostle calls for believers to live in the world, but not be of the world. Paul recognized the power of "this age" and the power of "the world" negatively to shape the character and conduct of Christians. The letter to the Christians in Rome teaches that they must be responsible for how much they conform to the society and culture around them. Paul calls on them to find wise ways to be members of the city and of the Roman Empire while at the same time remaining faithful citizens of Christ's exodus community of the cross and Christ's Promised Land of the resurrection.

This is my question: How do we as a Christian community support each other as we seek not to conform to the world around us, while also remaining in the world? How do we support and encourage each other to be transformed into the likeness of Jesus Christ, rather than into the likeness of the larger culture? A corollary question follows: How do we move beyond isolation and withdrawal so that we can be people who, as Mininger calls for, "are for the world"?

I think there are three steps in the process of living out Romans 12. The first is to affirm that indeed as Christians we do not want to allow ourselves to be molded and conformed primarily by the dominant culture around us. Our self-identify should be first as citizens of God's kingdom and only tangentially are we citizens of a nation state. Twenty-first century American Mennonites are immensely challenged by the change from isolation from the dominant culture to syncretizing our Christian faith and loyalty to the United States.

Secondly, the church needs to find ways to help us decide when, where, and how we will step out of the dominant cultural stream and live in contradiction to the culture around us.

Finally, the covenanted Christian community must support each member as they live out how they discern the Holy Spirit has called them to live.

Conformed to Jesus, Not the World

In his letter to the Christians in Rome, Paul appeals to the house churches to strive diligently to live faithfully in the dilemma of living and working within the culture of the Roman world. Paul admonishes the Christians to find ways of remaining faithful to their membership in Christ's family even as they live within the city of Rome. Paul is clear that the two are not the same—Roman society and Christianity are at times related but they are not one and the same. Early church leaders spent great pastoral capital on challenging those first and second century Christian believers to weigh carefully their accommodation with the larger culture.

An early church letter written sometime between the apostolic age and the Constantinian period, a Christian writer addressed a curious nonbeliever's desire to know about Christian faith. *The Letter to Diognetus* defined the Christian faith in this way:

> They live in both Greek and foreign cities wherever chance has put them. They follow local customs in clothing, food and other

aspects of life. But at the same time, they demonstrate to us the wonderful and certainly unusual form of their own citizenship. They live in their own native lands, but as aliens; as citizens they share all things with others; but like aliens, suffer all things. Every foreign country is to them as their native country and every native land as a foreign country . . . They are passing their days on earth, but are citizens of heaven. They obey the appointed laws, and go beyond the laws in their own lives . . . To put it simply -the soul is to the body as Christians are to the world. The soul is spread through all parts of the body and Christians through all cities of the world. The soul is in the body but is not of the body; Christians are in the world but not of the world. (Ehrman 73)

In Romans 12:2 Paul teaches believers to transform themselves by the renewing of their minds. The Greek word that Paul used for *transformed* is also the root word for *metamorphosis*. Paul uses a variant of that word in Galatians 4:19: "until Christ is formed in you." God desires transformation for us in a process of morphing into Christlikeness. Paul tells Christians in the Greek city of Corinth to meditate upon the glory of the Lord; "with unveiled faces," they "are being transformed into his likeness with ever-increasing glory" (2 Cor. 3:18). The apostle suggests that looking intently on Christ will bring about a metamorphosis into Christ's image.

The Christian Community Discerns Together

Through Bible study, prayer, and conversation within a faith community individual believers can decide how they will choose to live. In these faith communities members can wrestle with how much accommodation to make with "this age."

I believe that we can bring our faith struggle to the questions we are grappling with. Issues like the quagmire in Iraq should be addressed within the discerning community of faith. We have been through a year like I have not experienced before. The pressures to support a military answer to problems in the Middle East feel overwhelming. Likely the pressures will increase for those people out of step with the drumbeat of the militarism of the dominant culture. I fear that our children will face very difficult choices in school from teachers and their friends if they speak up for peace rather than war. Have we helped our children to be clear about what is right? I heard of a third grader whose class was told to wear red, white, and blue to school. With wonderful wisdom the third grader wore red, white, and blue, but also wore a button that read, "Pray for Peace."

How do we know when to speak and when to remain silent? How do we know when to act and when to remain on the sidelines? We need help! We need to know what the Bible teaches; we need prayer so that we can be wise. We need the counsel of sisters and brothers living day to day with one foot in the kingdom of God and one foot in this world. We need help recognizing God's call in our lives to go with Abraham and Sarah and Jesus into exodus searching for God's new Promised Land. The community helps each member discover what Frederick Buechner calls "true vocation" by finding the place where our deep gladness meets the world's deep need (Buechner 119).

In these perilous times, we need to be very intentional about forming and maintaining circles of Bible study, prayer, and discussion that move from theory to practice. We must pray for wisdom as we relate to the world around us.

Jesus warned his followers that they would suffer for being extraordinary people who were often out of step with the larger culture. But he also promised that the Holy Spirit would lead them; and when they need to make decisions the Holy Spirit would help them find just the right words to defend their extraordinary way of living.

This "being out of step"—this "being extraordinary people"—is not just about being opposed to violence and war. We must ask questions about all of life—all the things that the world assumes are normal. We are extraordinary people when as a family we prioritize attending church on Sunday over Sunday morning sports events. We are extraordinary people when we say that even if we lose money our businesses will not open on Sundays. We are extraordinary people when our business people speak up at a Chamber of Commerce meeting or at the Kiwanis Club when there is a racist comment or joke. We are extraordinary people when we speak out against the violence in Iraq, Colombia, and Palestine. We are extraordinary people when we joyfully welcome and genuinely include people of color in our community.

Parker Palmer writes in *Let Your Life Speak* about his own experience within a Christian community as he invited a "clearness committee" to help him decide about direction in his ownlife:

So as is the custom in the Quaker community, I called on a half dozen trusted friends to help me discern my vocation by means of a "clearness committee," a process in which the group refrains from giving you advice but spends three hours asking you honest, and open questions so you discover your own inner truth. (Palmer 44, 45)

Support for Nonconformity to the World

One of the most important aspects of the threefold process of living out the mandate of Romans 12:2 is the support offered to each other. As individual members live out their decisions about how not to conform to the world around them, they are encouraged and supported by the community of faith. In Romans 12:5 Paul says that even though the congregation consists of many different people it is actually one body. Different members bring different gifts that combine to make a strong and faithful community, living as citizens of God's kingdom.

♣

During the years our family lived on the farm along Indian Creek, we experienced community at a level that we have not found again. We had a powerful sense of "settledness." Our family had a connection to a church community that was profoundly nurturing. It was a contented and peaceful life but also a community that empowered us to move to a land we did not know so that we could worship and serve God there.

One community tradition during our years living on the banks of Indian Creek was going to church on Sunday morning and often hearing a sermon by John L. Ruth. Then in the afternoon John would lead any who wanted to tag along on walks beside the east Branch of the Perkiomen. Both the Sunday morning sermons and afternoon walking lectures were delightful lessons woven by John from strands of Scripture, local and world history, literature, and music. The cloth John would produce from these complementary strands was always a love poem to the beauty of God's gift of community. John has also been an honest preacher and so has not forgotten that every faithful community must experience from time to time exile and exodus. Yet the message never ends with exile and exodus. God never allows exile and exodus to last forever because God always continues leading his people to the Promised Land.

Works Cited

Bonhoeffer, Dietrich. 1974. *The Cost of Discipleship.* New York: Macmillan Publishing Company

Buechner, Frederick. 1973. *Wishful Thinking.* New York: Harper Collins.

"The Letter to Diognetus." In Ehrman, Bart D. 1999. *After the New Testament: A Reader in Early Christianity.* New York: Oxford University Press.

Hostetler, Beulah. 1987. *American Mennonites and Protestant Movements: A Community Paradigm.* Scottdale, Pa.: Herald Press.

Mininger, Paul. 1950, April. "The Limitations of Nonconformity." *Mennonite Quarterly Review*: 167-168.

Palmer, Parker. 2000. *Let Your Life Speak: Listening for the Voice of Vocation.* San Francisco: Jossey-Bass Inc.

Ruth, Jay. 1984. *Looking at Lower Salford: A Visual History of the Township 1717-1984.* Harleysville, Pa.: Harleysville National Bank and Trust Company.

Chapter 9

Preacher's Calling: For John Ruth, It Meant a Lot

Ervin R. Stutzman

"Take courage, brother; come forward." These are the words of a bishop, spoken to a group of candidates for ordination by lot. For those who were reluctant to accept the preacher's calling, the lot loomed large and foreboding. The congregation sat hushed and waiting for the first candidate to rise and step forward. Long minutes passed as candidates pondered their choice. The one who chose the book containing the lot slip would be ordained.

John Landis Ruth understands well the significance of ordination by lot. He knows from experience that ordination can introduce a dramatic shift in one's life direction. Just two years after graduating from high school, John was asked to share the lot with two other candidates. When he chose the book with the lot, he was ordained for life.

John also understands the significance of ordination by lot for Mennonite communal identity. His interpretive comments regarding this practice are woven throughout his narrative accounts of the two oldest conferences in the United States—*Maintaining the Right Fellowship* and *The Earth Is the Lord's*. Both the Franconia and Lancaster Conferences used the lot for two hundred-fifty years after bringing the custom to America. This longstanding practice predicated a constellation of values that lay at the core of their spiritual identity. The relatively recent abandonment of the practice reveals a radically different understanding of the preacher's calling in the Mennonite church today.

The hard reality of today's pastoral shortages begs for a re-examination of the way the church calls preachers. There are surely some lessons to be learned from our long history of calling people to church office. What did the preacher's calling reveal about the nature of Mennonite community at the time when it meant a lot? Why did the church abandon the practice, with what consequences? How can we apply the lessons from the past to our difficult realities today? These are the questions that beckoned me to write this essay. To light the way, I shall use many examples from Ruth's aforementioned books. I will indicate these books as follows: *Maintaining* and *The Earth*.

The spiritual values that supported ordination by lot cluster around an Anabaptist concept of discipleship, or following Jesus. Hans Denck, an early Anabaptist, insisted that "no one can truly know [Christ] unless he follow him in life, and no one may follow him unless he has first known him." This oft-quoted maxim reveals a spiritual conviction that led Anabaptists to develop a unique practice for the calling of preachers. Closely linked to the central motif of discipleship were the tripartite concepts of vocation (call), *Gelassenheit* (submission), and *Geimeinde* (community).

An Anabaptist Theology of Vocation or Call

An early Anabaptist, when asked about his vocation, is reputed to have answered: "My vocation is to follow Christ. To make a living I am a tailor." In this way Anabaptists typically distinguished *vocation* (the call to follow Christ) from *occupation* (the means of livelihood). Any occupation might be deemed legitimate if it was consistent with one's primary vocation—following Jesus as a disciple.

God's call was understood to be expressed as both an *inner* and *outer* call. The inner call had to do with a direct or immediate call from God through the Holy Spirit. In Anabaptist theology as well as in practice, it was often equated with the general call to follow Christ as a disciple. By this definition, Christian conversion and vocational call are part of the same process, so that one's calling is directly rooted in baptism and church membership.

The outer call had to do with human agency, or the church. This conviction was expressed in the baptismal vows made in early Anabaptist settings. Candidates for baptism vowed to accept appointment to church leadership roles or offices if and when the church determined that God was calling them to meet a particular need. In this way, the church placed before new members (actually, men only) the potential implications of their public commitment to Jesus Christ. This explains why individuals were sometimes reluctant to join the church, particularly near the time when an ordination seemed imminent.

For several hundred years, the outer call in the Mennonite faith community was expressed through ordination by lot. Several weeks before the time for an ordination, the bishop announced the need for a person to fill a ministerial office, whether deacon, preacher, or bishop (elder or "full minister"). Then the bishop would preach a sermon emphasizing the biblical qualifications for a preacher. On the appointed day, the congregation was invited to give nominations for the office. All persons with sufficient nominations (at times only one) were placed into a "class" for examination by the bishops (the regular bishop assisted by guest bishops). At this point, any person in the class could be dismissed by the bishops if deemed unacceptable for the role. The most common causes for dismissal were a perceived inconsistency in Christian lifestyle or an unwillingness to adhere to or enforce the church's *Ordnung* (order or rules).

After the members of the class were confirmed by examination, the congregation gathered for the ordination service. The lot itself consisted of the selection by each nominee of a book from among those placed on a table. The number of books matched the number of candidates for ordination. One of the books contained a slip upon which was printed a saying such as Proverbs 16:33 "The lot is cast into the lap; but the whole disposing thereof is of the Lord" (KJV).

This manner of calling leaders reflected both a high view of ministerial office and the conviction that persons are called directly by God. Therefore, ordination services were often highly dramatic events filled with an aura of mystery and suspense. The services drew large crowds, including many visitors. When Jonas Hershey Martin was ordained a minister at Weaverland in 1875, a huge crowd assembled to witness one of eleven men draw the lot. "I never saw more people than on that day," wrote one of the participants who had been named for the lot (*The Earth* 597). It proved to be an historical moment, for it was Jonas, (commonly called "Joni") who two decades later led a conservative group of churches out of the Lancaster Conference.

Again, when Menno Zimmerman was ordained at Weaverland near Lancaster in 1884, some twenty men were in the class. Although it was a spring day when the mud roads were "awful," more than 1,200 people packed the meeting house by eight o'clock in the morning. During the fifteen minutes it took to draw the lot, the suspense mounted until "men and women were weeping aloud all over the church." A visiting newspaper correspondent could only compare the emotional intensity of the audience to that of an execution he had attended (*The Earth* 645).

Gelassenheit and Gemeinde

Perhaps much of the emotion was prompted by the sense of suspense. But the willingness for candidates to submit to such an ordeal was prompted by *Gelassenheit* (submission) and deep commitment to the *Geimeinde*, or church community. In his attempt to explain adherence to church rules in that era, Ruth writes "Simply put, the long story of this book is about a spiritual family striving to persist and extend itself. That communal struggle in turn was felt in thousands of individual soul struggles over yielding one's will to the 'will of Christ' as defined by the spiritual community."

Although Ruth was writing under the rubric of "'yielding' and plain dress" (*The Earth* 839), these words apply equally to ordination by lot. The system of ordination by lot could only be sustained by the willingness of individuals to submit to God's call through the church. Few of the preachers in Ruth's accounts would have volunteered for the preaching task. Yet they were willing to submit to the communal process of calling by lot. Therefore, "taking this risk of obedience was often a definitive experience in the spiritual life of nominees for ordination and their wives." "The sense of shared yielding . . . was close to the core of what it meant to be part of the covenanted Mennonite fellowship." (*The Earth* 837)

The ordination of Jacob Cassel Clemens for the Plains congregation in Franconia Conference in 1906 clearly illustrates this truth. As Ruth tells the story, Jacob was a "fancy young violin-playing banker in the congregation" whose name was submitted late in the nomination process. Although somewhat dubious, the bishop allowed Jacob's name to stand with others in the class. When the lot fell on Jacob, he and his wife Hanna were stunned, as was the congregation. The young couple was so shaken that they "had to be helped out of the meetinghouse by friends." Consequently, Jacob turned down the opportunity to be a bank cashier and took up a humbler mode of life, cultivating a small farm along the Allentown Road. In his prime, avers Ruth, Jacob "was the conference's most memorable and gracious preacher." Without the use of the lot, he would never have been ordained. (*Maintaining* 420-421)

In his gentle way, Ruth lets us see that many men were ordained who seemed ill equipped for the preaching task. For example, when Sam Detweiler of the Rockhill congregation was ordained in 1876, he could not read or preach. When he first stood in the pulpit, no words came. After paging through the Bible, he blurted through his tears, "I give it up" and sat down. Yet his wife taught him to read and he was advanced to the office of bishop some twenty years later." (*Maintaining* 361-362)

The persons who were chosen by lot didn't always adapt as well as Jacob Clemens or Sam Detweiler. Consider, for example, the cases of Jacob Ramer of Juniata County in 1895 or Joseph Gehman at Bowmansville in 1843. As Ruth tells the story (*The Earth* 709) Ramer was placed in the class by mistake when the bishop misunderstood the pronunciation of the nominee's last name as it was given orally. Although the mistake was discovered before the lot was drawn, the bishop did not remove Ramer from the class. In the end, Ramer was chosen by the lot without ever having been nominated by a fellow member. Like Sam Detweiler, he could not read, and preaching proved to be a continual struggle. Ten years Ramer learned about the mistake that had placed him in the lot. Apparently he was so shocked that he stopped preaching altogether and quit coming to church for a time.

Although Joseph Gehman was chosen by legitimate means, he could say little more than *Thut Busse* (repent). After ten years of no seeming progress in his preaching, a fellow member commented that the congregation would be ready to hear more. He is said to have replied, "*Dunet mohl sell, no sag' ich euch meh*' (do that once, then I'll tell you more)." In 1855, twelve years after his ordination, Gehman gave up preaching. His request to serve instead in the deacon's role was affirmed by unanimous vote of the congregation (*The Earth* 518).

The ethos of the lot system made it very difficult for men like Ramer and Gehman to refuse the call to preach, even if they severely dreaded ordination. There were a few cases where a man refused to preach after being chosen by lot. Enos Beidler of the Swamp congregation is a notable example of this. He was so shocked when the lot fell on him that he "went out into the woods, and sat on a stump to grieve over his situation." He contended that his call was not legitimate since a somewhat "retarded" woman, as he understood it, had nominated him. Although the congregation insisted that he had some teaching ability, he steadfastly refused to preach. He insisted that his ordination had been a mistake. And though the conference sent two deacons to persuade him, he refused to change his mind. When three of Enos' children died of disease in a short time, some people interpreted it as divine punishment for his refusal to assume the office. Convinced that the lot could not make a mistake, the congregation waited for thirty years before ordaining another minister.

In a footnote (*Maintaining* 575), Ruth explains that family lore depicted Beidler as a proud man. In this case, Beidler disproved the common belief that a man would be humbled by participation in the lot. Apparently, church members sometimes nominated men for the lot in an attempt to increase their loyalty to the church.

The surprises and disappointments produced by the lot demonstrated the need for the virtue of Gelassenheit on every hand, including candidates, spouses and families, and congregation. All demonstrated submission to God by consenting to the use of the lot. Rather than exerting their own human wisdom or political power through the use of an election, they left the final choice to God. And when God spoke through the lot, the people did not readily release the chosen person from responsibility, as the story of Enos Beidler clearly shows.

The sense of divine mystery in the lot was enhanced by stories of ordination where God seemed to intervene in a particular way. Such was the case with Noah Mack, who was ordained at Groffdale in 1900. Because the gruff-voiced Franconia Conference native had passed through the lot several times, he struggled to submit himself again. On this occasion, however, he "fell into a trance" during the choosing of the lot, and the covers of the books became transparent to him. He declared later that he could see that the book he chose was the one with the lot slip in it. He experienced the strong hand of the divine in the process. Thus he became a strong "advocate" of the lot (*The Earth* 763).

The lot may well have demonstrated Mennonite commitment to Gelassenheit by helping persons deal with conflicts. By letting God choose their leader through the lot, some congregations averted or settled disputes within the fellowship. In the days when many members of the congregations were blood relatives, the choice of a minister could dramatically shift the power relationships among family systems. Perhaps that is why they often quoted the verse from Proverbs 18:19: "The lot causeth contentions to cease, and parteth between the mighty." (KJV) As long as the congregation was willing to accept the outcome of the lot, the preachers chosen in this way were authorized to lead despite political differences in the church. Furthermore, since nominations were given by members of the congregation, the laity could not blame the leaders for "stacking the deck" or choosing their own assistants or successors.

There may be another reason why Mennonites depended so heavily upon the use of the lot to choose their ministers. It provided a safeguard against the presumption of men who would readily have volunteered to be a preacher. In other words, the Mennonite sense of Gelassenheit cut both ways. On the one hand, it nearly forced men to serve if they were called by the congregation. On the other, it discouraged men from volunteering. To publicly voice a sense of call to ministry might well invite the accusation that one had the *Prediger-Geist* (the preaching spirit). In the community that relied on the lot, God's will and the community's will towered over the individual's will.

The influence of Gelassenheit was manifested not only in the choosing of a preacher, but in the preaching task itself. The congregation expected the preacher to speak in a humble manner, even to the point of self-deprecation. The congregation placed the highest spiritual value on extemporaneous sermons laced with abundant Scripture references. A preacher was expected to be prepared to speak upon a moment's notice. In fact, many bishops notified the preacher of his assignment in the early moments of the worship service as the congregation sang their opening songs. The congregation frowned upon "studied sermons" that relied upon the use of commentaries or sermon notes. No wonder that a woman once commented that it may take ten years to make a preacher. Yet no one was particularly bothered if a new preacher couldn't finish his first sermons; someone from the "bench" would simply step up to assist. Members viewed ordination as the beginning of a journey of apprenticeship. Some ministers eventually excelled in preaching, while others did not.

Consequently, some members of the church were lured away by more expressive preaching in neighboring churches. For example, the revivalist emphasis of Methodists and the evangelistic preaching of the Church of the Brethren stood in stark contrast to the humble preaching in many Mennonite churches. It only served to exacerbate the tension between individual salvation and communal discipline. This tension had been present for years on the frontiers of American life.

No one symbolized this tension more clearly than Martin Boehm. Boehm had been a reluctant participant in the lot at New Danville in 1756. The shock of his being chosen left him with deeply conflicting emotions. Although he had experience in speaking as a lay person, he felt ill equipped for the preaching task. Consequently, when he stammered in his preaching and had to sit down without delivering a sermon, he entertained the thought that something was deeply wrong. Eventually, he concluded that the reason he could not confidently preach the gospel was because he was "lost." After fervent prayer, he experienced an emotional conversion. His preaching changed dramatically, such that his listeners often wept. His preaching was a call to repentance and an invitation to experience God's gracious mercy, resulting in assurance of salvation. In this vein, he perhaps reflected the style of his pietistic ancestors from Europe. Thus, Boehm's preaching was more akin to Moravians and Methodists than to his fellow Mennonites.

Many ordained men before and after Boehm struggled with deep feelings of inadequacy for the task. He dealt with that humiliation by seeking a spiritual experience to validate his calling and equip him for the task. He was convinced that God answered his plea.

Boehm's preaching clashed with the values in the Mennonite community. Whereas Boehm emphasized the individual's responsibility before God, they emphasized humility and willingness to follow the order of the church. While he emphasized the necessity of a personal experience with God, they emphasized the importance of obedience. Boehm served the Mennonites as a preacher and bishop for nearly two decades. But when he seemed unwilling to respond to the bishops' admonitions, they excommunicated him from the Mennonite fellowship. He became a well-known United Brethren preacher (*The Earth* 333).

Moving Away from Ordination by Lot

Two centuries later, it would become much more difficult for the bishops to exercise authority over ministers. The rise of individualism, accompanied by a breakdown of conference authority, eventually undermined the authority of the bishops. This same trajectory eventually led to the abandonment of the lot.

These trends were already evident by the mid 1800s, when John Oberholtzer of the Swamp congregation in Franconia rose to prominence as a leader. Although he himself had been ordained by lot, the young minister was dissatisfied by the quality of preachers who were called by this system. Goaded in his convictions by a politically savvy preacher named Abraham Hunsicker, Oberholtzer envisioned a change in procedures that would call forth more highly qualified ministers.

In 1847, Oberholtzer drew up a sequence of seventy "articles" for discussion of "the guidance and government" of the Mennonite "brotherhood." The effect of this action was akin to Martin Luther's posting of his ninety-five theses on the Wittenberg Door. Oberholtzer's articles created deep consternation and resistance among the conservative leaders in the Franconia Conference. In a community that valued humility and self-deprecation, Oberholtzer's uninvited proposal and the call for public debate must have seemed like a flagrant violation of implicit rules based on Gelassenheit.

The paper called for changes to the most deeply ingrained leadership practices in the conference. For example, Oberholtzer stressed the importance of a preacher's ability to teach and speak publicly. At first, Oberholtzer did not call for the elimination of the lot. Rather, he suggested that the congregation take a special vote to choose the two best suited candidates from among those who had been nominated through the regular procedure. His opponents argued that this would be usurping God's place.

Soon after Oberholtzer's proposals were rejected he left the Franconia Conference with a group of supporters. They founded the Eastern District, which eventually became part of the larger General Conference Mennonite Church. Today Oberholzer's proposals seem eminently reasonable, even conservative. Over time, the Franconia Conference adopted most of the changes he proposed. The mindset that most Mennonites bring to the calling of preachers today is more akin to Oberholtzer's thinking than that of his conservative resisters.

By the early 1900s, some Mennonite conferences were ordaining men without using the lot. They allowed or even encouraged individuals to volunteer for ministerial roles. This put pressure on the more traditional conferences such as Franconia and Lancaster, who sensed grave dangers of individualism in this approach. The Franconia Conference was particularly alert to the dangers of "forwardness" in individuals who wanted to be preachers. Nowhere was this more evident than in their thinly veiled response to the assertive Clayton F. Derstine.

They determined that young Derstine had a case of the *Prediger-Geist*, demonstrated by his eagerness to speak at teachers' and "cottage meetings" shortly after his baptism. Frustrated by the barriers to ordination in Franconia Conference, Derstine moved to the Old Mennonite Mission in Altoona, Pennsylvania, where he was ordained by another conference without the lot. He soon learned that his authority as a minister did not readily extend back to the Franconia Conference. The October 1915 session of the conference resolved that "If any Brother leaves the Conference District and is ordained different from our conference rules, his office is not recognized by this Conference District, except by consent of Conference." Because Derstine was considered too self-promotional and insufficiently subject to conference authority, he remained a *persona non grata* in most Franconia Conference pulpits for the rest of his life (*Maintaining* 430, 433).

About the same time, a similar process was taking place in the Lancaster Conference, when revival preachers came from the West. One of the most significant among them was Amos Daniel Wenger. Born in Virginia, he traveled about in Ohio, Iowa, Nebraska, Kansas, and Missouri as a young man. In his late twenties, he was ordained (apparently without the lot) to serve a number of struggling congregations in Missouri. When he heard about the dire spiritual condition of young people in Lancaster, the young bachelor preached his way east, arriving at harvest-time in July 1896. Although he was warned that the conference did not allow protracted meetings, he preached a series of nineteen meetings by moving from one meetinghouse to another.

The meetings proved to be such a success that he was invited to address the upcoming quarterly meeting of the Sunday school mission at Paradise. Just two days after that meeting, an accident at Bird-in-Hand killed a young couple on the way home from a party. This event proved to be the catalyst for a memorable harvest of young people in "Methodist style" "revival meetings." Wenger continued his revival preaching in the Virginia and Franconia conferences, always under the watchful eye of dubious bishops.

Four years later, in 1900, after having been married and widowed, Wenger returned to the Lancaster area, speaking to rapt audiences about his six months of travel in the Holy Lands. As a result of this speaking circuit, he met and married a schoolteacher from Millersville. A week later, in its spring session, the Lancaster Conference gave him permission to preach in area churches, although he was not "seated" on the "bench" in the Millersville-Roherstown circuit, where he lived.

Three years later, the Millersville congregation received Wenger as a minister by a good majority. This affirmation surprised Wenger's Midwestern friends, who doubted that the Lancaster conference would be willing to accept an evangelist who had not been ordained from a Lancaster-area church in the prescribed way. They viewed it as a hard won victory against the staid and authoritarian Lancaster bishops. (*The Earth* 761)

Although changes came slowly in both Franconia and Lancaster, they both adapted to a more individual emphasis for salvation. Eventually, revival services became standard fare in Mennonite congregations, and even bishops such as Noah Mack gained notoriety as revival preachers. To supply the needs of a growing mission movement in the 1900s, church planters and missionaries were encouraged to volunteer. Conference leaders began issuing ministerial licenses, giving individuals the freedom to preach in local congregations. A license allowed people to try their hand at ministry before being ordained. Today the majority of ministers are licensed for a period of time before being ordained. Nearly all are ordained without the use of the lot.

Benefits and Liabilities of the Lot

In retrospect, one can see several spiritual and practical benefits for using the lot. Not only did it reflect the spiritual values of discipleship, vocation, Gelassenheit, and Gemeinde. It also provided the preachers that congregations needed. Except in unusual circumstances, the congregation always had a full supply of ministers. When there were candidates who were willing but reluctant to serve, the lot provided the means to bring them into ministerial leadership. Finally, those who were called felt the strong blessing of God through the climactic casting of the lot. The memory of the ordination service carried many a preacher through hard times.

Yet with all of these advantages, there were good reasons for the church to move away from this system. For one, the virtues of humility and submission were emphasized to the point where the preacher's individual will was unduly suppressed. In light of the believers church's emphasis on voluntarily following Christ, there could have been more room for nominated individuals to voice their reservations. The New Testament emphasis on spiritual gifts and calling suggests individual initiative as well as communal discernment.

Secondly, the use of the lot functioned to the exclusion of other biblical means of choosing leaders. The leaders who held rigidly to the old way seemed to ignore abundant scriptural evidence for multiple ways to commission leaders.

Thirdly, the administration of the lot seemed to short-circuit the congregation's discernment process. Should not a man like Ramer have been dismissed from the lot when it was discovered that he had not even been nominated? Without an openness to such discernment, the congregations may indeed have been tempting God. The congregation would have done well to take an additional step between the nomination of candidates and their participation in choosing the lot. Oberholtzer suggested that a congregational vote narrow the lot to two candidates. Lacking that, the leaders could have required a congregational "vote of confidence" for each candidate before he was placed in the lot. Finally, the lot system ignored the ministry gifts and calling of women. Except for the role of deaconess among descendants of Dutch and German Mennonites, women were not even perceived as candidates for pastoral ministry.

A Contemporary Dynamic Equivalent for the Lot

Although we now encourage both men and women to consider pastoral ministry, the church faces an increasing shortage of preachers. Along with other faith communities, we are desperately searching for the means to arrest or reverse this trend. Amid this quest, we would do well to reevaluate how preachers are called. What can we learn from the way preachers were called in the past?

Although it was appropriate to abandon the indiscriminate use of the lot, we would do well to adapt the best aspects of that system. It may even be possible to create a "dynamic equivalent" of the lot that is well

suited to our day. I suggest the following spiritual principles be received from the old tradition:
- an emphasis on both inner call and outer call
- a definition of vocation as Christ's call to discipleship
- a close link between baptism and call to ministry
- a definition of occupation as the concrete application of Christian vocation
- an opportunity for congregational members to name potential pastoral leaders
- a congregational process of discernment to select the best suited candidates
- an openness to transcendence and mystery in the choice of a candidate

Further, I suggest the following adaptations to the tradition to achieve a more fully orbed process of "calling the called." Each of them provides for meaningful interaction between the individual and the church community:
- Congregations should seek to create a "culture of call" that encourages individual members to listen for Christ's call to Christian service, whether for pastoral office or for other concrete expressions of ministry.
- Congregations should provide occasions where members may either volunteer or nominate others to be considered for pastoral ministry, not necessarily linked to a particular need in that congregation.
- Women should be considered on par with men for congregational nomination and discernment.
- Nominees should be given appropriate opportunity to serve in various church roles, including supervised internships, to test their gifts and skills as part of a process of communal discernment.
- The communal discernment process should allow for a variety of methods to select or confirm individuals for specific ministry assignments, such as a process of consensus in a small group, a clearness committee in the Quaker tradition, or by a vote of affirmation after a period of testing.
- The congregation should help selected persons to receive training for their ministry tasks.

The tasks of ministry are daunting in a postmodern world. Individuals need the affirmation and support of the community as they explore a call to ministry. They need to hear both leaders and other members of the church saying, "Take courage, brother. Take courage, sister. Come forward."

Works Cited

Ruth, John. L. 1984. *Maintaining the Right Fellowship: A Narrative Account of Life in the Oldest Mennonite Community in North America.* Scottdale, Pa.: Herald Press.

_____. 2001. *The Earth Is the Lord's: A Narrative History of the Lancaster Mennonite Conference.* Scottdale, Pa.: Herald Press.

Chapter 10

Communion as a Gathered Body: Or the Body of Christ, Mystical and Sacramental

John D. Rempel

The Issue

One of the underlying tensions of church life today is between the communal and outward expressions of faith, on the one hand, and the individual, inward ones, on the other hand. The Lord's Supper is often understood only as the individual's inward encounter with Christ. Yet each believer's encounter with Christ in communion is set within a larger reality: that of the body of Christ. The breaking of bread has to do with the ongoing recreation of community, with the tangible coming together of the church. "Body of Christ" is the essential concept we need to grasp the meaning of the Lord's Supper and how it creates community. The "body of Christ" signifies three realities, related but not the same; all of them are astonishing and unsettling.

First of all, "body of Christ" refers to Jesus' body of flesh and bones. In the accounts of the Last Supper this term stands parallel to the term, "blood of Christ" (Matt. 26:26-29). Together they describe Christ's self-giving—they tell us in the most vivid possible way that he is sacrificing his very life for others. The ritual of broken bread and poured cup enacts what Christ will do.

Second, "body of Christ" refers to the self-giving of Christ in the Lord's Supper, the re-presenting through the Holy Spirit of *what Christ has already done (Confession* 50). Paul writes, and we pray, "Let the bread we break and the cup we drink be a communion of the body and blood of Christ" (*Minister's Manual* 76; based on 1 Cor. 10:16). This reality is a great mystery. Over the centuries the church has gone to two extremes in interpreting it. One extreme tends in the direction of magic: with the proper blessing, the bread becomes flesh like the flesh of Jesus' earthly body.

The other extreme goes in the direction of reductionism: since the bread is obviously not flesh to our senses it must be a 'mere symbol,' a sign of something else. Through the centuries the church has sought to balance these tendencies. The Reformation tried to correct the first extreme but set in motion ways of thinking that were in danger of going to the second extreme. Most Protestant traditions then, and increasingly again today, agree that when bread and wine are shared in faith and love by the gathered community the bread and wine become a communion of the body and blood of Christ. In other words, in this communal act of breaking bread the Holy Spirit unites the church and individual believers with Christ and one another.

Third, "body of Christ" describes the church. Paul makes the case that the community of believers is Jesus' extension in history. In other words, in its visible life the church prolongs the presence of Christ in the world. The term is more than a metaphor in Paul's thought: Christ is our head and we are his members. (1 Cor. 12:4-31) This notion is at the heart of Pilgram Marpeck's view of the church and the basis for his mature theology of the Lord's Supper. (See "Pilgram Marpeck's Response to Caspar Schwenckfeld's Judgment," 168-157.) The church is not merely a collection of individuals or an institution but an organic reality, an extension of eternity in time. Marpeck talks about the church as the ongoing humanity of Jesus on earth. When we commune in Christ we are remade as his body on earth.

In the early centuries it became common to say that the church was the "sacramental" body of Christ (because it extended his physicality in the world) and the Eucharist his "mystical" body (because of his intangible presence in the breaking of bread). How this view was inverted offers a rarely explored insight into the nature of sacramental reality.

How the Issue Changed

Already in the second century seeds were being sown for this premise to be turned inside out. (See for example H. de Lubac, *Corpus Mysticum: L'Eucharistie et L'Eglise au Moyen Age*, summarized by W. Crockett in *Eucharist: Symbol of Transformation*; also P. Fitzpatrick, *In the Breaking of Bread: Eucharist and Ritual*, 176ff.) It began in a healthy way. Critics of the gospel found the teaching of the incarnation, that God had taken on flesh, difficult to accept. In the courtroom of contested arguments the Lord's Supper became exhibit number one for the gospel. Defenders of the faith began to press the analogy between the Word becoming flesh and the presence of Christ in the Eucharist. This analogy drew attention to the elements of bread and wine themselves. It was fed by the thinking of Christians whose background lay in mystery religions which taught that human substances could be transformed into divine ones.

Thus began one of the two most significant—but seldom recognized—changes in the church's understanding of communion. There was a movement away from an event—(a communal breaking of bread in faith and love) in which a relationship (the church's oneness with Christ) is renewed—to a reality contained in a venerated object. Slowly, it began to matter as much what happens to the elements as what happens to the people who share them. Augustine was one of the theologians who tried to hold both positions in a positive tension. At the Lord's table he proclaimed to communicants, "Become what you have eaten."

By this time another factor had arisen to undermine a belief in the church as the sacramental body of Christ and communion as his mystical body. The church had become a "mixed multitude," an institution that included everyone in society by means of infant baptism. The visible church was no longer a community made up only of people who had come to faith and obedience in Christ. And so the church seemed less and less like a sacrament, in the sense of a concrete reality that is a living sign of Christ, evidence of what he is like.

People yearned for a sure sign that the same Christ who had lived and died for them was present to them in the course of history. They wanted to know that his sacrifice on the cross was powerful enough to save them now. In the first centuries the church had been the primal sign of this incredible claim; it was a new humanity, evidence that the wall of alienation had been broken down (Eph. 2). Increasingly ordinary people as well as theologians sought the evidence for their salvation not in a community that was overcoming alienation but in a reality beyond the limits of human relationships, in the Eucharist.

By the sixth century the breaking of bread was a highly developed liturgical event but it was becoming less and less congregational in nature. Increasingly the priest alone was the actor; far from the congregation he carried out a transaction with God that concerned objects more than people. Developments in architecture document what happened. The apse of an early Romanesque church had a table at the front. The presiders sat in a semicircle around the back of the table. In the nave the worshippers stood opposite their leaders in full view of the able. Later on the table moved closer and closer to the East wall of the church and was separated from the congregation, in the west by a long choir and rood screen, and in the east by a massive iconostasis. This "sanctuary" was holy ground to which the people had no access. Reinforcing the emphasis on sacred space was an emphasis on sacred objects. By the eleventh century a decree was passed in the Western church that lay people could not receive the cup for fear that in spilling a drop of wine they would profane the blood of Christ. This is a far cry from the ancient church in Corinth where Paul says that profaning the blood of Christ has to do with being out of relationship with one's sisters and brothers (1 Cor 11).

Yet the early view of the two expressions of the body of Christ was not entirely lost. Catholic reformers, like Berengar of Tours, tried to hold back, if not reverse, this inversion. There is also evidence of pastoral practice reflecting the old view. One piece of it is a sixteenth century case on record in England where a priest invites the congregation to come forward during a Holy Week penitential service in preparation for communion to declare to him that they are at peace with God and their neighbor. As one woman comes forward another follows her and accuses her of slander. The priest tries in vain to reconcile the women on the spot. In the end he warns them that unless they make peace with each other they cannot take communion on Easter Sunday (Rubin 149). (Many Mennonites will recognize this rite of preparation because it was carried over into Swiss and South German Mennonite eucharistic life and is still practiced today!)

By the time of the high middle ages, the inversion of the two meanings of the term "body of Christ" was almost complete. The sacramental body of Christ, that which prolongs Christ's humanity in time and space, had become the Eucharist. The mystical body, the intangible, heavenly reality had become the church. The body of Christ in history no longer transformed people but transformed bread.

What the Reformation Did About It

The Reformation overturned the notion that priests were the exclusive mediators of God's grace and the belief that by their power a sacrament would become what it signified, independent of its reception in faith and love. The Reformation as a whole restored faith as the condition (not the cause) of grace in a sacrament. It was less successful in restoring love (making peace with each other) as the co-condition of eucharistic reality since the new churches of the sixteenth century remained "mixed multitudes" because they were each the official church of a political realm.

One notion that gained currency in parts of the Anabaptist, as well as the Reformed and Anglican reformations, was a restoration of the ancient teaching that the transformation that happens in the sacrament is one of people and not things. This is particularly clear in the teaching of Ulrich Zwingli and Thomas Cranmer—in the Supper the liturgy prays for the Spirit to come upon the people. In Anabaptism this notion of a transformation of character received literal enactment in footwashing, which it took over from monasticism. At the same time these movements all gave the memorial of Christ's death heightened emphasis. This was to make unmistakable the fact that his "once for all" sacrifice is the source of life; nothing can be added to it by the church. The Spirit makes the past sacrifice of Jesus present now: that is the reality to which the sacrament is the door. We receive Christ in a devout act of human recollection but it is not we who make the Supper happen: it is the Spirit mediating Christ to us through bread and wine shared in faith and love.

Overall, the reform of the Eucharist in the sixteenth century brought it much closer to Jesus' table fellowship in the New Testament. Again, the change in architecture is indicative. What had become an altar inaccessible to the congregation, on which a transaction between a priest and God was carried out, became the Lord's table amid the congregation from which they ate a holy meal. At the same time this restoration was also an innovation because it brought about a crack in the "sacramental universe," in the world as it had come to be understood in light of the incarnation—a place in which matter had the potential to bear grace. All that was needed for that potential to become actual was an intervention by the Holy Spirit. This was provided for in the Catholic scheme of things by speaking the words of institution as an act of consecration. A sacrament was an object infused by grace which infused people with grace. In Protestant movements the divine intervention took place not in objects, like bread and wine, but in people. Nature was a means of grace not in and of itself but only to the believing community and individual. The infusion of the human spirit with grace replaced the infusion of nature with it. This was the crack in the sacramental universe. It changed the experience of Protestant worshippers; increasingly the inward and subjective approach to God became more real and more to be relied on than the outward and objective.

Distinctive Anabaptist Emphases

The sixteenth century had some success in reversing the medieval inversion of what was signified by the "sacramental" and "mystical" body of Christ. At one point, that of the church being made up only of believers, this restoration was most complete in Anabaptism. Because of this ecclesiology the interpretive key for Marpeck's sacramental theology was the notion of "the humanity of Christ." Because the church was made up of believers it rang true to Anabaptists that this visible body was the sacramental extension of the Lord's presence in the world. And the breaking of bread made sense as his mystical presence.

Such an understanding was fostered by the notion of the church as a priesthood of believers rather than a hierarchy. This notion worked itself out liturgically: for the Anabaptists the celebration of communion went from being the work of a priest without a congregation to that of a congregation without a priest. The actors in this drama were Christ and the whole congregation. The minister was present as a presider but his role was that of a representative of the congregation not a mediator of grace distinct from that of any other Christian.

Later Mennonitism

What happened in later Mennonite history becomes more difficult to gauge because the record is surprisingly diverse. The three original emphases of what happens in the breaking of bread (remembrance, union, transformation) shifted in emphasis. For example, the High German Confession of 1660, the mother confession of North German Mennonites, lays the weight on individual union with Christ, "the life-giving bread of the soul in spiritual communion." The Shorter Confession of 1690, in the Swiss tradition, shows a high view of the sacrament when it claims that, "through faith there is a communion of the body and blood of Christ." But the Dordrecht Confession of 1632, the most widely accepted confession of all, has only the memorial and a meager reference to the fellowship of believers. Is this because the other emphases were assumed and didn't have to be argued, because such a toned down claim reflects its character as a compromise document, or because these people held no teaching of union with Christ in communion? From these fragmentary references we see that there is a broad, uneven, and largely unexplored eucharistic theology in our tradition.

One of the defining concerns of a Mennonite understanding of the church has been that of a holy people "without spot and wrinkle" (Eph.5:27). An upcoming communion service became the surpassing occasion for self-examination: are we really perfected in love? The response of the congregation was meticulous preparation for the Lord's table. The relationship with one's sister and brother was inseparable from one's relationship with Christ. Here the sacramental body of Christ was indeed the church. Traditional Mennonites would have been at home in the sixteenth century service where the two women had it out with each other and the priest warned them about coming to the table if they were not at peace. The danger in this high view of discipleship, whether in the sixteenth or twentieth century, is that the human effort at holy living so dominates that there is little room for the collective experience of grace, for the divine role in the remaking of Christians as the Lord's body in his supper.

The second great innovation in the church's eucharistic theology was yet to come. The rationalism of the Enlightenment and the popularization of scientific thinking in the nineteenth century reduced ritual to human action—to our act of remembering, our act of creating community. If the sixteenth century put a crack into the sacramental universe, the nineteenth century unraveled it. People no longer saw God's presence in the material world. This development had direct consequences for their understanding of sacraments. Where a place for God's action was maintained at all it happened outside the material world, to the soul and the invisible church.

Modern thinkers argued that ritual—outward, communal actions—belonged to primitive cultures; true religion was inward, between God and the soul. William James' *The Varieties of Religious Experience* is the classic declaration of that creed. Scientific thinking discredited God's presence in outward things, his effect on the material world. To science sacraments were magic. (Something in that accusation echoed a voice from the past for Protestants but nineteenth-century rationalism was not the position of the Reformation.) Free churches like ours, without encompassing structures of dogma and liturgy to guard them, had nowhere to flee from the attacks of science except inwards.

There is a third, and surprising, actor in this drama of emptying the material world of God. In its emphasis on individual and inward experience, Evangelicalism (whose importance for church renewal in the nineteenth century is unmistakable) became an unwitting accomplice of science and rationalism in undermining religious community and the outward signs by which it communicates.

Communal Worship in Our Time

I have tried to sketch out two profound shifts in the theology and practice of the Lord's Supper. The first one concerns the inversion of the notion of "the body of Christ." In the early centuries it meant the church as the sacramental extension of Christ's presence in history. Later the sacramental reality had to do with the transformation of bread and wine. The second shift began in the sixteenth century but came into its own in the nineteenth. In it the Lord's Supper was restricted to a subjective and individual reality and lost its sacramental and collective character.

To bemoan these shifts is not to say that the collective side of sacramental life has not been at fault. It has sometimes tyrannized the soul in its preoccupation with outward reality. It has sometimes placed the onus for transformation so strongly on us that God's action is forgotten—and so, if there was any spot or wrinkle you were shut out from the Lord's table.

It should also be pointed out that there have been trends in the past generation to reclaim the church as the body of Christ and its centrality to the meaning of the Lord's Supper. As a whole, I find them too subjective in orientation, too little grounded in the transcendent. In mainstream Mennonite congregations much emphasis is now placed on human fellowship, the voluntary gathering of people who want to live as Christians. The good thing is that they begin with reality as people know it—developing relationships, witnessing to experienced grace, undertaking social service or political advocacy. But something is missing: the sacramental basis for community. The church is the prolongation of the body of Christ, the Lord's Supper is the prototypical event in which this body is renewed. These are supernatural realities, divinely given.

Sometimes it seems as if we celebrate community as our creation. And how we worship betrays how we think. I have been dismayed in recent years at the number of communion services I've been part of in various Mennonite settings in which there has been no general communion prayer (recalling the work of Christ and praying for the Spirit) or even prayers of thanks for the bread and cup. The whole weight of the occasion falls on its human actors.

How can we restore a balance between what God does and what the church does in our theology and practice of the Holy Supper? I propose working with four aspects, in pairs of two, and three characteristics in that quest. The first pair is the mystical and sacramental aspects of the Eucharist. It is "mystical" in that as we visibly eat bread and drink wine we invisibly receive the body and blood—the very person—of Christ. It is "sacramental" in that this presence of Christ is given, in Marpeck's language, through the union of inner and outer: the sign participates in the reality to which it points.

The second pair is the Supper's communal and individual aspects. It is "communal" in that the body of Christ, the church, is a collective reality. Communion is not an event in which autonomous individuals have parallel religious experiences. We do not come to Christ alone but with and through one another. The meaning of the term "priesthood of all believers" is not that we can come to God privately but that we come to him on one another's behalf: each is a priest for the other. This corporate personality of the church is hard for people in the age of individualism to accept. It is also hard for free church Protestants to grasp. We fear a collective participation in acts of worship which seems to substitute for the direct involvement of every worshipper through her personal relationship with Christ.

Catholic worship relies on the collective; evangelical worship insists on the individual. In my view this is a false dichotomy. Believers church ecclesiology holds them together. In conversion and baptism I die to myself and am born in Christ (Rom. 6). I live, but it is "Christ lives who in me" (Gal. 2:19-20). While conversion is a profoundly personal experience of grace it is not an isolated one, in that to be in Christ is to be in his body. I dwell on this point because, in my experience, the two trends in Mennonite worship each focus on one aspect: the liturgical side is communal, the charismatic side individual. In communion these two are inseparable. The breaking of bread is a collective encounter but, at the same time, each of us meets Christ personally, "that I may gain Christ and be found in him, not having a righteousness of my own." (Phil. 3:8-9)

We turn now to the three characteristics of the Lord's Supper. They make up the content of the communion prayer: memorial of Christ's death, prayer to the Spirit to "represent" him to us now (*Confession of Faith* 50), transformation of the community. I use the term *communion* rather than 'eucharistic prayer" because the latter has the same content but in such elaborate (a long rendition of salvation history) and fixed (always a *sanctus* and *benedictus*) form that it seems out of keeping with the Free Church ethos.

The first of these characteristics is the memorial of Christ's passion. In the power of the Spirit we recall the saving works of God culminating in the sacrifice of Jesus' life, whose end was a broken body and shed blood. His death was a sacrifice for our sin and a victory over evil. We stand in awe and devotion. Then we pray for the Spirit to come upon the assembly and grant us a communion of the body and blood of Christ (1 Cor. 10:17). We are united with the living Christ in the breaking of bread, as were his disciples at the inn of Emmaus (Luke 24:28-35). In this surpassing collective reality of union with Christ and Christ's people we are remade into his body—its bones are reset. It is people who are transformed. Footwashing is a remarkable and concrete expression of this transformation, the sign that this is how we want to live our lives when we take the presence of Christ with us out into the world.

All along I have worked with an assumption that requires acknowledgement. It is the real presence of Christ in the Supper. I have made a historical and theological defense of it in the New Testament and Anabaptism elsewhere (e.g., "Communion, *Mennonite Encyclopedia* 5: 170-172). In our tradition I have found that Pilgram Marpeck has the most to offer. He joined in the critique the Reformation made of Catholic sacramentalism. He corrected it from the vantage point of a believers church ecclesiology. Then, when he saw that this corrective was leading to a total spiritualizing of God's work (a trend that has dogged the free churches ever since), he corrected that trend with a believers church sacramentalism. His great insight was that the Lord's Supper was an event rather than an object. There is no moment of consecration in his theology in which bread becomes body. But when believers gather in faith and love and share bread and wine in the Spirit, there Christ is received, surpassingly and tangibly—in this event. The Spirit is the agent, the people are the medium, the bread is the sign. It's a complicated formula but it provides the most satisfying answer I have found to the question, "How is Christ present in the breaking of bread?"

Our *Minister's Manual* (1998) was compiled to reclaim for our church a fuller worship life using resources from our own tradition and that of others. The principle on which its materials, particularly for communion, are based is the importance of a recognizable pattern for worshippers and worship planners to build on. Traditionally the Lord's Supper was an invariable service in which everything was done the same way each time. We have now had two generations in which effort has been made never to do anything the same way twice. The manual lifts up the value of a pattern which can take different forms. For example, on one occasion the act of preparation for communion might be a confession of sin; on another it might be a pledge of love, and so forth. But the act of preparation is part of the pattern of worship.

What is required to make liturgical sense out of the tug between tradition and innovation, order and improvisation, is a deeper understanding of the nature of ritual. Ritual depends on pattern; it is the language that speaks through repetition. The goal of ritual is to draw us into what is universal rather than what is particular to a given occasion. Its power lies in the subconscious, preverbal level to which it takes us. Bad ritual (rote repetition, fear of innovation) is confining. Good ritual (improvising on patterns that everyone knows and that don't need to be explained) is liberating. Good ritual is simple and recognizable—it stylizes and acts out the gift of salvation in a way that invites unself-conscious participation. In my ideal, worshippers from three very diverse Mennonite congregations in New York—King of Glory in the Bronx, First in Brooklyn, and the Manhattan Fellowship should be able to recognize the basics of their own service in that of the others and be able to participate in them without being distracted. Underneath the differences in language, music, and piety there should be a single pattern.

Early in this chapter I drew attention to the breakdown in Christians' confidence in the church as the primal sacrament of the body of Christ. In the New Testament the church was the evidence of the incarnation, of a new humanity, of the fact that the wall of alienation had been broken down. The Lord's Supper was the moment in which that reality was renewed. Nothing expresses the Anabaptist understanding of the church as fully as this double claim. The task before us is to learn how to live it out as children of the age of reductionism and individualism.

Appendix on Ritual Patterns

What follows is the pattern for the breaking of bread found in the *Minister's Manual* (1998). It is based both on the typical movement of worship in historic Mennonite and free church practice (not uniform at various times and places but with common elements) and on the worship of other denominations, especially those whose worship has been shaped by the liturgical movement of the twentieth century.

(1) We prepare for communion by individual and corporate self-examination before and during the service. We open ourselves to God's grace and offer it to others, especially those who have something against us (Matt. 5:23-24).

(2) The breaking of bread is always a service of Word (Bible reading and proclaiming) and sacrament.

(3) There is an invitation to the table of covenant renewal on the basis of baptism, the mark of the covenant.

(4) The communion prayer is a grateful recitation of the story of salvation and a plea for the Spirit to bring us into communion with Christ now.

(5) The words of institution are read as the warrant for our action and the ritual core we share with every other Christian community.

(6) Prayers of thanks for the bread and cup are offered in imitation

of Jesus' prayers at the Last Supper in gratitude for the breaking of his body and the shedding of his blood for us.

(7) The bread and cup are shared.

(8) We give thanks for the gift of salvation and the call to discipleship. Footwashing is one expression of this response. It is a striking way of enacting how we mean to live our lives yet it is so intimate that it can be best practiced once or twice a year.

(9) We are sent forth to give up our lives for our neighbors as Christ gave up his life for us.

WORKS CITED

Confession of Faith in a Mennonite Perspective. 1995. Scottdale, Pa.: Herald Press.

de Lubac, H. 1989. *Corpus Mysticum: L'Eucharistie et L'Eglise au Moyen Age*, Paris: Aubier, 1949; summarized by W. Crockett in *Eucharist: Symbol of Transformation*, New York: Pueblo, 1989.

Fitzpatrick, P., 1993. *In the Breaking of Bread: Eucharist and Ritual*, Cambridge, Mass.: Cambridge University Press.

Marpeck, Pilgram, 1992. "Pilgram Marpeck's Response to Caspar Schwenckfeld's Judgment." In *Later Writings of Pilgram Marpeck and His Circle, trans.* Walter Klaasen, Werner Packull, and John Rempel. Kitchener, Ont.: Pandora Press.

Minister's Manual. 1998. Scottdale, Pa.: Herald Press.

Rubin, M. 1991. *Corpus Christi: The Eucharist in Late Medieval Culture.* Cambridge, Mass.: Cambridge University Press.

Chapter 11

Feed the Hungry and Run for Relief: Mennonite Relief Sale as Folk Festival

Ervin Beck

It still remains difficult to reconcile participation in festival with being a "serious" person. . . Traditional preindustrial people, of course, understand otherwise." —Richard Bauman

The Michiana Mennonite Relief Sale, held the fourth Saturday in September at the Elkhart County (Ind.) Fairgrounds in Goshen, does not (yet) appear among the 614 festivals listed in "Enjoy Indiana," a booklet published by the Indiana Department of Commerce, Division of Tourism. But many people who attend the relief sale have at least a hunch that it is more than an MCC (Mennonite Central Committee)-sponsored way of relieving human suffering. Some try to put the genius of the relief sale into words: "It's like a fair, except there are no rides. You buy things instead" (Benjamin Rohrer, eleven years, 1999).[1] "Coming here is like a very large family reunion" (Joan Hockman, 1999). "We're not here to make money. We're here to make people happy" (pie-seller, 1999).

What these people sense—and what the folklorist knows—is that the Mennonite Relief Sale is also a folk festival. It is an unselfconscious expressive performance by Mennonites of their ethnic identity.[2] The relief sale, as festival, strengthens the Michiana Mennonite community as much as it relieves suffering in the wider world.

Definitions of "folk festival" by folklorists embrace what has taken place since 1966 at the Elkhart County Fairgrounds near Goshen, Indiana every fourth Saturday in September: "[Festivals] occur at calendrically regulated intervals and are public in nature, participatory in ethos, complex in structure, and multiple in voice, scene and purpose. Festivals are collective phenomena and serve purposes rooted in group life" (Stoeltje 161). The relief sale, as festival, is "a community expression suspending the rules of everyday life." It "reaffirms the cohesion of a social group to its communitarian structure through participation in a time of revitalization," which is "cosmic" as well as social and cultural (Mesnil 186).

The main difference between the relief sale and most festivals in the "Enjoy Indiana" list is that the relief sale is a "carnivalesque" festival, rather than a "folklorized" festival, to use Marianne Mesnil's terminology. Folklorized festivals often serve "the commercial, ideological, or political purposes of self-interested authorities or entrepreneurs" (Stoeltje 161). However, the relief sale is a festival prepared "by the people for the people" (Falassi 3)—not by the establishment for itself, or by the people for the establishment, or by the establishment for the people, or by the people versus the establishment (Falassi 3). Oddly, because Mennonites do not regard the relief sale as a "festival," and in fact think they are engaged in an entirely other enterprise, the relief sale is a more "authentic" festival than if Mennonites "folklorized" it—that is, than if they self-consciously planned it as a festival.

Folklorized festivals emphasize performances for the entertainment of passive audiences. But the seeming chaos of the carnivalesque Mennonite relief sale results from the fact that all attendees are participants, not passive audience. Because the sale emphasizes purchasing things, everyone can participate as fully as they like. They can eat the pancakes and sausages. They can bid on quilts. They can Run for Relief. They can buy shoofly pie to take home. If a folklorized festival emphasizes "make-see," then the relief sale, as carnivalized festival, emphasizes "make-do" (Mesnil 192) since all in attendance contribute to the festive activities.

An overwhelming majority of the estimated 30,000 people who attend the Michiana relief sale are Mennonites—which makes it an in-group festival. But since it is publicly advertised, strangers are also welcome and create some of the exotic element that "carnies" add to other kinds of festivals. Some visiting strangers are well-heeled urban tourists—from Detroit, Chicago, or Indianapolis—who come to look at the natives and to join the festive proceedings by buying quilts. Others are Mennonites from distant communities who have heard about the big sale by word of mouth and sometimes arrive in campers that they park on the fairgrounds for the duration. The worldwide crafts sold from the Ten Thousand Villages tables also bring a foreign, exotic element to the festival.

Although such widespread participation brings to festival behavior a sense of chaos, and although the various kinds of festivals in world cultures differ widely from each other, certain predictable events and sequences make up a kind of "morphology," or ritual structure, for the folklore genre of festival. I will blend insights from folklorists Beverly Stoeltje and Alessandro Falassi to discuss the archetypal festival elements found in the Michiana Mennonite Relief Sale: "rites" (to use Falassi's term) of valorization and devalorization, display, consumption, competition, and exchange.

RITES OF VALORIZATION AND DEVALORIZATION

Festivals create a "time out of time"—a liminal experience—by claiming or re-claiming an otherwise ordinary time and space for the special carnivalesque needs of festival: "An area is reclaimed, cleared, delimited, blessed, adored, forbidden to normal activities" (Falassi 3). Consequently, festivals are usually framed by opening events that "valorize" the holiday time and place and by concluding events that "devalorize" it and return it and the participants to an everyday time and place.

For the Michiana relief sale, valorizing means sacralizing the otherwise secular Elkhart County Fairgrounds. Especially for the more conservative Mennonite-related groups, as well as for older Mennonites who recall that attendance at county fairs used to be forbidden, sacralizing the fairgrounds is an important step. However, that task has been more easily accomplished since the 1980s, when the local relief sale board paid for and, with volunteers, constructed the large fairgrounds building that now houses the quilt auction. Nowadays, in sacralizing the fairgrounds, Mennonites are, in effect, reclaiming the building that was once their own.

Valorization occurs most obviously in the opening program of the sale, the Friday evening worship service in the quilt building. In recent years the program in the early part of the evening has featured a "sacred concert" by the inter-congregational MCC Relief Sale Men's Chorus. In 1999 the program theme was "Healer of Our Every Ill," which called attention to the world needs that the sale responds to. The event opened with a welcome by the sale's vice-president, then a prayer that emphasized not the needs of the world but the need for Mennonites to "come together as a community." Choir and audience then sang "606," the Mennonite ethnic anthem ("Praise God from Whom All Blessings Flow"), before the choir concert. In 2002 the choir concluded their program with "606," although then the audience itself sang it again—standing spontaneously—following which, all applauded each other in a kind of tribal ritual.

However, this program—with its official, decorous content and intention—was so often disrupted by sale-goers milling around on the edges of the large meeting, especially to look at the quilts in their maze of racks, that some men were posted on the fringes of the crowd, holding large printed signs that read: "Please be quiet. Thank you."

The meaning of the sale is again valorized the next day at 8:00 a.m. in the quilt building, when the first two items auctioned off are loaves of whole wheat bread (selling for $200 a loaf in 1999). The auctioning of the bread becomes a ritualistic symbol both of the worldwide need for basic food and of communion by sale-goers with each other as well as with the needy. Valorization occurs most dramatically at 12:00 noon, when the quilt sale stops, the audience is quieted, and someone leads in the singing of a hymn and someone else offers a prayer—not to bless the food eaten but to invoke the values of the sale.

The "official," valorizing motive for the sale is reinforced by the Mennonite Central Committee's information booth, located in a tent or building in a prime location on the grounds. It offers information on MCC and the Mennonite Church through videotapes, printed materials, displays, and well informed interpreters. Although the MCC booth is intended to orient strangers to those subjects, it seems to attract visits mainly by persons who have had or would like to have MCC assignments.

So that sale-goers would not forget what should motivate their behavior, valorizing signs used to be posted in the various areas of the sale, stating such Christian admonitions as these:

Feed the hungry.
Blessed are the peacemakers, for they shall be called the sons of God.

If someone strikes you on the right cheek, turn to him the other one.
God is love. Whoever lives in love, lives in God, and God in him.

The serious contents of those signs jostled with the festive activity that surrounded them.

Valorization occurs behind the scenes, too. A relief sale "kick-off" supper and program is held in the spring of each year, open to the public but intended to launch work on the year's sale and inspire midlevel administrators. In 2002 the event was held on April 25 at Clinton Frame Mennonite Church in rural Goshen and included a devotional by pastor Terry Diener, who spoke about his MCC service in Brazil; and a longer talk by Rick Hostetler, medical doctor, on his recent visit to Iraq on behalf of MCC.

The official reason, or sanction, for the relief sale festival is presented more often and more intensively than is usually the case at festivals. On one level, that is because the sale has a basically religious motivation. As one organizer emphasized at Clinton Frame, it's "not just food and quilts!" If organizers of the sale "protest too much," it may be because some elements of festival—as with the milling crowds during the Friday worship service, and other features to be described below—threaten to overwhelm the stated reason for the event.

As with most festivals, the devalorization of the relief sale occurs in a modest, low-ritual way: at the end of the quilt auction a prayer is offered, people are thanked, and the quilt building reverts to being just another empty fairgrounds building. Elsewhere, roughly simultaneous with the quilt sale, the festival dwindles gradually and anticlimactically, as one activity after another closes down, chairs and equipment are put away, and litter is cleared up. Devalorizing used to culminate the following day in Sunday worship services in local congregations, when out-of-town visitors to the sale were acknowledged and welcomed and the total proceeds of the sale were announced—usually to the audible approval of worshippers.

Many congregations have done away with that too-materialistic, too festive moment. Nowadays, the final event is an informal meeting of sale officers and board members on the Monday following the sale. It is a kind of debriefing session, mainly with stories and accounts of "how the sale went" in areas and activities that administrators were unable to visit. A one-page financial report concludes the annual relief sale cycle.

Rites of Conspicuous Display

Festivals typically feature parades or other processional presentations of items that express the sponsoring community's identity or self-image. Some festivals elevate and exhibit individuals—the homecoming king or queen, the grand marshal, the holiday saint—who temporarily embody the community's best values (Falassi 4). Neither kind of display is literally found at the relief sale. Even the winner of the 5K Run for Relief goes virtually unheralded—and wins only a pie. The closest one gets to "procession" is the line for the sausage and pancake breakfast that slowly wends its way into the dark tent. The closest one gets to king or queen of the sale are the people (mostly women) who preside over the quilt auction and the auctioneers (mostly men) who work in the several auctions. The auctioneers are rendered especially conspicuous by their costume, many being dressed in coats and ties and some in cowboy hats and boots and bright coats. Serious quilt-buyers also go on conspicuous display by paying to obtain prime seats in the first few rows of the quilt sale building.

Of course, the dominant "conspicuous display" of the relief sale is of the commodities offered for sale. In fact, the main appeal of the Friday night program is to let the next day's sale-goers get a preliminary survey of items for sale, so that they can be at the right place at the right time on Saturday. Most elaborately displayed are the quilts, in their labyrinth of racks, carefully numbered and tabulated—the touring of which establishes its own very elaborate in-and-out, snakelike procession. The same element of display can be found, to a lesser degree, in the buildings that house the crafts and the three other auctions.

Rites of Conspicuous Consumption

Festival-goers not only display their identity, they also ingest it—heartily (Falassi 4). However, unlike at most festivals, no alcoholic drinks are consumed at the Mennonite relief sale. The "conspicuous consumption" consists of food. And more food. In 2001 the fifty different food stands earned about $130,000, or 35% of total sale proceeds. In 1999, 25,000 apple fritters were sold. Eighty-two donated hogs were butchered to make sausage, headcheese, scrapple, and pork sandwiches. And sale-goers consumed 2,000 halves of Nelson's Golden Glo chicken.

Certain foods are consumed by sale-goers mainly—or only—at the relief sale and therefore constitute "festival" foods. The more exotic ones are funnel cakes, rosettes, elephant ears, and half-moon pies, none of which have been traditional foods of widespread use in Michiana Mennonite homes. As with festival foods in general, many foods that used to be everyday foods, especially in rural Mennonite households, are now consumed only once a year, at the relief sale, because the Mennonite economy and culture have changed so much.

These festival foods include sausage and pancakes for breakfast, mush, headcheese, scrapple, shoofly pie, apple fritters, and apple butter (which continues to be home-made on the sale grounds). The sausage consumed at the sale probably represents the most direct connection with Mennonites' European origins, since it is locally made according to a traditional family recipe maintained by the Mishler family.

The changing nature of the Mennonite community, as revealed by foods, includes the presence in recent years of a few non-European food stands, namely egg rolls (from the influence of Asian refugees) and Mexican food items (from the growing Hispanic Mennonite Church in northern Indiana). Even pluma moos, representing Russian Mennonite culture, has been added to the menu in recent years. In light of some Mennonites' diet consciousness, some stands now offer salads, fruits, and diet drinks. But they are "for the fanatical" and take "all the fun out of it" (Andrea Zuercher, 1982). "It has to be fattening [made with lard] to be good, you know," said one pie-seller in 1999.

The sale puts so much emphasis on the preparing, buying, and eating of food that official sale sponsors try hard to squelch the sale-goers' tendency to reinterpret in a perverse way the Michiana Mennonite Relief Sale motto: "Dedicated to feeding the hungry in the name of Jesus Christ." A second meaning of "feeding the hungry" refers to sale goers' own indulgence as they graze on goodies from building to building, booth to booth. "This is the Mennonite FOOD sale" (shortcake seller 1999). "This is pig-out day" (woman in pancake line, 1999). "I begin at one gate and eat my way through the camp, then start back" (Martha Liechty Conrad, 1984). "I consumed two egg rolls, a knee patch, an apple fritter, a dish of strawberry shortcake, a sausage sandwich, and two glasses of orange drink and bought a roll of bologna to take home" (Twila Yoder, 1982). "Feeding the hungry" becomes a joking proverbial saying in many conversational exchanges. Among other variants are these:

"Eating to help the starving" (John Liechty, 1982).

"Boy, that guy's *really* dedicated to feeding the hungry" (Randy Jacobs, 1982).

"Get fat for Jesus" (Karl Shelley).

The grim paradox of rich Americans stuffing themselves to contribute money for food relief troubles some sale organizers. In 1991 MCC, for instance, formulated an expanded mission statement for relief sales that avoids the word "feeding" altogether: "This sale is dedicated to helping the hungry, homeless, war-torn, sick, handicapped, jobless, and illiterate around the world in the name of Jesus Christ." However, the shorter statement, "Dedicated to feeding the hungry in the name of Jesus Christ," remains the one used by the Michiana sale committee on its brochure and on the banner that hangs above the quilt auction.

Rites of Competition

Festivals offer participants the thrill of observing and, better yet, participating in contests and competitions that serve to encourage skills associated with the community's everyday work and to reaffirm the group's important values (Falassi 5). The literal competitions in the relief sale are minor events that attract little attention and involve few participants: the five-kilometer "Run for Relief" and the three-on-three basketball tournament.

The true competition of the sale—its agon, or drama—resides in the four auctions: of quilts, of miscellaneous new and used items, of antiques, and of items for child bidders. The most important competition is the quilt auction, which contributed $151,220 (41 percent) of the total proceeds in 2001. The quilt auction so dominates the event that, as far as the Elkhart County Convention and Visitors Bureau is concerned, the day is "The Quilt Auction" rather than the "Michiana Mennonite Relief Sale."

The quilt auction is a democratic competition, since any one person in the audience of over 1,500 people may compete for a quilt, or for paying the highest price for a quilt, or for buying the designated "sale" quilt of unique design. In 1999 when 364 items were auctioned, there were 364 different scenes of competition between 8 a.m. to 4 p.m. (about 46 per hour), some short and quiet but others—the ones the crowd waits for—being very dramatic indeed. The skilled auctioneer gradually becomes more intense and persuasive, and his "spotters" range up and down the six aisles, gesturing broadly and shouting out loudly the bids they receive. "Duane Troyer of Goshen, Indiana, the most flamboyant of all aisle auctioneers . . . [was] kneeling with bidders, putting his arm around them, sitting beside them and always making eye contact, which had the effect of pressuring the audience" (Tim Kennel and Andre King, 1999).

The final "Sold!" sometimes brings laughter, cheers, and applause from the audience and smiles of triumph from auctioneer and cohorts. It is a cathartic experience, in a kind of impromptu comedy, for all concerned. That kind of dramatic competition is repeated hundreds of additional times, usually in a more muted way, in the other three auctions.

More subtle competition occurs behind the scenes of the sale. Individual food stalls compete with their neighbors for higher total proceeds, and even with themselves from one year to another. Each sale, in effect, is in competition to exceed all previous sales in total income—and indeed until 1999 that was the case, with each sale yielding an ever-increasing total. Now that sale proceeds have begun to taper off—total sales peaked in 1999 but total proceeds for MCC had peaked already in 1992—the sense of competition has become more grim and less is made of total income than used to be the case. Finally, one area relief sale competes with other, more distant area sales for the largest proceeds, with the Michiana sale being one of the top three in North America in net income.

Rites of Exchange

One major outcome of festival is the exchange, or redistribution, of wealth. Insofar as festivals repay "the community or the gods for what [has been] received in excess" (Falassi 5), this important feature distinguishes the Mennonite Relief Sale from most other festivals.

The redistribution occurs on two levels. First, of course, the main goal of the festival is to redistribute the world's resources—taking money from middle-class people in mid-north-central Indiana to needy people throughout the world.

A second redistribution—or perhaps redefinition—of wealth also occurs within the sponsoring Mennonite community. The poor members of the church contribute a lot of work and time, some materials and a lesser amount of cash. The wealthy members of the church contribute excessive amounts of cash: $200 for a loaf of bread, $1,500 for a marble roller, or $7,000 for a quilt. As one non-Mennonite said in the quilt tent, upon seeing a quilt sold for $6,700: "This is a millionaire's hall." And as one quilter with talent but little cash said, "I can make them for myself . . . for less than I would pay for one here. The ones buying them have lots of money" (Mary Shafer, 1984). "Bid with your heart," says the sale brochure. In 2001, $310,000 left Indiana coffers and went to the needy world; at the peak of the sale's success in 1999, $440,000 of excess was redistributed.

Rites of Reversal or Extension?

A continuing issue in the study of festival behavior by anthropologists and folklorists is whether a festival constitutes a *reversal* of the everyday behavior and values of the participants (as in the New Orleans Mardi Gras) or an *extension* of everyday behavior and values. The Mennonite Relief Sale does illustrate some radical shifting of the Mennonite community's priorities and hierarchies, thereby fulfilling Victor Turner's claim that festival is a time when people are allowed to violate everyday norms.

Perhaps the most immediately obvious reversal is in attitude toward getting and spending. At the relief sale otherwise frugal, simple-living Mennonites spend their money with abandon—often for things they do not really need. As one non-Mennonite put it, "On this day these people who are known for their frugalness, can't seem to part with their money fast enough" (Ginger Miller, 1982). And as one auctioneer encouraged his audience in 2002: "It's only money. You can't take it with you, so spend away!" If carnival is a "time out of time" that sanctions extraordinary behavior, this fiscal abandonment is most impressive, even if it is "for a good cause."

Gender roles also undergo reversal at the sale. The relief sale is a predominantly women's operation. Women, supervised by other women, prepared the quilts, food, and handicrafts that accounted for 79% of the sale's proceeds in 2001. On the day of the sale they are publicly prominent, since they present the quilts in the big auction, they stand behind the handicrafts for sale, and they dominate most of the food stalls. However, such gender reversal must be qualified with some persisting evidences of traditional Mennonite patriarchy. The opening program Friday night establishes the norms for the community and the sale by offering a very traditional men's chorus and other leadership by men, with women being virtually absent from the stage. The male auctioneers ultimately dominate and control the quilt sale. And, oddly, men decidedly dominate in preparing and serving the pancake and sausage breakfast—the largest food sale—as well as in some other food stalls. Perhaps this latter kind of gender reversal—men displacing women—helps compensate to some degree for the reversal accomplished more impressively by women elsewhere in the sale.

The sale also reverses the hierarchies of the clergy and the laity and the intellectuals and the less well educated. Mennonite Church affairs have traditionally been directed and dominated by ministers, who are definitely not in leadership positions at the relief sale, and some of whom are even displeased by the time and effort their members give to it. And if intellectuals conduct the affairs of the Mennonite Church at large, they do not dominate the relief sale, which tends—also like MDS (Mennonite Disaster Service) and MCC meat-canning—to rely more on grass-roots laborers than on persons with advanced degrees. In fact, well educated Mennonites tend to stay at home and criticize the relief sale on theological grounds.[3]

In addition to raising money, how do Mennonites benefit from the festival experience that the relief sale offers? If the relief sale is essentially a "reversal" of everyday life, then it yields to the analysis of functional anthropologists who, following Freud, see such festivals as being therapeutic for their participants. That is, participating in rituals of reversal enables otherwise oppressed festival-goers to experience a temporary release that makes it possible for them to return the next day—oppositional feelings defused—to their normal activity. Their culture remains unchanged, and festival thereby "functions" to conserve tradition by allowing people to harmlessly experience its opposite values. Victor Turner gives this temporary reprieve a more positive interpretation by claiming that the *communitas*, or democratic leveling, that occurs during the festival temporarily attains the higher political values of the community that sponsors it, even though during the rest of the year they submit to the hierarchies required by practical survival.

From a less deterministic perspective, especially that of the Christian cultural theorist Bakhtin, carnival's ritual of reversal—even though it exists for only a short time—does, by degrees and over time, subvert, critique, and transform the everyday culture in the direction of the reversed culture that temporarily exists during the festival. It is interesting to notice that during the forty-odd years of the relief sale's history, Mennonite churches have indeed tended to evolve in the direction of the reversals noted above: Mennonites have become more prosperous and less frugal, Mennonite women have gained in equality with men, and the laity's participation in and direction of church affairs has increased. If the relief sale has not helped bring about those changes, it at least mirrors them.

I think it is more important to see the relief sale as not mainly a reversal but as a natural extension, writ large, of many "festivities" that Mennonites have traditionally sponsored and participated in. The most obvious connection is with the household auction, which constitutes a practical Saturday entertainment for many Mennonites and Amish and also often includes homemade food served as a benefit for a parochial school or a family in need. The relief sale thus continues to dignify the folk skill of auctioneering, which has always been one of three public performance skills sanctioned by Mennonite and Amish communities—the others being preaching and song-leading.

The decline in MCC relief sale revenue may be a sign of the sale's success, not its failure. One reason for its recent decline is the number of smaller charity auctions that Mennonite and other church groups in Michiana have begun to sponsor: for Haiti relief (which perhaps attracts Old Order Amish and other conservative groups away from the MCC relief sale), for the Goldenrod Community, for Bethany and Clinton Christian High Schools, and for individual Amish families suffering from catastrophic health care costs. How many quilts can Mennonite and Amish quilters make in trying to support all of these sales? Each such spin-off auction is a relief sale in miniature, testifying to the thriving health of such folk festivals in Michiana. The relief sale has served to reinvigorate the auction as a festive tradition within Mennonite communities.

The relief sale is also an extension of the barn-raising bee, in the "Shalom" house usually built by men before the sale. Quilts and other handicrafts are extensions of Mennonite women's "sewing circles," which have always been associated with local and world relief efforts. The quilt auction has certainly revived and even expanded the folk art of quilting in Mennonite circles. The food resembles a giant potluck, offering foods that Swiss Mennonites in the U.S. have traditionally preferred. And in being a gathering of the Mennonite community the relief sale becomes a glorified family, or denominational, reunion.

Finally, its calendric location near the end of September associates it with the universal phenomenon of the harvest festival.[4] Of course, it is not literally so—except perhaps in some of the seasonal foods offered for sale, such as molasses, apple butter, apple fritters, ground cherries, and the "harvest" of fattened pigs (usually butchered in the winter). But the celebration of excess that the sale emphasizes and the erstwhile agricultural life that Mennonites have lived do turn it into a recognizable harvest festival.

Folk customs, including festivals, are performances of identity; that is, the traditional physical practices of social groups express deeply held values and convictions that are given embodied form in festival activity. As publicly expressed by the relief sale, Mennonite ethnic identity includes such traits as generosity; hard work; organizational skills and cooperation; practical technical expertise; modesty in self-display; plain aesthetic (in the sale itself, not the quilts and other crafts); communal association; a service ethic; self-sacrifice; and concern for the needs of the wider world. Or as Dan Beachy, a former president of the Michiana relief sale, put it more succinctly: the sale shows that Mennonites are "industrious, honest, faithful, communal."

The relief sale may critique and transform Mennonite culture, but it most obviously extends and enlarges traditional activities and attitudes to reaffirm and celebrate essentials of Mennonite identity, especially at a time when the community is coping with rapid change and increasing diversity.

Official and Unofficial Culture at the Relief Sale

One thumbnail definition of folklore is "unofficial culture," meaning aspects of culture that are based on unspoken but commonly held values, whether or not those values are also articulated by authorities who control official hierarchies in a community.

Some elements of the relief sale discussed previously, such as the disruption of the Friday night choral program, point to a subversion of the officially announced norms of the sale. In this regard, the relief sale festival becomes "the people vs. the establishment." The playful reinterpretation of "Feeding the Hungry" is a prime example of the folk asserting their own value in opposition to official pronouncements, as festival-goers pay more attention to feeding themselves than to feeding the destitute of the world.

"Run for Relief" has also assumed a subversive proverbial meaning. Its scatological connotation is best captured by this anecdote:

> I was in the quilt auction tent when they switched auctioneers. The new man was apparently recently elected for the auctioneers' hall of fame. Here's what he said as soon as he got to the mike and before he started auctioning: "There's lots of hungry people in the world . . . and as I found out this morning, also lots of hungry people here at the sale [audience laughs]. I had to wait in line for an hour this morning for my pancakes and sausage, only to find out in the end that it was the line for the ladies' restroom [more laughter]. Maybe that's why they call it a 'relief' auction [audience in uproar]." (Tim Manickam, 1982)

In reinterpreting those two proverbs, "feeding the hungry" and "run for relief," sale-goers assert festival norms in opposition to the official value placed on the sale by organizers.

Actually, from the time of the earliest sales, thoughtful leaders have perceived certain endemic "problems" with the relief sale, springing from the difficulty of rationalizing actual behavior with stated norms. The persistent problems have to do with (1) eating so others may be fed and (2) contributing money but expecting merchandise in return. The more recently articulated problem concerns (3) the sale's failure to reach non-Mennonite audiences.[5] An interesting response to the first two problems can be found in a feature article that John Bender, on behalf of the Michiana sale committee, wrote about the relief sale for the *South Bend Tribune* in 1979.

Bender said that the first problem, of "overeating so that others may be fed," constitutes a "paradox at best," since the two actions are "mutually exclusive" (11). Although he cites the connection of the sale to the well-supplied tables, pantries, and smokehouses of traditional Mennonite households, he cannot resolve the contradiction. Accepting that sale-time indulgence in fattening food is wrong, he defends Mennonites by citing their emergent discussions of wellness and ecology. He also cites the *More-with-Less Cookbook* (1976), which was derived from author Doris Janzen Longacre's experience with MCC and which shows how to eat well and deplete fewer of the world's resources.[6]

Nor can Bender resolve the second problem—that Mennonites seem to be able to give money to MCC, not by making an outright voluntary contribution but only by selfishly obtaining quilts, rosettes, or marble rollers in return. Bender sidesteps the issue by saying that, after all, money is not the essence of the relief sale, the *attitude* of service is: "What makes a relief sale tick is not money but people willingly giving themselves and their time" (13). Even the quilts have value only insofar as they represent "the interest of a service rendered and the satisfaction of a skill put to use" (13). Finally, Bender quotes an official statement by MCC: "Relief and service have validity for us only as the motivation, spirit and methods of work are in keeping with the Bible" (13). Hence, Bender ignores the hard materiality of the relief sale—the juicy sausage, the Carolina Lily quilts, the $440,000—in favor of abstract, essentialist ideas *about* the sale, which the average salegoer might agree with, upon reflection, although not by behavior at the sale.

Bender's attempt to rationalize festival activity fulfills the quotation from Richard Bauman in the headnote to this essay, which stresses the puritan notion that carnivalesque indulgence does not characterize "serious" people. Mennonite intellectuals and administrators clearly tend to be uncomfortable with the carnality of the relief festival.

The third problem—that the sale appeals mainly to Mennonites rather than outsiders—has both a practical and a theological side. As sale revenues decline, sales need to reach new audiences to generate more income. And in order for sales also to communicate Mennonite values to others, they need to be made to appeal to more than members of an ethnic in-group. Recently, therefore, MCC consultants have been encouraging local sale committees to respond to these new realities. The Southwest Pennsylvania relief sale—serving the geographic corner formed by the boundaries of Pennsylvania, Maryland, and West Virginia—has responded in two ways: by moving the sale away from the Mennonite community to a fairgrounds near a non-Mennonite resort area, and by offering more performer-audience programming. Their revenue has increased by 30% (Berg). Encouraged by MCC, some sale organizers increasingly regard and plan the sale as a "festival," even to the point of using "festival" as part of the name for the relief sales in Oregon, Southern California, Winnipeg, and Central Fraser Valley (British Columbia). For the 2002 sales throughout Canada and the U.S., MCC tried to strengthen the witnessing aspect of the sale by suggesting that each sale stress the motto, "Come, follow me," as an evangelical invitation consonant with the "missional" vision of the newly merged Mennonite Church.

Both impulses—to "improve" the sale by resisting its carnality and to turn it into a more "folklorized" festival that presents programs for a public audience—certainly threaten the relief sale's current nature and function and perhaps its very continuing existence. Such reforms threaten to domesticate the event and turn it into a more calculated performance that will present Mennonites as they *think* they are, or as they *want* to be, rather than as they *really are*.

The genius of Mennonite relief sales is that they have not been subject to official control "from above," as it were. Relief sales originated in a Morgantown, Pennsylvania, barnyard in 1957 and have since then grown abundantly—but with little direction from MCC officials in Akron, Pennsylvania. All of the forty-six sales throughout the U.S. and Canada are under full local control; no MCC directives guide them. MCC even allows local committees to designate to what worthy project the proceeds of their local sale should go.

In recent years, however, the "Resource Generation" staff at MCC-Akron has made more gestures toward unifying the work of local committees. Since 1997 there has been a North American Relief Sale Board, consisting of five regional representatives and led by "coordinators" on half-time salary from MCC. The board and coordinators have begun to sponsor international (U.S. and Canada) meetings of representatives of local relief sale committees, both for encouragement and for exchanging ideas and information. A recent suggestion emanating from MCC is that relief sales provide more self-consciously designed "festival" activities, such as demonstrations, story-telling programs, and so forth. Such programming, especially for a non-Mennonite audience, threatens to change the relief sale from a carnivalesque event for a close-knit community into a more pretentious, performance oriented, folklorized event for outsiders.

It may not be possible for "enlightened Mennonites" to resolve the paradoxes found in relief sales. After all, relief sales are like the ocean—they are there, probably not easily changed, and perhaps even indestructible. Selling food and quilts to raise money for world relief is inherent in this very successful Mennonite communal endeavor. The sale is best justified and rationalized for what it is—an ethnic festival—not for what it should be, according to official thinking.

Recent postmodern and feminist thinking about the body, about embodiment, and about the materiality of human life is also important for any interpretation of relief sale activity. In recent years *The Mennonite Quarterly Review* has published important essays by Rudy Wiebe, Julia Kasdorf, Beth Martin Birky, and Pamela Classen on how "the body knows," as Wiebe put it. Classen's work is directly relevant to theologizing the relief sale as festival, since she points out that Mennonite women, although traditionally barred from implementing the official worship rituals of the church upstairs, nevertheless performed corresponding rituals with food downstairs to sustain both the human body and the body of Christ, the church.

The word *carnival*, of course, derives from the Latin *carne*, a word that means "flesh," which was dignified most significantly for Christians in the *incarnation*—the Word become Flesh. The relief sale as festival, specifically "carnivalesque" festivity, legitimately exploits the fleshly, physical, carnal body, and material existence of everyone who participates. As folklorist Erin Roth points out ("Quilts"), there is a kind of appropriateness in using (Mennonite) *material culture* at one end of the conduit (such as in Goshen) to generate *material aid* at the other end (Afghanistan).

Furthermore, folklorists and anthropologists agree that the rationalization of faith and practice that occurred with the Reformation also split off *festival* from *worship* in Protestant cultures (Bauman 95; Stoeltje 161; Abrahams). Iconoclastic, puritanical groups like Quakers and Anabaptists created the greatest divides between festival and religious ritual behavior, both by prohibiting festivals, in general, and by not regarding as particularly religious the festivities that are a part of their culture— auctions, barn-raisings, family reunions, and now relief sales. Since Mennonites have been deprived of church-sponsored festivals for almost 500 years, it is not surprising that they are loath to abandon or change the very successful one that they have recently developed.

The relief sale in Mennonite culture is certainly not a worship service, but its connection with explicit and implicit Mennonite norms helps bridge the historical schism of festival and ritual, brings the body back into Anabaptist theology and—if only for eight hours a year—integrates body and soul, individual and community in service "in the name of Christ."

Then God's servant John Ruth enters the gateway to the Great Festival, Franconia history in one hand and Lancaster history in the other. On his glorified body he wears his plain coat without a necktie, as he did as a teenager even before he was required to, thus respecting his father, and long after he no longer needed to—to witness to his faith at Salford Church, Eastern College, and Harvard University. He understands that ethnic expressions of faith are not to be scorned, that ethnicity can be a witness, that the body also speaks.

Notes

A version of this chapter has been published in Ervin Beck, *MennoFolk: Mennonite and Amish Folk Traditions* (Herald Press, 2004).

1. Quotations by relief sale participants come from field observation reports completed by students in my Folklore classes at Goshen College, especially in 1982, 1984, and 1999. "The 1999 Michiana Mennonite Relief Sale as Folk Festival," a loose-leaf notebook surveying eight different aspects of the sale, has been deposited in the Mennonite Historical Library at Goshen College. The manila folder, "Relief Sale Field Observations," has been deposited in the Goshen Archives of the Mennonite Church USA. I am indebted to my former students for these materials.

2. The relationship between the relief sale and folk festival has been noted by Robert S. Kreider and Rachel Waltner Goossen, Griselda Shelly and Erin Roth, although not explored in detail.

3. Kreider and Waltner Goossen (367) cite one vociferous critic of relief sales who has never attended a sale.

4. The fourth weekend in September, which is the annual date of the Michiana Relief Sale, always falls near September 29, which is the festival of St. Michael, or Michaelmas, in the traditional church year. The Amish of Lancaster County, Pennsylvania, observe Michaelmas as a holiday for rest and fasting prior to a communion service. When Amish and Mennonites lived in Europe, Michaelmas was the day when rents were due, following harvest, and was also an occasion for giving some of one's wealth to the poor. I am indebted for these insights to Julia Kasdorf.

5. Shelley cites the objections to relief sales as being "commercialism and undercutting voluntary giving" and the fact that they do "little to promote a responsible Christian lifestyle" (760).

6. There are at least three ways to rationalize the eating of food at the sale in order to feed the hungry elsewhere. First, "grazing" from one food booth to another may be a more typical consumption pattern than actual overindulgence. Second, if one divides proceeds from food booths by the number of persons in attendance, the consumption per person is reasonable, especially since sale-goers also purchase food to eat

at home. Finally, people in the food-deprived cultures to which MCC relief aid goes are themselves likely to celebrate with feasting when food is abundant, rather than save it for times of scarcity. Also, MCC now emphasizes general assistance rather than hunger relief—"helping" rather than "feeding"—which somewhat defuses the food issue.

Works Cited

Abrahams, Roger D. 1987. "An American Vocabulary of Celebrations." In Falassi, 173-83.

Bakhtin, Mikhail. 1968. *Rabelais and His World*. Translated by Helene Iswolsky. Cambridge, Mass.: MIT Press.

Bauman, Richard. 1987. "The Place of Festival in the Worldview of Seventeenth-Century Quakers." In Falassi, 93-98.

Beachy, Dan. 2003, July. Interview. Goshen, Ind.

Bender, John. 1979, Sept. 16. "Down-Home Hospitality Pervades Mennonite Relief Sale" In "Michiana" section, *South Bend (Ind.) Tribune*, 10-13.

Berg, Douglas. 2002, Aug. 27. Telephone interview.

Birky, Beth Martin. 1998, Oct. "When Flesh Becomes Word: Creating Space for the Female Body in Mennonite Women's Poetry." In *Mennonite Quarterly Review*, 72.4: 677-88.

Classen, Pamela. 1994, April. "What's Bre(a)d in the Bone: The Bodily Heritage of Mennonite Women." In *Mennonite Quarterly Review*, 68.2: 229-47.

Falassi, Alessandro, ed. 1987. In *Time Out of Time: Essays on the Festival*. Albuquerque: University of New Mexico Press.

Kasdorf, Julia. 1997, April. "Bakhtin, Boundaries, and Bodies." In *Mennonite Quarterly Review*, 71.2: 169-88.

Kreider, Robert and Rachel Waltner Goossen. 1988. "Organizing Festivals for MCC: Relief Sales" in their *Hungry, Thirsty, a Stranger: The MCC Experience*. Scottdale, Pa.: Herald Press, 361-69.

Mesnil, Marianne. 1987. "Place and Time in the Carnivalesque Festival." In Falassi, 184-95.

Roth, Erin. 2001, Oct. 20. "Quilts, Zwiebach, and Oak Furniture: Mennonite Material Culture as Material Aid." Paper presented at the meeting of the American Folklore Society, Anchorage, Alaska.

―――. "Relief Sales in the Midwest" in *Encyclopedia of Midwestern Folklore* (forthcoming).

Shelley, Griselda. 1990. "Relief Sales." In *Mennonite Encyclopedia*, vol 5. Scottdale, Pa.: Herald Press, 759-60.

Stoeltje, Beverly J. C. 1989. "Festival." In *International Encyclopedia of Communications*, ed. Eric Barnouw. New York: Oxford University Press, 2:161-65.

Turner, Victor. 1969. "Humility and Hierarchy: The Liminality of Status Elevation and Reversal." Chapter 5 in his *The Ritual Process: Structure and Anti-Structure*. Ithaca, N.Y.: Cornell University Press.

Wiebe, Rudy. 1997, April. "The Body Knows as Much as the Soul: On the Human Reality of Being a Writer." In *Mennonite Quarterly Review* 71.2: 189-200.

Chapter 12

Husk and Kernel: Anabaptist-Mennonite Essence Revisited

Leonard Gross

Poking at the Husks

Never doubt that a small group of thoughtful, committed citizens can change the world—indeed, it's the only thing that ever has! —Margaret Mead

We are born into this world, alone; we leave this existence, alone—alone with our conscience, alone with our Creator. This given provides a central clue to existence itself, namely, that each of us is responsible for self. I am myself responsible for my actions, decisions, thought processes—vis-à-vis other human beings, other forms of life, all of reality: vis-à-vis the whole spiritual-physical realm called existence and life.

I can only go by conscience; I have no other option. My conscience may be ill-taught and faulty, but so may the conscience and thought-processes of the other who is trying to convince me I am wrong. No, I can only go by my own conscience, always attempting at the same time to be open to the wisdom, counsel, and best intentions of others.

Conscience tells me I am here for a purpose, one I must enter and respond to, as I try to fulfill that for which I have been born. Central here lies the idea of relating, one to another, myself to others. I will have need of certain types of individuals to help me, to complement me, to enrich me. Slowly I also might find the wherewithal to reach out to others in need of relating, and to accept another's so reaching out to me.

No president, bishop, guru, or spouse, no male or female authority-figure may take away my ultimate singular responsibility of living and acting out of conscience. This fact is as true for women as it is for men, as true for the wealthy as it is for the poor. It is as true for the one who has known little love as it is for the one who has known parental love as a child, and close friendship as an adult.

How do we brave this—in the face of the myriad forces and persons of ambition, attempting to put us in our place and telling us what to buy, how to live, what to think, how to act? This is where conscience enters the scene, complemented with learning and the essential mind-set of reaching out to others. Indeed, developing positive human relations is also part-and-parcel of the very foundation of life's meaning, centered in the mystery of the Eternal, and the spiritual forces that are part of life and existence. For to be sure, faith, hope, and love are the core abiding spiritual realities that serve us well as we reach out to the other. In this regard, we discover elements of such faith, hope, and love in the process of conquering inner doubt, despair, and inimical attitudes and acts. And if we are fortunate, we discover the additional spiritual-existential reality and power of the "two or three": two or three (or more) disciples, together, intent on living out Christ's gospel of peace.

♣

I didn't always understand life in terms of individuality and conscience. In my early years as a child, I was naturally dependent on my parents—secure in Mother's arms and on Dad's lap. I always thought ours was a strong congregation, with many a person in our midst taking on the role of leader in one fashion or another. I generally looked forward to the tutelage of sympathetic and creative Sunday school teachers, some of whom were my own aunts. I looked up to our fine congregational song leaders, Timothy Thut and Millard Detweiler, who over the years taught us to appreciate the whole spectrum of traditional hymnology. I remember singing "Before Jehovah's Awful Throne," in that earlier, majestic, even-half-note mode, Sunday after Sunday during that year of 1945, until we mastered this gem as a congregation. The hymn slowly grew on us, as Millard helped us enter this hymn's spirit and mystery. I would later come to realize the strength of the singing tradition of our Doylestown Mennonite congregation. I can also still picture vividly in our Sunday evening young people's meeting those returning missionaries from India in strange garb, as they interwove sparkling artifacts and tales from foreign lands with biblical story.

After I was baptized at the early age of eleven, my view of church changed. The church no longer seemed to be "us," the congregation, but "they," the ordained ministry—those who insisted they were carrying out "the will of the church." Then during my teens, one day it came to me that I had been wrong. The church was not "they," but "it." For whenever I asked "they" the reason for this or that, "they" the ministry always referred me to "it," the Rules and Discipline of the Franconia Mennonite Conference, which proclaimed, among other things, "Thou shalt not go to parks." You see, I once needed to confess to the whole congregation during a communion preparatory service for attending an end-of-the-year public school picnic at Chalfont Park. I had found out, personally, that conference Rules and Discipline were for real, seemingly carved in granite.

Fortunately, the Doylestown congregation did not swallow this without a murmur—something which certainly helped me along in being a Mennonite to this day: During that very same preparatory service, just after the moment I was obliged to confess my wrong (I was told I would not need to speak, just nod affirmatively at the appropriate moment), a woman, Barbara Leatherman, never before known to be in any manner outspoken, stood up and said that something was wrong: A twelve-year-old boy needs to confess the sin of going to a school picnic at a small park where there is a merry-go-round and mixed bathing, but two couples from our congregation who were at the Ocean City boardwalk last Saturday do not need to confess, since Ocean City is not a park—even though merry-go-rounds are there in abundance!

♣

It would not be until college days and beyond that I was finally able to sort all this out. I slowly discovered, through the study of church history, the intention of the Anabaptists. Harold S. Bender, dean of Goshen (Ind.) College, was central in this regard, but only one of a large number of teachers who together helped make this vision something of a reality for us as students. Guy Hershberger was strong on community, formed upon Christ's teachings. President emeritus Sanford C. Yoder exemplified his quiet message of tending to the spiritual needs within—that the "outer" then tends to take care of itself. J. D. Graber was college evangelist during my junior year, one of the few evangelists I experienced who did not have an altar call. He exerted a positive and unusually powerful influence on campus that year, because of his sensitivities and deep respect for others.

Donovan (Don E.) Smucker, summer guest professor, introduced us to the complex Troeltschian world of social-religious typology. Robert Friedmann, another guest professor, made sense when he talked about existential Christianity, rather than doctrine, as comprising the very foundation of Anabaptism. In German class, Elizabeth Bender introduced us to Martin Luther's masterful translation of the Bible. I remember the living "story" qualities of the first chapters of Genesis.

In short, I discovered the hermeneutical community, where no one person was claiming the ability of defining truth, yet where the many, together, were living out the spirit, in complementarity.

The Anabaptist triad of ideas was alive—as ideas—during my 1949-1953 college days. For those who have forgotten, here are quotes from central paragraphs within Bender's essay, *The Anabaptist Vision*:

> First and fundamental in the Anabaptist vision was the conception of the essence of Christianity as discipleship. It was a concept which meant the transformation of the entire way of life of the individual believer and of society so that it should be fashioned after the teachings and example of Christ....
>
> As a second major element in the Anabaptist vision, a new concept of the church was created by the central principle of newness of life and applied Christianity. Voluntary church membership based upon true conversion and involving a commitment to holy living and discipleship was the absolutely essential heart of this concept....
>
> The third great element in the Anabaptist vision was the ethic of love and nonresistance as applied to all human relationships. The Brethren understood this to mean complete abandonment of all warfare, strife, and violence, and of the taking of human life.... (Bender, 1944, 78, 82, 85-86)

The impact of my Goshen College experience also colored my world outlook. I caught the international spirit on campus, occasioned in large part by the experiences of many a faculty member who had served abroad in relief work after the Second World War. I, too, set my sights on MCC Europe, and for three years, 1955-1957, helped out in youth work among the North German Mennonites—mostly refugees.

Yet, I was but one of many who experienced such a church that was indeed "we," and not "they" or "it." This Mennonite spirit, informed by the *Anabaptist Vision*, slowly extended itself in the 1950s and 1960s into many a corner of the Mennonite Church, being in tune as it was with *Nachfolge Christi*, or "discipleship," as Bender would translate this reality for the great majority of Mennonites who no longer knew German. Mennonites continued to feel in their bones this traditional approach to faith, going back as it did for four and more centuries, even after a brand-new doctrinal stance suddenly entered its ranks in the 1890s, at the time of a veritable Mennonite revolution when the German language gave way to English.

Mennonites needed a "quick fix." They no longer knew what the words *Nachfolge Christi* meant in German. So when Daniel Kauffman came along—one of the few central Mennonite leaders who could write in "good English"—his *Manual of Bible Doctrines* (1898) was accepted by many as truth, at least for the short term. And it was this doctrinal stance, the "it," which Bender questioned, and countered, with his formulation of the *Anabaptist Vision* in 1943.[1]

♣

The impact of another veritable revolution, this time from without, fell upon all Mennonites in the mid-1960s, when the Vietnam Era (1964-78) engulfed us. For a while, Mennonites wondered if anything we believed would survive: would we survive as a people? Institutional attempts to stem the tide notwithstanding, the power of the people—mainly youth—not only emerged socially and culturally within general society, it also had a revolutionary impact on Mennonites in particular. Franconia Mennonite Conference was actually without its Rules and Discipline for a time, when the old Rules and Discipline was rescinded but no new discipline enacted to take its place. Women's prayer veilings came off throughout most of the (Old) Mennonite Church during the height of the Vietnam Era. Mennonites, who just a few years earlier could be recognized as Mennonites on the highways and byways, all of a sudden disappeared, culturally, at least, in matters of distinctive dress.

The Mennonite Church reorganized in 1971 on the basis of congregationalism, weakening the hierarchical structures that had entered its ranks over a seventy-five-year period. And many Mennonites, throughout this whole era, went along with the general societal theme of "changing Washington" to bring about needed reform: the answer lies in changing Washington policy! The assumption all too often was that "placing the right people in Washington will take care of things."

It was only natural that a new era of interpretive Mennonite writing also came along, attempting to make some sense out of the brand-new Vietnam Era. Revisionism could be found on all levels, popular and scholarly, within the Mennonite Church, and without. Articles and books on liberation theology and revolutionary Anabaptism were soon to appear. *The Anabaptist Vision*, too, was placed under the critical scrutiny of revisionism.

Was there anything out of our Anabaptist-Mennonite traditions going back 450 years that could be salvaged honestly by modern Mennonites?

The Mennonite Church did not come apart. Even Franconia Conference survived its hiatus without Rules and Discipline—in fact, remained quite healthy and together congregationally, during and after this time. Many of the cultural strictures as defined in Kauffman's *Manual of Bible Doctrines* did not survive. But Bender's *The Anabaptist Vision* would fare better.

I mark the end of the Vietnam Era—at least at Goshen College—with 1978, when a student, John D. Roth, posted a note on the Peace Society board, suggesting that perhaps Washington is not in fact capable of "doing it all." Let's begin placing our efforts, time, and money, he said, with our own denominational programs, such as the Mennonite Central Committee, where we have had a better track record by far.

Then came the 1980s and 1990s, a time of North American prosperity when, alas, avarice set in. Here, too, Mennonites were deeply affected, many along with most everybody else tuned in to the Dow as it rose daily, miraculously, to ever-new heights of glory, forevermore.

Given such a milieu, aspects of my own childhood experiences with Rules and Discipline must sound strange to the ears of contemporary Mennonites. And indeed, there are no longer those seemingly harsh Rules and Discipline to impede current faithfulness. Some lament loss of the certainty of the old days.

Yet the Mennonite Church somehow did manage to survive many of the outside influences, sometimes needing to learn a few things the hard way. And we somehow continued—imperfectly to be sure—to gather together as earnest seekers and followers of the way of Christ.

♣

The clock does not stop, and we American Mennonites entered yet another era. The national emergency, September 11, 2001, came and went, spilling over into its uncertain aftermath. The Dow lost its dazzle, and a "minority" president declared all-out war on terrorism and pressed hard, mustering all his strength and forces upon a seemingly singular goal of toppling one evil man and his régime. Significantly, those advisors who had seen war were far more hesitant to enter the fray than were other key defense secretaries and under-secretaries. Experience is its own unique teacher, and historically, many a war commander and battlefield observer has turned peacemaker—after the fact. Ben Franklin was one such observer, close in to war, who in 1783 wrote, hoping "that mankind will at length, as they call themselves reasonable creatures, have reason and sense enough to settle their differences without cutting throats: For in my opinion there never was a good war, or a bad peace." (*Mennonite Historical Bulletin*, April 1990, 23). Too bad Franklin's eloquent words were uttered only after the fact. How much better had they been proclaimed eight years earlier in 1775, when the rush to war was only in its beginning stages!

Exactly on this point a minority group, for nearly five centuries, has attempted to maintain a concerted voice against all violence, including every form of warfare—at least for the church as the body of Christ. Such has been recognized far and wide, perhaps most recently in the World Council of Churches' *Current Dialogue* on what major world religions have to say about violence. One article deals with "Religion and Violence: A Protestant Christian Perspective," by S. Wesley Ariarajah, who summarizes well the Old and New Testament ideas that emerge on violence and nonviolence. He reviews how Jesus advocated radical nonviolence and how the early church espoused a nonviolent stance vis-à-vis the Roman Empire up to the time of Emperor Constantine. Another subsection, entitled, "Christian Approaches to War and Violence," begins as follows:

> Even though Christianity eventually developed into a religion that in principle rejected violence, both in the Middle Ages, as also today, Christian discussions on violence have centered mainly on one issue of whether there are situations in which some measure of violence is justified. Some are very clear that, in accordance with Jesus' own teachings, violence is not justified under any circumstance. Within the mainstream of the Church, "the historic Peace Churches" (mainly the Mennonites and the Quakers) have adopted the pacifist position of rejecting war and violence for any reason. (Ariarajah 21)

That Mennonites are viewed in this World Council of Churches journal as being "mainstream" suggests a major transformation that has taken place within the Mennonite Church over the past half-century. General society sees us culturally as being definitely "in the world" these days, an explicit change in perspective, and justifiably so. On the other hand—at least from the standpoint of our continuing rejection of war and violence—we still stand out as a group, not "of the world," in our taking exception to the majority views of general society on the justifiable use of military force by Christians.

Mennonites were not traditionally seen as being "within the mainstream of the church." Such a transformation came about, within scholarly circles, largely due to the impact, beginning in 1927, of the *Mennonite Quarterly Review* on North American scholarship, the brainchild of Harold S. Bender. Yet such a pronouncement was certainly capped throughout much of the Christian world by the monumental work of John Howard Yoder, best known for his *Politics of Jesus* (1972). What Bender and a host of *MQR* interpretive authors accomplished historically, Yoder accomplished theologically and hermeneutically. The *MQR* provided the context for scholarly conversation about things Anabaptist and Mennonite. Yoder's keen mind, combined with his prodigious volume of scholarship, founded as it was on an implicit believers church hermeneutic, caught on in Catholic, Protestant, and Mennonite scholarly circles and beyond, worldwide.

♣

In the light of radical Mennonite transformation that has come over the Mennonite Church since the 1890s, how much of the original Anabaptist kernel still remains? If we, indeed, are able to isolate the kernel! This quest now takes us to the concluding section of this essay.

Probing the Kernel

What the Western Christian establishment has so often regarded as the marginal issue of "social tactics" (as opposed to "doctrine") is not only inextricable from the faith, but the very arena in which the meaning of Christ's cross—the criterion of the faith—becomes clear. —John L. Ruth

The task of separating out husk from kernel is always fraught with the critical point and counterpoint, interpreted through the eye of the beholder. For our purposes here, we go back to the decade of the 1940s, when a small group of thoughtful, committed citizens of the kingdom got their heads together at Goshen College and penned some powerful words. One trio of personalities, especially, stands out in this regard: Robert Friedmann, Harold S. Bender, and Guy F. Hershberger.

It was probably the Austrian, Robert Friedmann, who first suggested that Anabaptism could best be interpreted descriptively, and not definitionally. His 1939 essay, "Anabaptism and Pietism," translated by Harold and Elizabeth Bender themselves and almost immediately published in 1940 in the *Mennonite Quarterly Review,* lay as the foundation of something new in the air. When Friedmann then came to Goshen soon thereafter, his presence was felt, centrally, in a manner that would transform Anabaptist scholarship. An example of Friedmann's spirit and influence may be seen in his 1942 essay, "The Anabaptist Genius and Its Influence on Mennonites Today," a lengthy segment of which merits full quotation:

> [Many seekers for a true Christianity] wanted not only the first step but also a true . . . [community] of the reborn as a nucleus in a heathen world. They wanted a Christian church in the proper sense of the word. So they ventured the hard and narrow way of nonconformity to the "world" that is a consistent life of earnest discipleship of Christ. It became in fact a "Christian revolution." A simple, untheological biblicism prevailed and gave the solid foundation. The brethren did not speak so much about salvation or justification by faith (although they believed in both), they did not use the Paulinic language as the Reformers mostly did, their primary concern was the keeping of the commandments of

Christ, or to say it in one word, *obedience*. Without obedience, simple and untwisted, there cannot be discipleship. *Faith* is no private matter of unrelated individuals; faith exists only as far as it leads to evidencing in life.

    The brethren, as they called themselves, tried to follow two great principles, well known to every Christian, but rarely actualized in history: *Love* and the *Cross*. The Anabaptists understood obedience of true discipleship consisting of nothing but these two principles which were very little taught in the official churches. Love leads to . . . [community], to a close and permanent fellowship which is unknown in the world at large, while the Cross is the unavoidable consequence of such contradiction to the world as it was taught by Christ. Of course, the Cross must never be sought for its own sake, but will inevitably be faced by those who do not compromise in things which matter. (21)[2]

Friedmann penned this in 1942. The triad of ideas that Harold Bender would acknowledge as being central in the *Anabaptist Vision*, written a year later, are all expressed in this Friedmann passage, ideas which Bender most likely picked up from Friedmann. "Faith is no private matter." "Love leads to . . . [community]." And the cross must be understood as something not only for the Jesus of history, but equally for his disciples as well. John Ruth, many years later, would lay out this same insight about the cross, that the issue of "'social tactics' (as opposed to 'doctrine') is not only inextricable from the faith, but the very arena in which the meaning of Christ's cross—the criterion of the faith—becomes clear" (Ruth 148). To be sure, the influence of Robert Friedmann on the developments of Anabaptist ideas and their interpretation dare not be minimized.

    Guy F. Hershberger, too, was an integral part of the small Goshen group working at Anabaptist interpretation. His master's thesis had been on Anabaptism, and in the very first issue of the *Mennonite Quarterly Review* in 1927 his solid ideas on "False Patriotism" appeared, spilling over as well into the second issue. By 1942, Hershberger also understood the Anabaptist nature of the church as something essential for a deeper understanding of our peace position. We save one of his vital ideas for the very end of this essay.

    Harold S. Bender certainly would have agreed with Friedmann that love leads to community, and with Hershberger, on the power of group testimony—and for that matter, with Margaret Mead's dictum, "Never doubt that a small group of thoughtful, committed citizens can change the world—indeed, it's the only thing that ever has!" Yet there was no doubt in Bender's mind as to what comes first, in this triad of vital elements that together describe the Anabaptist faith and life. Unless one begins with discipleship, the rest—whether the church as the body of Christ, or the idea of love—does not become reality. Bender's singular convictions are significant enough to quote *in extenso*:

> Does it not seem that every time we have sought the essence of Anabaptism in one of the other major ideas, such as the Scriptures, the church, or the principle of love, we are driven a step further into the ultimate relationship of the individual Christian to Christ? I would therefore propose that we pursue our search further down this road, for I believe that if we do so we shall find the answer in the concept of discipleship as the most characteristic, most central, most essential and regulative concept in Anabaptist thought, which largely determines all else. We shall also find at this point the parting of the ways between various forms of Christianity, and various types of theology and ethics. (Bender, 1950, 27)

> The character of the church is determined by something beyond the church itself, for it ultimately derives from the concept of the nature of the Christian experience and the Christian life. The concept of the church is actually a derivative idea. (Bender, 1950, 26)

> In the last analysis the meaning of love for the Anabaptist flows from the understanding of the nature and example of Jesus. (Bender, 1950, 27)

Here Bender understands Christianity to be more than (systematic) theology, more than ethics. Still he leaves no doubt that the beginning point is that of the individual as disciple, who existentially knows the inseparability of belief and practice, and of faith and life.

Bender goes on, convinced that discipleship, however, is far broader than the mere individual. Discipleship has societal ramifications, not only for the gathered believers but also for all of society and its culture:

> In essence the discipleship which the Anabaptists proclaimed was simply the bringing of the whole of life under the Lordship of

Christ, and the transformation of this life, both personal and social, after his image. From this point of view they subjected not only the church but the whole social and cultural order to criticism, rejected what they found to be contrary to Christ, and attempted to put into actual practice his teachings as they understood them both ethically and sociologically. (Bender, 1950, 29)

♣

For our purposes here it is highly instructive to note what exactly Harold S. Bender chose as his intellectual grid, in his now-classic portrayal of the primary motifs of Christianity as exemplified by some early Swiss Anabaptists. He did not go the route of defining faith through theological categories, as does systematic theology and dogmatics, but instead he made use of three "scientific" categories, as handles. Bender began very consciously with the individual; then stepped into the framework of multiple individuals who relate, one to another; and finally, capped all this—the individual, within a group—with an analysis of the quality of such interaction. In this regard, scientifically, one speaks of psychology, sociology, and (cultural) anthropology—whereby the individual, significant in his or her own right, becomes part of a group of individuals who, together, create a common culture and way of life.

Equally significant is what Bender tied each of these elements to, in his existential triad. The individual is bound inexorably to the Jesus of history and the Christ of faith. The group is tied to the corporate and gathered body of Christ, going back historically to Pentecost, where God's Spirit came to abide. The quality of group interaction is tied to Christ's gospel of peace (Matt. 5-7, Eph. 6), centering in love of God and neighbor.

Each of the elements in Bender's existential triad transcends the discipline of ethics, and is far removed from certain sociological concepts, such as a secular "social contract." For in following Christ we develop a living reality which is more than—indeed, other than—ethics. Such a following after is also more than—indeed, other than—(systematic) theology. In being a living part of the body of Christ, we enter a living corporate body that transcends mere secular societal covenants. In experiencing the gospel of peace and responding to the love of God by loving our neighbor, we come to know an existential and spiritual way that is again a reality set apart from ethics and (systematic) theology.

Also highly instructive is where Bender began in his triad of spheres: he did not begin with the body of Christ, nor with the gospel of peace, but rather with discipleship—and this, for a very good reason. The Mennonite Church had taken to a theological sidetrack that began largely with the concept of the church. It was, in addition, doctrinal in nature, which changed the very character of Mennonitism. To have begun with the concept of the church had the potential of lessening the visibility and God-given individual worth of each disciple. And to have begun with the idea of peace had the potential of attempting peace without acknowledging the necessity of the power of the spirit that makes peace possible: Spirit, that is, as experienced within the body of Christ—a body, composed of Christ's gathered disciples who, together, reflect on and then enact what it means to be a disciple.

By no means did Bender invent this triad. He, along with others, rediscovered it within the Swiss Anabaptist tradition, and helped a whole generation of members of the Mennonite Church to rediscover for themselves what they felt in their bones. True, Bender's delineation has rightfully been criticized as being too all-inclusive, since Anabaptist groups in the Low Countries and parts of Germany arose, based on somewhat different polities and theologies. Yet the *Anabaptist Vision* triad holds true for those whose tradition goes back to early Swiss Anabaptism. Examples abound, from Felix Manz, Michael Sattler, Andreas Castelberger, to Conrad Grebel (at least as long as he was part of the Zurich Anabaptist hermeneutical community)[3] (Gross, 2000).

What Harold S. Bender accomplished in 1943 with his *Anabaptist Vision*, was truly a return to a normative (Swiss) Anabaptist-Mennonite theology, as it had been articulated over the centuries, whereby discipleship found its fulfillment within the gathered community. Such a return to the idea of discipleship brought to an end the doctrinal interlude of the Mennonite Church, extending from the 1890s to the mid-twentieth century, that the Mennonite Church had bought into, and, which, with its emphasis on sometimes sterile and definitional doctrinal categories, stood at odds with a more existential and descriptive Anabaptist approach to faith and life.

♣

Bender, along with Friedmann and Hershberger, I think, had it right: biblically (the new life in Christ, beginning with the individual), historically (an accurate description of Swiss Anabaptism), and scientifically (using social-science categories of the individual, group, and quality of life together), as the most appropriate way of describing the faith and life of the early Anabaptists—rather than defining the movement in more traditional theological terms.

John Howard Yoder accepted much of this foundation, then took it the next logical step, developing many an Anabaptist biblical theme in hermeneutical fashion, in keeping with the existential nature of the Anabaptist movement in its early decades.

The *Anabaptist Vision* is true today for many Mennonites, to the same degree that it was true for many earlier generations of early Anabaptists and later Mennonites. Certainly, Bender's interpretation flows more naturally out of the Swiss Brethren tradition than it does out of Dutch Anabaptism. For the church polity of Menno Simons (a bit episcopal) contrasted with that of the Swiss Brethren (more thoroughly congregational). Yet we would be remiss not to mention that two traditions, the Swiss and the Dutch, came together in 1591 at the Anabaptist conference that produced the *Concept of Cologne*. And Mennonite Church Unites States in its present form has as its common *Confession of Faith in a Mennonite Perspective* and *Vision: Healing and Hope,* documents that are in tune with Bender's *Anabaptist Vision*. Both of these expressly incorporate the ideas of discipleship, community, and the gospel of peace.

♣

We look back into our Anabaptist-Mennonite history, three centuries, to the preface of *Golden Apples in Silver Bowls,* written in 1702. Times then were also tenuous, and the Swiss Mennonites had just experienced a shattering schism. It drove them again to look backwards from 1702, back to 1525 and following, to see where we had come from.

Something of this same backward look is apropos also for us today, as we ponder how to step into our own Mennonite future. We do well to look back from whence we have come, to steer our course in the positive direction we intend to go. Here is my summary of that 1702 preface:

> We disciples of Jesus are gathered together in faith and in the Spirit, as part of Christ's kingdom of love, looking to Christ our king. Currently, we are finding life to be unusually easy, and devoid of outward persecution. Many of us are therefore asking, as we look to the future: wherein lies our lot, what might we expect?

In answer to this question, we see in the book of Revelation that for God's people, persecution is to continue throughout history. Yet victory is assured for those who are prepared. May we Anabaptists, with all the rest who desire this route, "fill our lamps with the oil of the Spirit, in faith and love," and remain awake "from all sloth, love of the world, security and lusts of the flesh," and in addition, continue to bear witness to all these things.

There is to be sure something new and completely unexpected on the horizon, however. The themes of discipleship and Christ's kingdom of love in general, and the Anabaptist fellowship in particular, are being accepted as biblical among many from within mainstream churches. With such an open door, we Anabaptists need all the more to be on the cutting edge of witness and mission; for it is we who have suffered, even unto death; we therefore have a genuine witness to proclaim.

Yet we need to note, in the same breath, there are also dangers accompanying the current situation of relative tolerance by general society that we find ourselves in as a people. To counter the negative effects of such ease and prosperity, we need, therefore, to undergird one another in speaking and in writing, and so, mutually admonish and encourage each other, so that each of us may be living examples of what it means to be Christ's disciples. For separation from the evils of this world needs to continue, and is part and parcel of what it means to be prepared to go meet the Bridegroom, Jesus the King.

And in this regard, it may well be that suffering provides the ultimate clue to preparedness, where each of us bears his or her own cross, experiencing the same testing that our Master endured.

And so, let us as Anabaptists remain resolute in our life together, and in witness and mission, also focusing upon the new generation of believers among us who need to know how God has led us over a period of almost two centuries—youth, who need to know about our ancestors whose hope it was that "the true faith of the heart . . . [might] fulfill itself in love." We hope "we may find ourselves reflected in the footsteps of our Anointed One, and will thus find the means to stir our hearts in obedience to the truth."

We hope other godly minded readers will also benefit from

this witness, and so help fulfill Christ's kingdom of love. (Gross, 1999, 8-9)

In conclusion, we note in the summary just above that three centuries ago an unnamed Anabaptist author also attempted to sort out the husk from the kernel. He described, way back in 1702, the same Anabaptist triad Robert Friedmann and Harold Bender selected as the core idea behind Anabaptism: the obedient disciple, gathered together in fellowship with other disciples, attempting to live out Christ's kingdom of love. The visibility of the individual disciple living in tune with his or her conscience is paramount. Such visibility dare never be compromised "for the sake of the church," since Christ's kingdom of love is indeed to be understood as the "we" and not the "they." On the other hand, the other two vital parts of the Anabaptist Vision are also essential qualities, without which the Anabaptist tradition would come apart. Guy F. Hershberger spoke eloquently to this back in 1942, a statement which remains to this day as a powerful rationale for our coming together in social interaction—that Mennonites need to continue to congregate:

> We must remember that the most effective testimony of the Mennonites in times past has been given through the group, and not merely as individuals. It has not been a matter of a few individuals here and there preaching their message, but rather of the entire . . . [community] maintaining a faith and living a life, collectively, which was a testimony to the entire world. In the [First] World War it was not merely the conscientious objector in the military camp who testified to the principle of nonresistance. It was rather the entire church standing together that gave this testimony to the world. (Hershberger 56)

Notes

1. Bender's own carefully-chosen words in this regard are found in his editorial accompanying the publication of his "Anabaptist Vision" in 1944, and deserve to be quoted in full:

> Modern Mennonitism in America without doubt carries within its soul much of authentic original Anabaptism, but this authentic Anabaptist heritage is overlaid with the deposits of numerous and varied spiritual influences which have entered into the life of the group during the past four hundred years. Perhaps, in some quarters, even the very essence of that heritage has been transmuted or perverted into something quite different from its original content. Some might say that such

a change or modification is not only inevitable, but desirable, and should not be opposed. Whether one agrees with this position or not, certainly it is essential to know and understand what original Anabaptism was, but all too often this understanding is hindered by the overlay. 'The Anabaptist Vision,' which appears in this issue, is an attempt to define the spirit and purposes of the original Anabaptists in the light of the latest research in the hope that a fresh definition may enable a better evaluation and appraisal, not only of sixteenth century Anabaptism but of modern Mennonitism. (66)

2. In 1944, Friedmann could say that in Anabaptism, "one cannot find salvation without caring for his brother"; that it consisted in an "intimate caring for each other, as it was commanded to the disciples of Christ as the way to God's kingdom"; that it was not "'mere' fellowship that constitutes the Anabaptist *Gemeinden*," but rather "an *essential fellowship*, something which to a certain extent might be compared with family relations where the 'I' and the 'we' supplement each other" (121).

3. Grebel may have deviated somewhat from some of the convictions to emerge through the process of group discernment in Zurich in the years 1523 to early 1525, but the testimony of the others, as identified above, remained in keeping with the ideas of a peaceable discipleship, entered into and finding its fulfillment through group process.

WORKS CITED

Ariarajah, S. Wesley. 2002, June. "Religion and Violence: A Protestant Christian Perspective." In *Current Dialogue* 39.

Bender, Harold S., 1944, April. "The Anabaptist Vision." In *Mennonite Quarterly Review* 18. See also as booklet: 1944, with many reprints, *The Anabaptist Vision*. Scottdale, Pa.: Herald Press.

———,1950, Jan. "The Anabaptist Theology of Discipleship," *Mennonite Quarterly Review* 24.

Franklin, Ben. Cited in 1990, April. *Mennonite Historical Bulletin* 51:4.

Friedmann, Robert. 1942. "The Anabaptist Genius and Its Influence on Mennonites Today." *Proceedings of the First Conference on Mennonite Cultural Problems* (North Newton, Kan.: Bethel College Press).

———. 1944, April. "On Mennonite Historiography and on Individualism and Brotherhood." *Mennonite Quarterly Review* 18.

Gross, Leonard. 2000. "Anabaptist-Mennonite Group Dynamics," http://history.mennonite.net/articles/apolity.html; copy also in Mennonite Historical Library, Goshen (Ind.) College.

———, ed. 1999. *Golden Apples in Silver Bowls*. Lancaster, Pa.: Lancaster Mennonite Historical Society.

Hershberger, Guy. 1942. "Suggestions for Improving the Small Christian Community." In *Proceedings of the First Conference on Mennonite Cultural Problems*. North Newton, Kan.: Bethel College Press.

Ruth, John L. 1975. *Conrad Grebel, Son of Zurich*. Scottdale, Pa.: Herald Press.

Chapter 13

The Peculiar Beauty of *Gelassenheit*: An Interview with Amos B. Hoover

Joe Miller

Joe: Amos, you've spent a lot of time studying Old Order Mennonites, I'm wondering how you define the difference between an Old Order Mennonite and those, sometimes called conference Mennonites?

Amos: Well, conference Mennonites are primarily Mennonites around here who are a part of the Lancaster Mennonite Conference. We also bump into the Franconia Conference people all the time, and some of the Maryland conference people as well. The conference Mennonites have called themselves Old Mennonites, as you know; yet we thought we were the Old Mennonites. I suspect, sometime around World War I someone coined the name Old Order to refer to our group of Mennonites. I do know the early date stones to our churches all say Old Mennonite rather than Old Order. For example the Weaverland meetinghouse was built in 1894, and the date stone says that it was built by the Old Mennonites, which meant the Jonas Martin branch of Mennonites. The descendants of that group are what is called today the Old Order Mennonites.

About the same time a Lancaster County atlas was published in 1899, and the editors came up with an intriguing name. They called our

Weaverland church the Defenseless Mennonites. We don't usually say that in English, but that could be one way of identifying our group in the German language. You never hear our group called Defenseless Mennonites in the English language. My grandfather always referred to our church as the *wehrlose Leit* (defenseless people), which for him meant pretty much—what are called today in English—the Old Order people.

At that time there was a strong dispute between two Mennonite groups in the Weaverland Valley of Lancaster County over the ownership of the meetinghouse. The Lancaster Mennonite Conference claimed it owned the meetinghouses, and the Old Order group felt it should have the meetinghouses. Feelings were not the best during those years immediately following the division. In fact in a way the argument over who owned the church buildings was almost worse than the actual division itself.

The Old Order people decided they would build a new meetinghouse just up the hill from the Weaverland meetinghouse, and it is that church which is listed in the atlas as the Defenseless Mennonites. I was impressed that the mapmaker called our church the Defenseless Mennonites. But then the next year, in 1895, we were obliged to build another meetinghouse at Groffdale. And the following year the Old Orders built yet another one in Pequea, in 1896. And I think each of those Old Order meetinghouses would have on the church sign that the building was built by the Old Order Mennonites. That says something about their own sense of who they were within the Mennonite world.

Joe: How do you define "Old Order Mennonite"?

Amos: It's very hard to get a handle on this, because usually, although we call ourselves Old Order Mennonites, this may not be part of the official name. Old Order is sort of an umbrella name. Some people had tried to reserve this name for the Mennonites who use horse and buggy—what we call the Groffdale Conference, or Wenger group. But I think most people by now accept "Old Order" as an umbrella name, meaning our group, which is the Weaverland Conference, as well as the Groffdale Conference, which is now larger than our group. In a sense even the Stauffer Mennonites and the Reidenbacher Mennonites also lay claim to the name Old Order.

The Wenger church is in many ways actually the closest to the old conference. But we Old Order people have to recognize we are a little bit ashamed that there are so many divisions within what is called the Old Order Mennonites. Within the Old Order community we have various Reidenbach groups, which broke away from the Groffdale church. Very early in our history we had the Stauffer division—the Stauffers of 1845 and 1846. They also call themselves Old Order. So the name Old Order really is an umbrella name that covers many different Mennonite groups.

Joe: You created a wonderful chart where you tried to delineate all the various Mennonite groups in Lancaster Country. That chart is amazing in its complexity.

Amos: That chart was my attempt to explain visually what I discovered as I worked on my book, *The Jonas Martin Era*. My chart, however, is today a little outdated. Going back to 1980 or 1982, the chart is now twenty years old. Some of the smaller groups have died out and a few new ones have come along. Basically, we think of the Old Order Mennonites as largely our group, and the horse-and-buggy group.

There are other ways of defining Old Orders, in contrast to the Lancaster Conference Mennonites. Clothing is the most obvious distinctive. Another difference that is very noticeable is that Old Order Mennonites have also very intentionally chosen not to have Sunday school as part of our Sunday morning worship. In our meetinghouses we have been satisfied with an ordinary table, serving as a place where our preachers speak. This is quite a contrast to the Mennonites in the Lancaster Conference, who have elevated their preachers away from the congregation and have their speakers teaching from nicely crafted lecterns and pulpits.

Preaching within the Old Order congregations is markedly different from the preaching in Mennonite conference churches. Old Order preachers will take a portion of New Testament Scripture, often a whole chapter, which is read by the deacon. Then the preacher will systematically preach from the whole chapter. Higher Mennonite churches often have preaching that is much more topical. The preacher will decide on a topic and then bring in different Scriptures to support the topical theme.

Here in Lancaster County, Old Order Mennonites work very hard to do their visiting and worshiping in the German language. Over the years, as conference Mennonites speak less and less German, a difference in language has become an obvious distinction, separating culturally the

Old Order people from conference Mennonites. I must say though that we also are struggling to keep our German language. Our members are tending more and more to use quite a bit of English even within our own circles, which is of considerable concern for us.

Becoming Old Order

Another crucial thing that sets us apart is our using the Dordrecht Confession of Faith. I am quite sure this is also true for the Old Orders in Ohio and Indiana, and it is also true for the Canadian Mennonites of the Markham-Waterloo Conference and for our conference, and for all the horse-and-buggy groups. All these groups would adhere to the Dordrecht Confession of 1632. That would be something that—well, if you don't mind my saying—the "higher" churches have long since abandoned.

Joe: What is it about that Dordrecht Confession of Faith that keeps those of us who are conference Mennonites from saying, we're part of the same church as the Old Order Mennonites?

Amos: Irvin B. Horst from Eastern Mennonite University keeps reminding me that—I think maybe when he was in his thirties—he was one of the last in the Lancaster Conference to be instructed on the basis of the Dordrecht Confession. I guess I can't really speak for the Lancaster Conference but I think they probably thought the Dordrecht Confession was just a little too awkward and old. In particular, there is the article on shunning which is a little tricky. We don't emphasize it very hard, but we still say that shunning has a role to play.

Now the Stauffer Mennonites, Reidenbacher Mennonites and the Amish are very rigid in not eating with individuals while they are being shunned. I guess we interpret the Bible and the confession of faith to be saying that if a man lives in gross sin, we need to avoid him while he lives in his sinful ways. For example if we have a situation where a man is living with a woman other than his wife, then we don't associate with those persons because of their sinful choices. But if they do repent and, say, they join a similar nonresistant group, then we just sort of forget about it.

Joe: A young adult person of Amish background had been attending our congregation for probably three years, and finally asked to become a member. I went out to the Amish bishop and inquired how best to proceed with the question of membership. I told him that as a Mennonite congregation we wanted to respect the Amish congregation. We just didn't want to take the person into membership without at least a conversation. The bishop said that we should simply take the person in as a member and then the Amish congregation would decide whether or not to lift the ban. It was important to the Amish bishop to find out if our Mennonite congregation practiced foot washing and whether we were nonresistant.

Amos: I think we would be similar. I remember people having asked about renting our church building in York County. We weren't using it very much but we still had ownership of the building. Our old bishop said, well, if they're nonresistant they could use our meetinghouse. I don't know if he had foot washing to go along with this or not. Anyway, I thought this interesting, that we would not rent our meetinghouse to the "state churches."

Actually, we have tested this same principle closer home. Within our group some of our congregations alternate holding services with the team (horse-and-buggy) congregations. One Sunday we use the meetinghouse and the next Sunday they use the same meetinghouse. That means we can't open the meetinghouse for our own group more than every other Sunday. This practice of having an off-Sunday has slightly fallen by the wayside for some congregations, although we think that an off-Sunday can be an important day for visiting other congregations within our group.

Right now we are so pressed for space in some of our churches that our Springville congregation has been meeting eleven Sundays in succession, then takes the twelfth Sunday as an off-Sunday. That means the surrounding churches are very full when the Springville congregation is closed, in order that its members may visit other congregations. The Lutheran people nearby observed that on the twelfth Sunday we did not open the meetinghouse, and they came and asked our bishop if they could use our meetinghouse for their centennial celebration. They told the bishop: "We're having a centennial and we want to dress up in old clothing, and we think your church would be more Old World for our centennial."

Well, it didn't take the bishop long to say no to their request. If the Lutherans would have been in dire need, say, like they would have been thrown out of their church, that would have felt different. We had that happen several times and we were glad to help out non-Mennonite congregations. Or if their church had been damaged by fire, we would have given them the use of our meetinghouse—but not to put on a costume drama!

Joe: How have artists and creative people found ways to remain among the Old Order Mennonites? Can a person belong and yet enter into the arts? Under what circumstances do artists or creative people have room to express themselves and their art as members of the Old Order group? Do people who are thinking creative new thoughts, or different thoughts, or are doing things in a little different way, or doing things especially well, have a place within the Old Order community?

Amos: I would think that this depends so much on the person. For example in 1964 we started a newsletter called the *Home Messenger*. It was our church's way of keeping in contact with our young men who had been drafted by the government and were in alternative service instead of in the military. There were a lot of people within the church who were critical of such a paper because it seemed too worldly.

This was not an official church paper; it was sort of unofficial. A lot of those who started the paper were very frustrated that the church did not see value in their attempts to reach out to our young men in the draft. It was so upsetting that some of the folks involved in starting the *Home Messenger* left the church. Ironically some who had been critical of the paper have since become supportive of the paper and have even helped with publishing the *Home Messenger*. The paper is now very much accepted as a worthwhile tool of the church's ministry.

I am reminded of one of our ministers who was a little bit more tolerant and not quite as critical as some of his peers. He was a person who was able to think about things differently than some of the more traditional leaders. But he was, well, I call it smart enough to see that what is modern isn't always good, and he decided to stay with the Old Order group. By staying, even when he did not always agree, he has been able to gently have a very big influence on the church.

He is a highly respected and valued member of our deacons meetings. There were 27 deacons that met the last time. These brothers are pretty influential. They talk things over and discuss the problems and then they may present solutions to the total conference. This deacons group also deals with the financial issues relating to our churches. This same man that I mentioned—he doesn't have nearly the seniority that some of the other leaders have— but when he speaks, people sit and listen. There's something about the man that people respect. He has a special giftedness and ability that he has offered to us as an Old Order group. He could have used that gift outside the church but he stayed and slowly, over time, has made a huge contribution.

The other thing this man has is endurance. When he was criticized, he didn't just throw up his hands and give up or leave our church. I think it depends on the person. We believe totally that all gifts belong to the community and are best shaped by the community. This man is an example of submitting his abilities for the building of the church. He still is promoting mission work in a gentle way and on a limited basis, and slowly this is being accepted as well. He knew how far to go and how far not to go.

Joe: Amos, would it be fair to say that you are one of the people within the Old Order church who has been given a gift by God to understand history and theology? Haven't you chosen to use that gift within the framework of the Old Order community? Would you agree that at different times you have been pushing a little on the edges? Is that fair to say?

Amos: Well, maybe. Yes. I guess so. Back in the late fifties or early sixties a problem within the Old Order church certainly tested my resolve about whether to stay or to leave. There was a spontaneous Bible study group, and most of the ordained leaders viewed this as undermining the ministry. It was all laity, those who were involved in private Bible study, and our pastors made a rule against Bible study. Well, this sounded horrible, and I remember I was on the fence myself with that at that time. But I'm glad I stayed with the old group. Most of those people involved in the Bible studies have left our church and have become members of the Eastern Pennsylvania Mennonite Conference. They wanted to be a part of a church where they could have Sunday school and things like that.

Joe: Was your collecting a library of rare Mennonite and Anabaptist material, and your having connections with professors from all over the world a cause for concern within your church? How did the community view all those worldly people driving in your lane to visit and talk with you? Plus, you were traveling onto college campuses and visiting places where Old Order people did not usually go.

Old Orders and Education

Amos: A few brethren here and there were worried about me. They were concerned that I'd stray away. I took a correspondence course from the Knights of Columbus so that I could learn about the Catholic church. I wanted to know more about Catholic teaching. One brother within our church thought I'd get carried away and he was really upset with me. I don't think that little episode of my taking a correspondence course was generally discussed within my community. I don't know what all the people thought, but I guess that my taking things slow and easy helped a great deal.

Sometimes my wife and I conclude that we would not want to live our lives over again in the same manner. We would attempt to make this and that area better, but we realize that the temptations to be led astray from the church community are very strong. We conclude, if any good thing has come out of our lives, it was all by the grace of God. I remember approaching our old bishop, Joe Weaver, to get his counsel about whether I should accept an invitation by the Lancaster Conference to give a talk. Bishop Weaver wisely said to me, "I think you answered your own question—you're not sure if it's the right thing to do." So he said, "If you're not sure, then you'd better not accept the invitation to speak."

That was sound advice. I would never do anything like that at a regular morning worship service in a non-Old Order worship. I would not feel comfortable speaking in other people's church houses. If somebody asks me a question at a meeting of the Christian Aid Ministry building for example, which is sort of an inter-Mennonite relief organization, and they don't really go into doctrine, then I'd feel free to answer questions or speak our opinion.

For example, we will freely take part under such circumstances in inter-Mennonite relief projects. One of the first times that one of our ministers spoke publicly was when Clare Frey openly gave a speech. Up until then it would have been just a remark here and there. Now it's pretty well accepted that our leaders speak more publicly. Knowing how far you may go and still be in the good graces of the church community is the key, I think.

I might as well give you my personal testimony. I had a deep desire to go to school and I asked my grandfather for his counsel. At that time, when you passed the eighth grade it was expected that you were done with formal education. I was scarcely fourteen years old when I finished eighth grade and I said I'd like to go further. My grandfather asked me why I wanted more education. My response was that I probably could be a doctor and help other people.

He said no, that I'd never be a good doctor. He really talked me down. One of his lectures was enough for me, and I didn't challenge him. Not long after that, I had a new idea about finishing high school by mail. Once again my grandfather couldn't quite see even this idea as something positive. You see my parents weren't living, so I grew up with Grandfather, and my uncles were sort of the in-between generation. They felt that my idea of high school by mail probably wouldn't hurt me if I did all my studies at home. I guess the social contact of going to public high school was a big concern.

So I did take correspondence classes. I worked at it four years and finished from the American School in Chicago. So I guess I was pushing the edges, but I was always committed to doing things in a way that I was still well within the expectations of our church community. Staying within the wishes of my grandfather and the church was always more important to me than getting more formal education. But I found, with a gentle spirit and humility, a great deal could be accomplished

Today, we have some people doing correspondence courses in our group so that they can have a high school education. That is now more or less acceptable. Back when I was doing high school studies it was at the time the parochial schools run by our Old Order community were being discussed and getting started. I heard some people were saying, "Amos wants to study so that he can get a respectable job teaching school." I don't know who manufactured that idea, but it was simply not true. I had a hunger for formal learning, but I felt that this interest did not necessarily mean I was rejecting my church community. I felt hurt by those comments, in part because those people doing the talking should have come directly to me in the spirit of the teachings of Matthew 18.

I hope that those people's comments were their attempt at voicing a constructive criticism. But at one point, an observation was made that wasn't supposed to come back to me, but it did. Many years later, when I was nominated for the lot for the role of deacon, the old talk of my being too close to the world came up again. There were eleven of us in the lot for deacon, and during the period leading up to the casting of the lot there was some talk about who was acceptable to serve as the next deacon.

During the examination of our theology and lifestyle, and until the actual ordination took place, one of these older brethren told the bishop that Amos had been out too much with other groups. I guess these critics were skeptical of me being a deacon. But then it was also noted that I had at another level passed the acid test, which is whether your children stay within the church community. It is amazing to me that some of this was shared with the bishop and then that the bishop in turn shared it with me. I guess the bishop thought that if he shares it with me it will help me keep on track.

One of the important reasons I stayed within our church was how leaving has such a profound bearing on one's children and the grandchildren. Not being a part of the Old Order community would have just had an enormous impact on the family life that we have together. I suspect that if I would have gone off to the university and entered regular American life, my children might not even be Mennonites by now.

That for me would be too high a price to pay. I guess I was weighing all this when I made the choice to remain within the community. And also, I wasn't sure if I could take it mentally—you know—to declare openly that I am now leaving the community. I might well have been wrestling with these questions, but to be able to stand all that change in life was another matter. I also think that our marriage would have been a very unhappy experience if we had taken that course. In the end I think my grandfather's views were right on. Farm life certainly was the most ideal way for us to raise a family.

So with deep contentment and real joy I stayed within the community. I guess that's when I started collecting Mennonite books in a major way. I thought to myself, the cutoff point is going to an outside school in person. If you have a little correspondence, so what? That seemed partly acceptable. But to go in person, that was different.

Old Order Leadership

Joe: How does the community decide who has the gift for something, like serving as a song leader or preaching? How does the church call out and honor those gifts and yet at the same time not wanting to see that gifted person get too prideful?

Amos: There are usually about eight or ten or twelve people leading singing. These men sit at the singers' table and they whisper together what song would be appropriate and who's going to lead it. The truth is that someone's voice must lead out, but it is crucial to the song leaders and to the congregation that song leading is seen as serving the congregation with a sense of humility. It is not about showing off one's gifts, but rather, placing your ability at the service of the larger group.

We had one of the most gifted song leaders involved in a horrible chicken barn fire. Tragically, he was burned to death in that fire a couple of weeks ago. Now we're talking about seeking a replacement. He was gifted. Most of the song leaders are not singing-school teachers. The singing-school leaders are ones that go to the youth meetings and help the children, help the young people, the dating-age people, and so forth—help them learn singing skills. But you cannot bring everything they do at the singing schools back into the worship service—for example, four-part harmony. We're really happy if somebody can sing in parts, and if the young people learn this, that is good; but the Old Orders say that's something you don't do in real worship. You sing in unison. And that's why, although there would be many people ready to bring notation into our churches, they say no, we'll keep the old book.

Joe: But, Amos, help me understand more. Are there examples where a person was a song leader or a preacher—or where there were other artistic expressive gifts that someone had—that were, or were not, well accepted in the community? Were there, for example, ever song leaders that the community said were too proud of their voice?

Amos: Well, not of the voice. You don't talk about voice and make comparisons in that way. It's just understood. It's understood that if you have a monotone up there who can't keep a tune, you have a problem in that the congregation can't even sing right. So the church tries to select a song leader who knows a little bit about music. But we have quite a variety of talent. Some of the song leaders with more talent will help out if the hymn stays hanging—we have a saying that when a hymn is not going well, that it is "stuck in the mud"—then someone with a stronger voice will pick it up and lead the song to get it back to where it needs to be.

All this is done very subtly and no particular song leader is highlighted as doing a bad job in leading the hymn, or doing a good job in saving the hymn. So there are several song leaders who are always prepared, and you never do this alone, you know. To have one person on a pedestal, and stand up and lead, is just unthinkable for an Old Order worship service. That's acceptable for the young people who are singing together socially on a Saturday evening, but not in Sunday morning worship. My grandfather used to say in German, *"Stimmig singes is melodisch für die junge leit, awwer es g'höret net zum en Gottesdienst."* In English this means: "Singing in parts is fine for the young people. It's melodious, and it gives them something to do. They think it's something meaningful to do, but it does not belong to a real worship service."

So that was the old view, and I guess we still have this in part—although many of us like to sing in four-part harmony when we have weddings and anything other than the normal worship service.

Joe: You'll break into four-part harmony in gatherings outside of worship. What happens if—and I'm sorry to sort of stay on this—but let's say that you have a preacher or a song leader who is particularly gifted and eloquent. What happens if the song leader or the preacher might be too smooth? And what does the community do: do they value a good speaker or not?

Amos: There have been occasions where ministers have been silenced because they valued their own views too highly. I remember a song leader who caused a good bit of concern because he seemed to be too impressed with himself. Among our song leaders there are a variety of levels of how plain they dress. Some song leaders wear a frock coat, broadfall pants, and a plain vest. These clothes are required for all pastors in the Old Order church. Song leaders are encouraged to wear these plain clothes, but it is not mandatory.

I remember that in the case of this song leader where there was concern, it was felt he was too aggressive in new songs and so forth, and somebody said he could at least get his clothing in order. And then the deacon talked with him and said he needs to start wearing the plainer clothing that was worn by ministers.

It's really hard to pin down a person's motivation. You can't tell if somebody's proud, or if he simply has a real good voice. It's easier to pin his coat down than what is in a man's heart. So the person who would want to comply with church expectations is more apt to not be in the fore quite as much. In a sense, it worked. The crux of the matter is to keep the community in the fore, and play down individualism.

Eventually that song leader did start wearing the plainer clothing. But years later he left the church. Maybe he left for other reasons, but nonetheless he was not willing to remain a part of our congregation.

This was a person who couldn't quite take the community's direction. He still is a good friend of mine, but there was just a little difference in interpretation there. And he also was involved pretty heavy in this Bible study movement I mentioned earlier.

Joe: The average North American who is autonomous and independent would say, "How dare anyone tell me how to live or how to do anything?" Amos, do you see the dissonance that's between the Old Order church's value on submitting to community, and what the average North American feels about community?

Amos: I think there is a difference. I think there's a basic mentality difference. You know, we're trying to support the community and not talk about the individual so much. Now if someone would send me an application that they'd like to work for us in the new library and they send a resume—which I think is probably normal out in the world—of all the things they could do, sending us a resume would raise grave concerns for us about how they would fit into our community.

Joe: Most résumés are a glowing account of how wonderful and talented a person is.

Amos: To an Old Order this would be just nauseating. Because such a litany of self-promotion ends up being a great deal of talking about yourself too much. I think I'm doing too much of that right now.

Joe: Would you say more about the difference between the Old Order and regular North Americans? In being part of this community, you must experience something that in some ways restricts you. It probably sounds like a very North American question, but why would I want to stay in a community that limits me? What am I getting in return?

Amos: I think that sounds very American. Well, I'm quite happy to be in my great grandfather's faith, because he was one of the people that helped found the Old Orders, and his generation was faithful to the members of the faith—his forebears. So I'm glad to continue in the same profession of faith. Within our community there was a little discord some time ago, and several deacons were looking into the matter. One of the fellows made the statement that "the church is not going to tell me what I have to do." Despite his growing up within our church I don't think he understood the Old Order faith at all. There is a basic difference between what Billy Graham asks for when he calls on people to make a decision for Christ, and what the Old Order church asks of people wanting to be a Christian. For mainstream North American Christianity it is totally a private and individual transaction—you put your hand up and that's a decision for Christ.

On the other hand, if you would like to join our fellowship, you would first of all be encouraged to live among us and attend our worship services for a while to see if you could possibly adhere to the life of our faith community. We are very clear that the life of the Christian is a hard road that is out of step with modern popular culture.

A newcomer came who wanted to join immediately. Our bishop told him that a person needed the counsel of the church before joining. Everyone in the church has a voice in the matter and the whole church needed to agree that any new person would be able to be a faithful part of the church. The question the bishop asked the man was: "How do you expect the congregation to give its counsel in favor of your joining us if they don't know you? If you never have been, till now, a part of our life together, how can you really already be a part of our Old Order church? So, one needs to get used to the community, and the community needs to learn to know the candidate; and then we can discern together whether we are ready for mutual Christian commitment."

But then, when we have made a commitment to each other, we share a covenant that has the strength of connection like a family. I was telling you about the song leader who was killed in that tragic fire. Thousands of people came to his funeral or to the visitation before the service itself. During the clean-up of his barn, hundreds of people participated. I was there myself. But the song leader had burned to death within his chicken house, so there could be no viewing. It was really more than an average disaster, including the loss of a $150,000 building.

The sympathy that went along with everything else was just staggering. Members of the Old Order church were sending in money to help his family, some of which I received myself in my role as deacon, so that I could pass it on to the man's family. I think we experience an amazing amount of security in our brotherhood that one can't really measure.

Joe: Actually, you're referring to what we sometimes call in Mennonite circles "mutual aid." In addition to the generosity of the community in a time of physical need, I hear you mentioning spiritual mutual aid. Hundreds of people came out to help this poor man's family rebuild and grieve, but isn't it true that the community also steps in when there is a spiritual crisis by offering the spiritual discipline of giving and receiving counsel?

Old Order Community

Amos: There you used the right words: *giving* and *receiving*. It's not just one way—it is literally both giving and receiving. That is the genius of our church community. I think the great sadness I feel for the worldly culture is the terrible loneliness in which I see those people living.

When people join the Old Order church they may indeed be giving up some independence, but they gain richly in a depth of community that is rarely experienced in North America. There is a crucial question we ask people that I am sure would sound quite strange to the average North American. As individuals seek to become a part of the community, they come in the minister's room—it's usually the young people but it could be an older person, some older people join—and they'll say, "We'd like to join the fellowship."

The ministers will have only one question. They say, "This sounds good. We'll make known to the congregation that you are applying for membership." The minister also says, "In the intervening time [before the council meeting preceding communion] if anyone sees anything in your life that is not conducive to good church life, you are willing to be approached on the matter and make the necessary changes." All members are encouraged to speak with the individual if he or she is not in order.

The answer needs to be an unqualified yes, and that's the only question. They don't ask how much training you have, or what you like to do. But simply, would you be willing to be taught by the group how to walk in the footsteps of Jesus Christ. That's basically what we're saying. It has to be the consensus of the whole congregation before you are allowed to join. At a later point, if one or more persons become so arrogant that they say, nobody's telling me what to do, then they have lost their first love, and they're in deep trouble with the church community.

Some people don't realize how important that question is. We think, if someone decides a year later to leave the community, there's not much we can do. But that person has missed or misinterpreted the first question: would you be willing to be corrected? That's the only question, because we think all other issues can be worked at as long as members are open to the church's teaching.

The minister will come out after the worship service just before dismissal and report to the congregation, "We have three people who have come into the 'anteroom.' In great weakness we spoke with those seeking membership. We have ask them if they are willing to be shown a better way if something in their life does not comply [this is in general the wording; sometimes it's phrased a little bit differently]. We spoke in great weakness with the persons seeking membership, and they said they would be willing to be taught [they used to say, in German, 'to be admonished']."

When there is a spiritual concern, for example a woman's head covering isn't quite big enough, or someone has not gotten rid of a CB radio, then the deacon will visit the person and raise the matter with him or her. The deacon reminds the member of the promises made to give and receive the counsel of the church. He then asks if the member in question is willing to conform to the community's standards.

Sometimes, parents will threaten their children with the possibility of withdrawing their inheritance if a child were to leave the church. That seems to me not to be normal. It might be an unhappy home to start with. Then sometimes you hear the debate, well, is it actually wrong to leave the brotherhood and join the other group—and of course, the reason for joining is usually to join a group a little bit more liberal. So, something happened between the time they promised that they would agree to the community standards and lifestyle, and a later point in their life, when you start hearing that now they don't agree to what they promised. There was a shift in that person's commitment.

The story is told of Noah Mack, a Lancaster Conference bishop at Groffdale. I think his years of service continued through the 1920s. He was a church leader in the Lancaster area during the formative years of what became Eastern Mennonite University. His support was wanted for starting a Mennonite college in Virginia. Mack's response was what you might expect from a person with a farming background.

He observed that formal education, if used properly, can be a good thing but when formal education is something prideful it is like manure that is only on the surface and never works its way down to where it really can nourish the crops. Mack knew that manure can be good for a field. To raise excellent potatoes you need to use some manure. But if the manure stays only on the surface and never gets into the ground to nourish the roots of the plants, all the manure is going to do is stink!

The Old Order point of view is that some education is good, but that you shouldn't get too much formal education because it can separate you from your faith community. The problem isn't education, in and of itself, but our experience has been that too much formal education leads to pride and to a distancing from the rest of the people in the community. We say in German *"je gelehrter, je verkehrter"* which means that "The more educated people become, the more stupid they become."

I know it is difficult for the average North American to understand, but within the Old Order community we endeavor to place a higher value on the whole community than we do on the individual. The community is what is beautiful and sacred, not the individual. That is almost impossible for the average American person to grasp, let alone appreciate. To find other expressions of this way of living, I am guessing that you would need to look to other cultures outside of North America.

So, true beauty to the plain people is being part of the whole, and not setting oneself off from fellow members of the church. This often does become most obvious in outward forms, but we would suggest that the outward is a reflection of what is in the heart. So we have agreed to dress more or less alike and to dress plainly, as a way to express our desire for simplicity, and to celebrate our unity. So it is the truth that for me, beauty is people who do not crowd the boundary lines—like the size of a woman's prayer covering, for example, or the cut of a man's coat.

Some individuals really crowd the tolerance line; others are content to wear what is agreed on by the community. So, yes, beauty is in the eye of the beholder, isn't it? When someone asks me what I think is beautiful, I think it looks nice when women have the full-size prayer covering. Then there may be a few within our circles who have gone overboard with tradition because they are too prescriptive about outward things. I am not recommending being obsessive about clothing and lifestyle issues. What I'm talking about is that our shared and agreed-on culture is the norm of the old generation. That is what I call beautiful.

I believe church traditions are beautiful. I think of Pathway magazines. Their drawings of persons don't have literally realistic faces. The illustrations show impressions of faces. This is our attempt to honor God's call for humans not to make any image of people. We are free to have very detailed illustrations of other parts of God's nature. But that again comes back to the same question, not to exalt the individual. It is all right to have quite good pictures in our magazines of God's natural world, but not of people.

Here is something that is perhaps ironic. We would say that an illustration without a realistic face is a beautiful thing because it is not emphasizing the individual. I think the idea centers in not wanting to show a person too distinctly and invade his person. Our group as a whole doesn't like pictures of people if you display them or if you put them on the wall, it should not be too much of people—of people that you know. So if you put a calendar up of someone you don't know, that is better than of people you know. Anything that exalts the individual is what we seek to avoid.

Some among the Old Orders will accept having a picture of a family member or a close friend, but such a picture would have to be kept in the drawer. Years ago I asked my grandfather if I could take a picture of him. He said to me that it would be a great wrong, terribly wrong. He quoted the Bible verse that says, "Make no graven image, . . . [nor] fall down and worship it." However my guess is that the younger generation no longer holds this austere view and is satisfied simply not making a display of photographs or have a photograph appear in the newspaper.

The Old Order Chasm

Joe: Amos I'm struck by the fact that there's a huge cultural difference between Old Order people and North Americans. It seems that there are also significant differences between Old Order Mennonites and conference Mennonites.

Amos: I think you're right, and I'd say that the gap is getting wider. During the early times of the division in the later nineteenth century, there was a little bit of mission work and things that would have been different between Old Order Mennonites and conference Mennonites. But generally speaking, soon after the division, I think Lancaster Conference sort of had a revival in plain clothing and some of those things. In the first years after the division the differences between the Old Order people and conference people weren't that *auffallend* (noticeable). I would guess, during the first 30 or 40 years there would have been subtle changes, but not quite as evident. But I think, since the forties and beyond—in the last 60 years—the gap has gotten wider.

Joe: I've probably had more connection with Old Orders than most people, but I find that culturally there seems to a chasm between Old Order thinking and conference Mennonite thinking. It's hard to understand, in some ways, for a worldly person, how you give up everything for the community. I believe in community, and I've sacrificed some things for my church community; but I probably would draw the limit much sooner than you would.

Amos: There was a time that I was very vicious and hungry for education. At that time television would just have been coming into existence. Had I been left to my own decision, I would probably be using television. But church members agreed that we would not have television sets in our homes. Some things are negotiable, but television was a point that was not negotiable for us as a community. I'm so thankful now that we were not exposed to television.

Some of our members have fire department scanners. That is acceptable to the church because it helps members who are firemen to respond to emergencies. But in my mind they spend too much time abusively listening to every detail that is spoken by the fire and police on their radios. My wife and I are so happy that we're spared from television and sitting beside the scanner listening to everything. I pity those people who monitor the scanner all day long, hanging on to every detail. They want to know everything that's going on at all times.

Frankly, it can become addictive I'm so glad that as a church we agreed not to allow television, or for that matter, even regular radios.

Joe: Is that part of the beauty that we were talking about earlier? I'm not sure that the world, and even many conference Mennonites, have the capacity to see that kind of beauty.

Amos: I think there's a serenity that the world doesn't see. There are some people from outside the Old Order world whom I know, who have been able to see the beauty we see. I just got done speaking with Carolyn Wenger, and she really has an understanding and appreciation for all these nice things. So does John Ruth and a few others. But the numbers are not great among non-Old Order people who really have an appreciation for the old way.

Joe: Inversely, there can be sentimentality when outside people look at Old Orders. When tourists come to Lancaster County they observe the Old Order people and love how Old Order people seem quaint. These tourists can easily become sentimental about the plain way of life—for them it is something like a living Courier and Ives tableau.

Amos: We Old Order Mennonites are often looked upon as sort of mediocre Amish, but we just don't pay any attention to that. I've gotten to the point that if somebody asks me if we're Amish, I say, "Yes, just about. We're just about Amish."

The difference isn't great. Usually, I offer tourists as brief an answer as I can to get them off my back. I remember one time we had an acquaintance from New York visiting, and I went to great pains to explain to our visitor that the Amish and the Mennonites are not the same. I carefully explained that Amish and Old Order Mennonites have a different history, and so forth. And in the very next sentence, my New York acquaintance still talked about us as being Amish. There's no way you can change that mentality.

Joe: As tourists drive through Lancaster County and see the beautiful farms and the bucolic setting, they can be attracted to the Old Order lifestyle and they might think it's wonderful. Are they in that moment seeing some of the beauty? Is it possible that they recognize the beauty of lovely farms and horse-drawn buggies but that they usually can't see the hidden beauty of being a member of the Old Order community?

Amos: I think that is true. So often people come in from New York and say, "Hey, we'd like to move here." Their concept is that the farm always smells like freshly mown hay, which can be very sweet. But sometimes it's not so sweet, and they might not have lived through that, so they might have a surprise coming. That is, of course, true for all of life. The Amish have an expression of hanging out their dirty wash for everybody to see. Of course you don't really want to tell outsiders how hard being a part of community sometimes is. I don't think anybody that's humble would say that we have always lived in community correctly. We have made mistakes and we have failed sometimes and that is very painful to live through and to admit.

Old Order Stereotypes

Joe: There are stereotypes of the Old Order that I have seen portrayed in movies and literature. That image is of a severity within the Old Order community, and that anything that's creative or beautiful is totally squashed by the community. Is that also a stereotype? Have you seen those portrayals, or are you aware of people who would contend that anything that's beautiful or anything that's joyful—that the Old Order community cannot tolerate this? Have you run into people who feel that way?

Amos: Some people see nothing but the bad.

Joe: There are those who say no creativity is allowed because the church is a closed, cold, and brittle community. Why are some people feeling that?

Amos: I think there is some validity to that point. But you know a lot of those sources, especially the quick surveys that are made in one or two days, are about the people who have left our community. It is easy to find ex-members who are disgruntled, which is not always the best way to learn about Old Order Mennonites. It is important to listen to what they have to say, but ex-members' voices are certainly not a fully balanced view.

People who are a part of the popular culture have little ability to see how we delight in different ways to have recreation and enjoyment. I think one of the key ways for us to experience enjoyment is visiting. Sunday afternoon, it's almost a ritual that we go and visit fellow church members. Just visiting: plain, down, visiting. And then there are the public sales and quiltings, and things like that. The great part of the impetus behind the visiting is that it is a wonderful way to be connected, and to care about each other in the Old Order community. It is for us a great delight to learn about what fellow church members are doing and how their life is going. We are cared about and cared for, and we get to care about and for others within the Old Order community. This deep, deep sense of mutual care and concern feels wonderful and for me is beautiful. To outsiders, ours is a strange and peculiar beauty not easily understood or seen by non-Old Order people.

When we visit each other we are brought up to date, and it's the best way to know what's going on. This visiting and wanting to know about other members' lives is not being nosy about people, because mostly it is genuine interest. We grieve and celebrate other members' life experiences. It's maintaining the community. It also keeps you posted what's going on in the Old Order world. Right now we have a strong trend of people moving to Wisconsin. You wonder why, but the price of land here in the east dictates it. You find all those things out—what the land prices are in Wisconsin and what the land prices are here in Lancaster County. When the land here in Lancaster is 500 percent higher than in Wisconsin, it's almost irresistible for families to move west. You know, it's worth paying twice as much for a farm here in Lancaster, but is it worth paying five times the amount for a farm?

Joe: The Old Order way of thinking is just so different. It's somewhat like average Americans going to a whole other culture like Japan or

China and realizing they don't understand the culture—the Old Order community is like a foreign culture to most Americans. There's a different way of thinking here.

Amos: Yes, I think there is. One place you can notice this is in the preamble of our conference report. I can't send you a copy because it's sort of semi-restricted. This document is read by the bishop and no one else has a copy. But the first sentence in the conference report says, "We believe we are called to follow the example of our forefathers." I couldn't imagine that a normal North American would say such a thing. You know, worldly people want to find the latest. They have to be on the cutting edge of scientific developments. Within the popular culture of North America, what is new is assumed to be the best. Inversely, as Old Order people, we assume what is tried and tested is the best. There's so much contradicting evidence that seems to overwhelm modern people and we believe the older way is tried and proven. When it comes to matters of Christian faith we believe looking to the past is especially and truly of the essence and not negotiable.

Sometimes Old Order people say, "We have history on our side." This sounds like bragging, but someone else originated this. In my preamble to the book about Jonas Martin, I quote Sam Wenger who said that at the time of the division between Lancaster Conference and the Old Order Mennonites in 1893, there was a cry that we needed to worship in the English language and Sunday school to keep our young people. It was Sam Wenger, from the Lancaster Mennonite Conference, who said, the Old Orders have history on their side. So it didn't pan out the way the proponents of English and Sunday school claimed.

Wenger's contention was that if conference Mennonites count even their young people who have gone to the Church of the Brethren as still being Anabaptist-Mennonite, conference Mennonites were only retaining 40 percent of their young people. That's what he said 20 years ago. Wenger went on to say that the Old Orders were retaining 90 percent of their children. I think that's a little high, maybe, but our retention rate is quite good. The point is that Old Olders do have history on their side. So, I guess the Old Orders feel pretty good about that. And I tried to put that down in a humble way by quoting Sam Wenger. You can find it in the early pages of the *Jonas Martin Era* book.

Joe: I still am trying to come to grips with the chasm—the space between what the Old Order feels and what an average American feels. It seems to me there is a gap, there's this space that's hard to cross because of this significantly different worldview. I'm starting to understand that it's because the Old Order community sees value and beauty in things different from what almost all Americans in general do—but also many conference Mennonites. It becomes very difficult for us to understand you Old Order people. It doesn't make sense to us, the way you choose to live.

Old Orders and Postmodernity

Amos: One of your old Franconia buddies, Clarence Kulp, helped me understand the subtleties of the German language. Before I knew him, I tried hard to learn High German correctly. There's nothing wrong with that, but I discovered that I was missing the point, and Clarence helped me understand. I needed to value the Pennsylvania Dutch dialect that I learned from our parents. Clarence helped me understand how important their language was for me.

Giving up what has been taught by our parents and grandparents is not a thing that is beautiful to us. Whether it is giving up on our Pennsylvania Dutch language, or giving up on the way we have traditionally worshipped, is not beautiful.

I think the world would call giving up the past something that is beautiful, and they would claim that doing your own thing is beautiful. For me the ultimate example of this was my experience with a friend from Germany. We were writing letters back and forth for 55 years. On several occasions we visited each other for a number of weeks at a time. He was here one time and he saw exactly how we raise our children and he of course saw the weak spots, I imagine. He said, *"Du bist am vorsage, du bist dei Kinder am vorsage, was sie glauben sollen."* The English meaning is: "You are telling your children in advance what to believe. When your children grow up they will have no choice but to believe what you taught them."

He's a very modern person and he totally believes in doing your own thing the modern way. Ultimately, the most important thing for my friend was independence and individual choice. He explained to me very carefully how in the area of religion he does not prescribe to his children what they should believe. He said he's very careful he doesn't influence them—*sie beeinflusse.*

At best he would have pointed out to his children what their various options were. Nora and I could not convince him that the parents' duty is to teach their children what to choose. Nora and I often talk about how our friend is so careful not to influence his children in choices about life in general or even in religious matters.

I told my friend, what I see is that he doesn't want to influence or guide his own children, but he sends them away to a college where perfect strangers influence his children. At the university the professors and others push a lot of ideas on the students, and the professors influence my friends' children. Our German friend had a daughter who was just crazy about Elvis Presley. Once we were visiting in Germany with our friends. They were very nice and we had a wonderful time, but Nora and I just concluded that our friends were so careful not to influence their children—but then they allow perfect strangers to deluge their children with values. Their children were being drowned in all the influences from others. I think Europeans in general are more modern and almost post-Christian. These friends are simply ultramodern Christians.

Joe: I think it is very difficult for a person who has no familiarity with Mennonites' theology of "giving and receiving counsel" to understand this idea of Christian community. Can you look this way, from your vantage point as an Old Order, and try to understand the attraction of independence that many of us attempted to buy into?

Amos: Well, I think maybe I can do that slightly better than you can look my way, and in so doing, fully understand the beauty of the mutual dependence of our community. I've been exposed to the world more than you've been exposed to the Old Orders, maybe.

I think the more we're talking, the more I'm realizing there is a difference. There are just a few people outside the Old Order community whom I believe understand how we live. John Ruth is one of those unusual non-Old Order people who understands. We're on the same frequency. But, by and large, people cannot understand. I am amazed at my ministry, which is primarily not to people outside the Older Order community, but to my own people.

A portion of my understanding of the history and culture of Old Order people actually comes from people like John Ruth and Clarence Kulp. A great deal of what I have learned, and my love for the Old Order ways comes from my grandfather Burkholder. I have been grateful that a deeper appreciation and understanding of what it means to be an Old

Order person is continuing to be passed on to other people within our community.

Just yesterday, Robert Zimmerman, the man who farms the land where immigrants are buried said to me, "I live right in the heart of Weaverland, beside the little cemetery where all our ancestors are buried." His people are a part of the Lancaster Conference Weaverland brick church, which is only a stone's throw away from our Old Order Weaverland meetinghouse. He is now with the Eastern Pennsylvania group. He said that people are visiting that cemetery more than ever. He asked me, "What is going on?" He said they're coming into the cemetery by the busloads. My response was that I think it's a sign of the times. People in general are more interested in history now than they had been earlier.

Maybe it's partly, they have a little bit more spare time. You know, with the current average life expectancy, we don't have to work every minute quite as much as we used to, when life spans were shorter and the workload was heavier. Whatever the cause, there's definitely more interest in history. When I published my first Burkholder family history book in 1957, along with my wife and others' help, we charged $1.00 a book, and we almost had to press the book down people's throats. People were not sure it wasn't a waste of money.

Thirty years later, in 1980-81, a second edition came out, and I said I'm not going to print as many because it's my own money and I'm just not going to risk not being able to sell all the books. When the book came out, many of my relatives said, well, I want a case for all my children and grandchildren. Some actually ordered two cases, and in about six weeks we sold out.

So there is a shift in attitude. Irvin B. Horst tells the story of how as a teenager he was going to pick up a couple of extra dollars by selling door to door M. G. Weaver's history, *Mennonites of Lancaster Conference*, that came out in 1931. This was in the height of the Great Depression, and most of the people said, "No, we don't have money." The price back then for the book was $3.00. The folks that Irvin visited to sell the book told him, "We don't have that kind of money for a book!" Now today, they'll plunk down $30 and $50 for a good book. I guess John Ruth's book on the Lancaster Conference history [*The Earth Is the Lord's*, Scottdale, 2001] has now gone up to $70. The third printing is out and it went up $10.

Joe: Has John's Lancaster book been popular?

Amos: Yes. And our Old Order people read it more than do the Lancaster Conference people.

Joe: Much of the history in John's book would be shared history.

Amos: That's right, the early history is the same. Our bishop has a copy, and he tells stories from John's book. He said to me, "You know, the old way of 'keeping house' is still pretty much the same way as we have it in our Old Order community." So they're sort of feeling good about seeing this in John's history of the Lancaster Conference.

Old Orders in a Nutshell

Joe: Are you familiar with the term, "postmodernism"?

Amos: Not exactly. I could figure out what it means.

Joe: There are some people saying that we're entering a period called postmodern.

An oversimplification of postmodernism holds the point of view that there is no story or history that is normative. Everything's open, and your story and your faith and what you believe in is fine, but your faith and your story are not for everyone. There is no story, there are no rules, that are for everyone or that are universal.

Amos: I would call that ultra-modern—the same as postmodern. The Old Order community stands in contradiction to the proposition that there are no givens which are universally true. Many of us would say Christianity stands for and claims to be a normative story for every human. For members of the Old Order community, there is the strong possibility that they will have an anchor in their life. This stability comes from the fact that they belong to something bigger than themselves. Most members of the Old Order community delight in the knowledge of belonging to a community, to something that is normative.

The beauty of the Old Order community is the lack of loneliness and isolation as found among modern—or I guess I should say postmodern—people. I really do believe that the realities of the Old Order and the mainstream culture are a world apart, aren't they? Yes, there is indeed a huge chasm that stands between the Old Order person and people of the world.

In the Old Testament God says to Abraham that he was to be a blessing to the nations. Perhaps we Old Orders have a calling to be a witness to modern American culture. Our message is that their loneliness and isolation is not the only path. Maybe there are some gentle ways we Old Order people might share, through how we live out the beauty of community—Christian community.

Old Order people have identified themselves as a "strange and peculiar people." I think the Old Orders have a strange kind of beauty to share with the world. But like all real beauty, the deepest kind of beauty—a beauty that goes deeper than the surface is always difficult to see and understand. It is the strange beauty of submission of the self to the faith community.

Two old German words, *Gelassenheit* and *Demut* capture for us the special beauty of community better than any English word. Gelassenheit in English means the submission of oneself to God and to the church community. Demut suggests humility. The opposite of these two words is arrogance and self-assertion. That in a nutshell is how beauty is expressed in an Old Order community.

Chapter 14

Dancing on the Bridge: Creating Virtual Community Through Mennonite Literature

Ann Hostetler

In the late 1960s, when I was twelve, I attended Family Music Week at Laurelville Mennonite Church Center with my family. Just old enough to sing in the adult choir, that week I learned to sustain a melisma in such anthems as "Great Was the Company of the Preachers" under the expert and enthusiastic direction of Alice Parker, as we rehearsed the second part of Handel's Messiah. Parker, an arranger for the Robert Shaw Chorale, had grown interested in Mennonites after learning of their strong tradition of a cappella singing. John and Roma Ruth were also at the music week with their family, and in time John would collaborate with Parker on various projects such as "The Martyrs Mirror Oratorio" and a number of documentary films.

At Family Music Week I also learned about art as cultural critique. During the talent show the final evening of camp, pianist Peter Amstutz wowed us with a hilarious rendition of "I Could Have Danced All Night." Its alternate libretto continued "but I'm a Mennonite, and we don't think it's right." The fact that a Mennonite could sing—and laugh—about one of the taboos setting him apart from the larger culture left a lasting impression on me.

That event also showed me that many customs and taboos in local Mennonite congregations were relative. For instance, in my home congregation of Blooming Glen in Franconia Conference, Pennsylvania, the piano hadn't even been permanently moved to the sanctuary yet. It sat in the fellowship hall and made appearances only for weddings and special music, the congregation suspended between the traditional prohibitions against instruments in church and their eventual embrace.

Laurelville offered an opportunity for exchange with those outside of my home community. Laurelville's temporary gathering did not draw the fine distinctions of an identity based on place; rather it drew together from different places those who shared a love of music and wanted to listen to other voices. It included both those from the outside (Parker) whose contribution to the community was valued and those insiders who, because of their contact with the outside world, could offer new perspectives (Amstutz). I didn't realize it yet, but during Music Week I participated in the pleasures of "virtual community"—the exchange of ideas through language with others who shared a frame of reference but not the same physical territory.

In the latter half of the twentieth century, Mennonites have often created virtual communities. Although one might speculate that virtual community began with the tent meeting, it still flourishes in other forms: the church camp setting, such as the Music Camp in which I participated, the Mennonite World Conference, or in the communities of arts and letters, including a sequence of "Mennonite/s Writing Conferences" sponsored by either or both Conrad Grebel College or Goshen College. Such conferences, without denying the importance of landed community in all of its embodied specificity, suggest that the the ties that bind can be modes of discourse rather than a specific place. John Ruth made this association already in 1978 in his Herald Press pamphlet *Mennonite Identity and Art*, perhaps the first work of Mennonite literary criticism.

A virtual community of writers and artists at the Cincinnati Mennonite Fellowship's Mennonite Arts Weekend brought me back into conversation with the church after more than a decade away. Living in Milwaukee, Wisconsin, at the time, I was isolated from Mennonite community. I learned of the weekend and decided to attend with my daughter during the mid-1990s. There I found for the first time an open embrace and celebration of the arts in a Mennonite congregational setting. I stood weeping as Mary Oyer led hymns accompanied by Carol Ann Weaver on the piano and Brad Lehman on the saxophone. And I was introduced to the variety of Mennonite poets writing today. It was at the Cincinnati Mennonite arts weekend that I first was inspired to create an anthology of poetry by writers from Mennonite contexts.

In creating the anthology I had to raise such questions as "Who are Mennonites?" and "What is a Mennonite poet?" and answer them for both a Mennonite and a non-Mennonite audience simultaneously. This in itself took me about five years. The definition I arrived at was much broader than the parameters of even the largest Mennonite institution, the recently formed Mennonite Church USA. The anthology is regional (North American) but not circumscribed by national boundaries. It includes church members, those raised in a Mennonite community, and those who have had significant engagement with Mennonites. In fact the representation in the anthology is much more like the assembled bodies at a conference than the bodies who populate a particular congregation or conference located in a literal place. (On the other hand, I am the first to admit that the anthology, while representative, does not include all the worthy poets writing today.)

The twenty-four poets collected in *A Cappella: Mennonite Voices in Poetry* (University of Iowa Press, 2003) represent a wide array of Mennonite communities in both the United States and Canada. They write from the context of their experiences as Mennonites. But they also write for an audience beyond the community. In this way their work is founded on a creative tension not only between self and world, but between the community of faith and other communities of discourse. For some of these writers, the multiple intersecting communities of poetry and readers have come to substitute for the literal Mennonite community that once both nurtured and confined them. For others, the poetry is a way of expressing and celebrating their connection to Mennonite congregational life.

The Romance of Place and the Body of Believers

Community as the living embodiment of the church has long been a central, if not sacred, symbol of Mennonite faith and practice. Mennonites came to refer to themselves as "the quiet in the land," a people living simply, in mutuality with each other, and in relationship to an agricultural economy and the farmland they had come to own and bequeath to their descendants. Thus for centuries the gathering of the body of believers has been inextricably linked with the land and a sense of place. But for the European Anabaptist forbears of today's Mennonites, a community that identified itself in terms of place was often impossible. Intense persecution during the Reformation forced them to hide and flee. Anabaptist opposition to the union of church and state, refusal of military service, and insistence on adult baptism were political threats in nations using ecclesiastical authority to establish power.

Resistance to such markers of church loyalty as baptism was also a refusal of nationalistic identity; Anabaptist doctrine challenged the concept of nation as place and voted with the body for the right to migrate, move, and choose one's loyalty to a higher kingdom. Rather than identify themselves with the nation and a notion of place, early Anabaptists based their communities on a shared language and interpretation of a sacred text—the newly translated German Bible.

With persecution, most Mennonites (except for a significant group in Amsterdam) were driven into the hinterlands along with the larger number of peasants who had converted to this radical new faith. In a still largely feudal economy, military service was inextricably linked to land and place. Tenant farmers owed fealty to the princes who controlled land use. Thus some Anabaptists became successful stewards of estates in Alsace and Prussia but could not own their own land. The desire for land grew fervent among these people, prompting their emigration to the Americas or to the Russia of Catherine the Great.

Between the Reformation and the twentieth century the diligence, community ethic, and religious faith of Mennonites in Europe and North America earned them the reputation of productive and thrifty stewards of the land. Finally they were able to realize the desire for a landed community that had been an impossible dream for their ancestors. The rural, agricultural community gradually became the trope for Mennonite community among both Swiss and Russian Mennonite streams. Despite the growth of urban Mennonite communities since the 1960s, and the inception of Mennonite life in urban Holland in the sixteenth century, Mennonites have been represented as a rural people both by outsiders and by their own historians and dramatists.

Almost every Mennonite church I know of today is named for a place—from the three Yellow Creek Mennonite Churches and those named after small towns—Akron, Bart, Belleville, Blooming Glen, Mount Joy, Souderton, Strasburg—to urban congregations named after streets: Eighth Street, Willow Street, Diamond Street, Berkey Avenue, Prairie Street. Sometimes to differentiate between local churches it has been necessary to add building materials, as in Clinton Frame and Clinton Brick. Some Russian Mennonites who emigrated to this country a century ago are still associated with the names of the Russian communities from which they emigrated: Chortitza, Molotchna, and so forth. To a religious community that has become deeply imbued with a literal sense of place, the notion that a community might be "virtual" could be a bit unsettling. That community is created first by language, then by place, is perhaps also an unfamiliar concept to new generations of Mennonites who have shed the German dialects that once set them apart from their Russian or English-speaking neighbors.

In *Mennonite Identity and Literary Art*, John Ruth makes the point that Mennonites who stay in one "place" for generations can reject or ignore the stories that have brought them there. He calls for storyteller who will recognize, embrace, and interpret the narrative from past to present and future generations. Ruth himself has answered the call, most recently with his monumental history of Lancaster Mennonite Conference, *The Earth Is the Lord's* (Herald Press, 2001). In this volume he allows his readers to "experience the flavor of life" (35) and its complexity as lived in relation to place.

The romance of place, on the other hand, tends to obscure the history of Mennonites as a diasporic people. Several centuries of agricultural life in rural, patriarchal, community settings have certainly contributed to the Mennonite ties with place, but this sense of earth-bound roots is precious because it has also been threatened by a history of persecution. Therefore, while community has always been especially important to Mennonites, both because of a history of migration and exile, as well as an ideology of "separation from the world" and loyalty to the kingdom of God over that of the nation, the idea of landed community is secondary, as it was for the children of Israel, travelers who longed for a "promised land." This paradox is eloquently addressed in Jean Janzen's *Tasting the Dust* (Good Books, 2000), in which the poetry embraces her adopted California landscape after a life and history of movement.

The Virtual Community of Mennonite Literature

During the past several generations, as U.S. Mennonites have begun to leave their rural lifestyle—if not their rural image—a parallel phenomenon has occurred: a renaissance of Mennonite literature in the form of poetry. As ties to the land have become more tenuous, language again has come to bear the weight of creating community. While poetry may seem a slender thread, indeed, to bind up the fractious elements of (post)modern Mennonite experience, the recent meetings between poets and fiction writers of Mennonite background have served to create a space and a kind of virtual community in which the many factions of Mennonite identity can be sorted out and knit together in a new way. Literature can tolerate ambiguity much better than theology can. The discursive communities of poets do not aspire to one "true" definition of Mennonite community. Rather, the conversations and meetings between these creative writers in recent years have provided alternatives to institutional discourse, as well as an alternative form of connection, between those who care to imagine the faults as well as the future of Mennonite community.

In 1999 poet Julia Kasdorf said in a Goshen College lecture that she had begun to write poetry about the Amish and Mennonite community as a way of creating an imaginary bridge between the community of her birth and faith and her adult life in New York City. The lecture cautioned students both about the comforts and the dangers of community isolation. Kasdorf's title, "The Poet Is Not a Bridge," refers literally to Walt Whitman and the Walt Whitman bridge. While a poem can build a bridge that connects various communities, both for the writer and the reader, the poet herself cannot be the bridge across whom the entire ethnic group travels.

Kasdorf came to represent, during the 1990s, the poet who created a sturdy literary bridge between the Mennonite and the literary world, and who provided the fulcrum around which a community of U.S. Mennonite writers has created a literary conversation and community. But her work, as Laura Weaver suggests, also creates a space for others to do their own writing. The poem, not the poet, is the bridge. When enough Mennonites enter the discursive space of poetry, a new form of virtual community emerges.

From the beginning this community celebrates multiple perspectives and perceptions, honoring the interior voices within the communal body. Mennonites have consciously used the word *community* to invent a religious and historical identity. Dutch leader Menno Simons became known to Anabaptists in Switzerland through his writings, and Harold Bender, a twentieth-century American Mennonite scholar who studied at Princeton and in Basel, formulated the Anabaptist Vision. But only in recent decades have Mennonites produced serious poetry and fiction. The invention of a literary tradition within which to "place" these imaginative writers is, in some ways, infused with the same desires that the invention of community and place have been for Mennonites. The *Martyrs Mirror* is held up as the key document in this invented tradition that insists on literature as an act of witnessing. I use the word *invented* not to question the veracity of the martyr stories, but rather to suggest that traditions are narratives created in the present by those who need stories to connect themselves to the past in a meaningful way.

While community has often been connected with literal place or "landedness" in Mennonite thinking, as Mennonites become more mobile and the networks in which they are involved more complex, the connection of community and land has of necessity become more symbolic. The patriarchal, rural definition of landed community is, in fact, too limited in terms of human relationships and ideas to represent adequately the many forms of interaction taking place. In actual Mennonite communities members are, in fact, citizens of multiple nations as well as multiple communities created by work, social networks, and the media. Our virtual community is enriched when we attend to the stories and poems written from these acts of cultural crossing.

Bridges and Footings:
Place and Mennonite Literature

The rigid structures of a landed patriarchal community were the subject of Rudy Wiebe's critique in his first novel, *Peace Shall Destroy Many*, published in 1963 (Eerdmans). The first novel by a North American Mennonite writer to gain an international audience, it sparked a controversy among members of his Mennonite Brethren denomination—many of whom had not actually *read* it.

Although Wiebe remains a member of the Mennonite Brethren church, as well as a lay minister—and winner twice of the Governor

General's Award for fiction in Canada—the reception of his first novel dramatizes the difficulty of the Mennonite artist seeking to critique the landed community. Largely due to Wiebe's leadership and literary recognition, the literary community of Mennonite writers in Canada developed about a decade before that in the United States, as the continued tension between his art and his Mennonite membership created a context in which he has made a highly productive career as the novelist.

In the past two decades Mennonite poets and fiction writers (although the latter are more numerous in Canada than in the United States) have suddenly appeared in increasing numbers. But in the fall of 2002, when Wiebe's forty-year career as a distinguished novelist was honored at "Mennonite/s Writing: An International Conference," Wiebe remarked that he had never felt such a warm reception among Mennonites for his writing as he did among the gathered body of that "virtual community" of writers. In his career as a fiction writer, Wiebe has continued to explore place as one of his major subjects, interrogating it in ways that explode Mennonite fictions of "promised land." This land was the domain, it turns out, of native peoples whose religions or rights were little appreciated by production-oriented Mennonite farmers. Wiebe's fiction repays a debt to Cree and Metis people in its keen exploration of land and Indian culture, in an acknowledgement of the ways in which the Promised Land for Mennonites has been predicated, as immigration usually is, on the taking of the land of others.

One of the reasons that Kasdorf's poetry gained a community of readers among Mennonites so readily is the powerful sense of place(s) it evokes. At first glance, this appears to be the literal Amish and Mennonite community of Big Valley, Pennsylvania. But even in "Green Market," the first poem of Kasdorf's 1992 collection *Sleeping Preacher* (University of Pittsburgh Press), the notion of a pure and distant community is already an unattainable fiction for both the poet and the Amish woman she meets selling pies in New York City's Washington Square. By their very presence in New York, both the poet and the pie-seller belie the insular nature of the landed communities they long for. Both are travelers between worldly and unworldly places, and their travels will ultimately serve to transform their communities of origin. "Green Market" introduces the paradox of place in virtual space: that places mutually exclusive in the material realm, and that what they represent can coexist simultaneously in the virtual space of language.

The sense of place in *Sleeping Preacher* is really a sense of *places*, and the tension between them: an Amish/Mennonite community located in a narrow valley of the Northern Appalachian range—Big Valley, Pennsylvania—and a huge multicultural city—New York, in particular, Brooklyn. The tension between these two locations is also a "place" in which the reader of this volume spends a great deal of time. And, I believe, it is in this "tension between," where North American Mennonites live as urban or suburban, car-driving, cell-phoning, computer-owning, TV watching, NPR listening, movie-going citizens of the Western world. Even the plainest members of our sect drive in vanloads to shop at Wal-Mart. The idea of a literal, embodied community bounded by place has become a historical fiction, a trope that informs the ways in which we think about community and each other; but it is a concept that also severely limits and restricts the notion of how community operates for most of us. John Ruth's *The Earth Is the Lord's*, while rooted in a particular place, shows the many forces within that community propelling it into conversations with other denominations, citizens of other worlds.

The Virtual Community of Mennonite Poetry

With the advent of the Internet and the creation of such entities as Mennolink and Mennonite.net, the ways in which the strands of relationship bind communities at a distance from each other has acquired new metaphors. Poet Jeff Gundy has celebrated Mennonite artists, writing "In Praise of the Lurkers (Who Come Out to Speak" (*Mennonite Quarterly Review* 72.4 [Oct. 1998], 503-510). Certainly the creation of *A Cappella* would never have been possible without e-mail, as it enabled me to transcend the dictates of a physically bound life as mother and teacher in a place far from Mennonite community. But while talk of the global Mennonite community abounds in such organizations as MCC and Mennonite Mission Network, manifestations of global community beyond the four-color covers of Mennonite periodicals has resisted permeating our literal, place-bound communities, except perhaps for guest speakers on mission Sunday. Geographic separation from the world, once deemed desirable by a community that wished to express God's kingdom in a separatist manner, seems to run counter to the impulse to "connect" to larger virtual bodies within and beyond the church. Poetry can remind us that our inner lives can and do engage multiple words simultaneously.

For instance, Kasdorf's voice in *Sleeping Preacher* and *The Body and the Book* (Johns Hopkins, 2001) is situated not in the community but in the space between communities—that space created by leave-taking and the necessary reenvisioning of the relation of community to self. Kasdorf's articulation of the growing pains of individuals moving outward from traditional close-knit community into complex relationships with multiple communities of discourse portrays the experience of many Mennonites of the last several generations. Art that grows out of ethnic experience provides a chance for readers to reenter the collective wisdom of a community, its history, and to critically reflect on its assumptions and practices.

Jeff Gundy's prose memoir imagining the immigrant journeys of his great-great grandfather, *Community of Memory* (University of Illinois Press, 1996), loosely responds to Kasdorf's "Mennonites" as it questions how and whether we can know our ancestors. Gundy's "How to Write the New Mennonite Poem" warns any wanna-be-Mennonite poets away from the ethnic representations so easy to stereotype. In fact, Gundy's caveat has its own theological roots, as Mennonites are still very much a growing denomination with over half their numbers outside of North America and ethnic representations do not begin to represent these Mennonites. David Wright's poem, "A New Mennonite Replies to Julia Kasdorf," playfully uses images of soybean casseroles and Volvos from his urban Mennonite congregation to respond to the ethnic images from Russian and Swiss Mennonite traditions in Kasdorf's and Gundy's poems. Wright brings a new tone to the discussion as well. The ironic stance of Gundy and Kasdorf is replaced by a gentler, bemused earnestness reflecting the stance of a newcomer to an old tradition.

Such intertextuality within the Mennonite literary community serves to highlight the constructed nature of what cultural theorist Stuart Hall calls the "one true self" of cultural identity—the imposed homogeneity that one uses to present one's group to the outside, or which is imposed on the group when seen from outside. In other words, the intertextual references among these poems reveal an inner dialectic of different perspectives within the group itself. They also reveal a conversation among the poets. Jeff Gundy has written poems to Kasdorf and Janet Kauffman as well as Canadian poet Di Brandt. Jean Janzen has written poems to Julia Kasdorf and Rudy Wiebe. Kasdorf has written poems to Rudy Wiebe and to other Mennonite figures. While such intertextuality may be at the risk of losing readers outside the community, it has served to reinforce the sense that a virtual community of poets created through poetry may substitute for some of the shortcomings of living communities circumscribed by the wish for "one true identity" imposed by theological definitions and reinforced by tropes of community based on land rather than on language.

The Mennonite Writers' Conferences, reflecting the scholarship and vision of Hildi Frose Tiessen and Ervin Beck, have fostered a new sense of community among Mennonite writers, many of them alienated from the landed communities of their origin, in a new discourse that may transcend national borders and boundaries of church dispute, embodied so poignantly in the three "Yellow Creek" Mennonite congregations in Indiana that resulted from doctrinal church splits. At such conferences it is possible to have coffee, to share stories and laughter, with the grandchild of the man who excommunicated one's grandfather.

Dancing on the Bridge

When she spoke to Goshen College students on the theme of poets and bridges, Kasdorf urged her audience to create their own bridges, to write the poems they needed to write. Despite her protest that "the poet is not a bridge," the conversations among Mennonites stimulated by Kasdorf's poetic representations of Mennonite community have brought together readers from diverse places in an intertextual dialogue that reaches farther than one contained in an ecclesiastical setting. And one reason her work has been able to stimulate such conversations is that her poems and essays create bridges to the past as well as to the future. For instance, her work is informed by serious dialogue with her Mennonite literary forebears, including John Ruth, whose long productivity has also made him her publishing contemporary.

The virtual community created by and among poets and writers thrives on relationship and connection, a sense of play informed but not bounded by notions of history and place. As such, it can serve as a healthy antidote to the essentialist but often unarticulated narratives of community, purity, history, and place that have become vehicles for expressing our fears of mixing, of disappearance, of an imperfection that enables grace. On the other hand, poems need metaphors rooted in the material world, and place serves as one of the footings of the poetic bridge, even as virtual community serves as the other. On such a bridge, it may even be possible for Mennonites to dance with other Mennonites. The dance of community requires both distance and intimacy, the approach and retreat from each other that the elasticity of language allows.

In February 2003, along with poets Jeff Gundy, Julia Kasdorf, Keith Ratzlaff, and Betsy Sholl, I introduced *A Cappella: Mennonite Voices in Poetry* to the larger community of American poets and writers at the Associated Writing Programs annual conference in Baltimore, Maryland. At the end of the session, Keith Ratzlaff asked the capacity audience why *they* had come to hear about Mennonite and poetry. The answers were varied, and some voiced later to the poets individually, but among the audience were those who had come from Mennonite background or who had found Mennonites along the way. Our panel was an island in that large conference of nearly 3,000 people from across the United States, the virtual community of seventy-five minutes.

A few days later, after we had scattered to our geographic places and institutions both secular and Mennonite, we carried the sense of community with us. All the poets e-mailed me the next day. What surprised me the most was the strength the Mennonite or non-Mennonite poets in secular institutions derived from that moment of community. Perhaps the virtual community of Mennonite literature is not just a move away from the land, a gesture toward assimilation into a culture modeled on cyberspace, but can also serve as a palimpsestic network that enables its members to retain a sense of Mennonite identity and community in strange new lands.

Chapter 15

For Conscience' Sake? Examining a Commonplace

John Richard Burkholder

The voice of conscience is heard early in the first episode of John Ruth's massive historical narrative, *The Earth Is the Lord's*. When the Swiss Anabaptist leader Hans Landis was called before the civil authorities in Zurich in 1613, he explained that in "matters not involving conscience," such as paying taxes, he and his followers would be obedient and pray for God's blessing on their rulers (Ruth, 2001, 47). The point of contention, however, had to do with proper church order; the brothers and sisters were accused of setting up their own fellowship and rejecting the communion of the official church because they judged it to be unfaithful to Christ's teachings.

In the ensuing interrogation, claims of conscience were tossed back and forth between the officials and the simple believers. Mayor Rhan admonished the Anabaptists to go to the established church; that "will not hurt your conscience." Later, one of the prisoners asked how the lords could break up families "with a good conscience" (Ruth, 2001, 48-51). After months of threats, imprisonments, and even brief escapes, the grim outcome of this intense debate was the execution of Hans Landis on Michaelmas (September 29, 1614), the last Anabaptist victim of the sword in Switzerland.

The story of Hans Landis might well have been titled "For conscience' sake," a phrase that has been used frequently to describe the cost of remaining true to convictions in difficult circumstances. Ironically, the biblical source of that phrase is imbedded in what is perhaps the most troublesome New Testament passage for Anabaptist-minded readers, that is, Paul's admonition on being subject to the authorities in Romans 13:1-7. In the classic King James Version, we read: "Wherefore ye must needs be subject, not only for wrath, but also for conscience sake."

The other Pauline use of the phrase connects us to John Ruth's biblical title for the Lancaster Mennonite story. The Apostle Paul advises those at Corinth who are troubled about eating meat offered to idols: "Whatsoever is sold in the shambles, that eat, asking no questions for conscience sake; *for the earth is the Lord's*, and the fulness thereof" (1 Cor. 10:25-26, KJV, emphasis added). At this point we will avoid Paul's convoluted discussion of the problems in seeking to follow conscience; I simply wish to highlight the juxtaposition of themes. If we recognize "the earth is the Lord's" as a *Fraktur* representing John Ruth's body of work, then "for conscience' sake" will frame my exploration of some episodes in the sweep of Mennonite history that John embraces.

For some four decades, John Ruth has been exhibiting his affection for the Plain People—Amish, Hutterites, and Mennonites. Throughout his work in print and on film, he repeatedly emphasizes the importance of community and tradition, especially the church community and the tradition of faith. But John loves to tell stories, and a story is nothing without characters and conflict.

Thus despite his professed admiration of the stable enduring community, John Ruth as storyteller introduces unique individuals who engage and challenge the solidity of the group. His writings feature those distinctive personalities who break new ground, enlivening the narrative as they respond to the urgings of an unexpected voice, the voice of something sometimes called conscience, sometimes named as the very voice of God.

Look, for example, at the central figure in the major conflict in *Maintaining the Right Fellowship*, John Ruth's story of Mennonites in eastern Pennsylvania. The first token of change in traditional procedures occurs when John Oberholtzer, after his 1842 ordination by lot in the Franconia conference, follows his own inner voice and refuses to wear the regulation plain coat (Ruth, 1984, 242). That event triggered five years of agitation, as the progressives and conservatives became increasingly polarized. After reconstructing the dramatic scene of the October

1847 fall conference, when sixteen dissidents were silenced and then dismissed over their rejected proposal for a written constitution, Ruth speaks insightfully of the questions of conscience that must have been stirring on both sides (Ruth, 1984, 272-273). Each group claimed to be faithful to truth "for conscience' sake," yet they went separate ways.

Years before he embarked on his historical investigations, John Ruth tackled the elusive problem of conscience in a fictional mode. His first widely publicized work, the drama *Twilight Auction*, (we can't really call it a published work, because even though it was presented to the public a number of times, it exists now only in typescript) is built around a conflict of conscience that engages the extended family, the church community, and indeed the surrounding society.

In the "forward" (*sic*) to the 1966 text, John pleads with the audience/readers not to take sides too readily; he wants to portray both parties sympathetically. He even admits his own inner dilemma as he speaks of feeling guilty for stealing time from church, family, and school, but claims that "my conscience is partly quieted by the feeling of love for my home country . . . which drove me to write."

The drama is grounded in a generational conflict in the eastern Pennsylvania Mennonite Moyer family. Sam Moyer, a 23-year-old graduate student, makes a sudden trip home from Massachusetts with his Harvard roommate Morris Cohen, because he's learned that the family heirlooms are up for sale. The farm has been turned over to a housing development, the grandfather is moving to an old folk's home.

Sam's brief visit provokes intense conversations revealing underlying anxieties over the loss of land, changing patterns of behavior, and especially the threats to traditional expressions of faith.

When father Jacob Moyer learns that his son has taken part in an anti-war demonstration at the White House, he is dismayed. He judges such aggressive political activity as a serious departure from the conventional teaching of Mennonite nonresistance.

Sam, however, claims that "testifying in Washington" is also an expression of nonresistance. He silently observes the irony in the breakfast table Scripture reading (from Deuteronomy 8) with its focus on God's gift of productive land to the people of faith, even as the family land is slipping away. Sam is bothered not only by the family's apparent disregard for the importance of historic possessions, but also by their attraction to right-wing radio preaching. In conversations with his Jewish friend Morris, Sam reveals his anxiety: must he choose between his parents' approval, and claiming his own identity? Yet he's aware that his identity is deeply intertwined with heritage.

Later, two black-garbed Mennonite bishops arrive to inquire about the report they have heard of Sam's political protest, viewed by them as a transgression of church order. In the ensuing interaction, the bishops demand repentance, but Sam remonstrates "I can't repent when I'm doing exactly what my conscience tells me." Several times in the exchange, Sam alludes to the influence of his parents, who taught him to think for himself, and on that ground he claims the right to rethink the meaning of traditional nonresistance. He cannot accept their call for him to repent of his political activism, because, "You're asking me to do an impossible, unethical thing—go against my conscience" (Ruth, 1966, 44-48).

The dramatic climax of the play takes place at the evening auction, when Sam suddenly finds himself in a physical struggle with his father over possession of the prized family Bible. While the others are willing for it to go to the highest bidder, Sam aggressively claims it as a necessary token of his faith tradition, even incurring debt to do so. Other family members don't understand what's happening; they're worried about Sam's apparent rebellion against the received faith and don't recognize his way of claiming that tradition. He exclaims bitterly "I'm supposed to accept my heritage—and look at the help I get!" (Ruth, 1966, 62).

A poignant final exchange illuminates the gap between father and son. Sam exclaims: "You're gonna find out that I'm sincere," but father Jacob replies: "Yes, sincere. But what if you're sincerely wrong?" (Ruth, 1966, 65). The question hangs in the air as Sam and Morris head back to their other world of university life, the car loaded with the ransomed symbols of family heritage. The confused parents acknowledge to themselves: all that's left is to trust and pray.

Questions of conscience show up regularly in John Ruth's historical work. We encounter "freedom of conscience" early in *'Twas Seeding Time,* especially in the 1755 and 1775 declarations of conscience by the Lancaster area Mennonites (Ruth, 1976, 14, 22, 54ff). Those historic statements are recognized as the work of Bishop Benjamin Hirschi (Hershey) in *The Earth Is the Lord's,* as the Mennonists declared to the Pennsylvania authorities that they were "not at Liberty in Conscience to take up arms." (Ruth, 2001, 325)

In the Franconia history, "conscience" appears in the title of chapter 15, but the idea is present at other points along the way, both in the early colonial history and in the accounts of conscientious objectors to military service. Yet the stimulus of conscience, while usually admirable, can also be suspect in John Ruth's telling. He quotes Silas Grubb regarding the men of the Eastern District who went to war in 1917-18: "A man is answerable to his own conscience and not that of another" (Ruth, 1984, 531). The inference is that this elevation of individual conscience is a departure from the Anabaptist concept of church.

What we are learning from these brief samplings of John Ruth's extensive telling of Mennonite stories is that, interwoven with his strong emphasis on the solidarity of community, much of the energy that enlivens the narratives comes from distinctive personalities, from Hans Landis to Sam Moyer to Duane Shank (1970 draft resister in Lancaster), whose motivations have been described in the language of conscience.

We've observed that taking a stand "for conscience' sake" is a familiar Mennonite expression. Book titles abound (*For Conscience Sake, Conscience in Crisis, The Politics of Conscience*) but surprisingly, despite the pervasive use of the term, very little attention is given, in these books or other standard sources, to definition or explanation of what is really meant by "conscience." The topic is not found in the *Mennonite Encyclopedia* or the Swartley and Dyck A*nnotated Bibliography of Mennonite Writings on War and Peace, 1930-1980,* although one can find twenty-nine pages of references to "conscientious objection." According to the *Oxford English Dictionary*, the actual *conscientious objector* wording first appears only around World War I, although the phrase is used regularly in Mennonite and other writings with reference to earlier history.

Given the Anabaptist-Mennonite history of consistent witness against warfare, it's not surprising that Mennonites have centered on the adjectival form, as in "conscientious objection." But it is regrettable that there has been no significant attention to the explicit meaning of conscience from a distinctive Anabaptist perspective. So we are left wondering: what do we really mean by conscience?

The Complications of Conscience

Writing on the efforts of Lancaster Mennonites to counter the war spirit of the 1940s, John Ruth summed up the message of a pamphlet on nonresistance: its teaching gave "special stress on the example of Jesus, on following one's conscience, on being 'consistent,' and on being meekly submissive to both government and unfriendly critics" (Ruth, 2001, 973). But we must ask, is "following one's conscience" really what we should care about?

Our samplings from the Ruth corpus exposed some of the manifold meanings that the word "conscience" has had to bear. Introducing *Twilight Auction,* John himself spoke of his own uneasy conscience, perhaps the most ordinary usage—feeling guilty about something done or undone. Sam Moyer voices other common meanings—on one hand the steadfast holding to conviction, regardless of the cost; on the other, the implicit demand that one's sincerity, that is, one's "conscientiousness," is an adequate grounding. This claim to sincerity focuses one of the recurring problems in dealing with conscience. Simply stated, can matters of right and wrong be decided on the basis of sincerity? Doesn't this reduce the question of ethical discernment to a matter of emotional intensity? A related confusion is that sometimes "conscience" is used to mean merely the intention to do the right thing, but more often conscience is not just a nudge, but a moral compass, enabling one to determine just what is the right thing. Conscience is thus, in the classical definition from Thomas Aquinas, "the mind of man making moral judgments" (Preston 116)

Further, there's a fundamental contradiction in assessing the actual function of conscience. On one side is the classic view that conscience dare not be disobeyed; traditional moral theology states that one must always obey one's conscience. Yet at the same time, it's widely recognized that conscience is not infallible. Conscience can err, for all sorts of reasons: corrupted by self-interest, ignorant of relevant facts, inattentive to other human factors, faulty processes of reasoning, overwhelmed by emotion. Christian tradition, beginning with Paul the apostle, is fully aware that conscience is not trustworthy (1 Cor. 8,10; Romans 7).

What we know—or think we know—-about the function of conscience today is significantly different from earlier views. After more than a century of social scientific analysis, we are told that conscience cannot be the voice of God. It's a product of socialization, the result of a complicated nexus of interactions, all the way from rebellion against the parent to identification with significant authority figures. Whether as theologians or social psychologists, we can agree that human moral life exists in a context of community, the social matrix that shapes and molds the individual. But although we can't choose our parents, we can decide on the kind of reference group that helps form our developing conscience. And it is those choices of primary community that become a critical factor in ethical maturity, the forming of Christian conscience.

These tentative explorations of the problems inherent in the idea of conscience may help explain why a respected Presbyterian seminary president titled his 1978 book *Don't Let Your Conscience Be Your Guide*. Although conscience may be untrustworthy, however, it has been so pervasive a concept that we must give it more attention. The rest of this chapter selects instances from John Ruth's storytelling as starting points for probing more deeply the notion of conscience. The hope is to gain further understanding of how conscience can both illuminate and obscure important aspects of faith and life

Conscience and Religion in Colonial America

It's highly improbable that Mennonite Bishop Benedict Hirschi (1697-1789) and President Thomas Jefferson (1743-1826) ever met, although their lives in colonial America overlapped nearly half a century, and the active farmer-preacher from just west of Lancaster may have visited Philadelphia, where Jefferson first made history as the author of the Declaration of Independence. But for our purposes we can indulge historical fantasy and juxtapose the revolutionary philosopher-statesman and the immigrant sectarian minister in an imaginary dialogue around a key idea of the eighteenth century—liberty of conscience.

In John Ruth's Lancaster story, Benedict (also written as Benss, Bentz, or Benjamin) Hirschi (anglicized as Hershey) first appears on the public stage in 1725 as one of the signers of an English publication of the Dordrecht Confession. The document, intended to inform the authorities of the true nature of the oft-misunderstood Mennonist faith, included in its explanatory Appendix the charming phrase "our religion, the weaponless and revengeless Christendom" (Ruth, 2001, 213). Hirschi's signature suggests that he was already a confirmed minister in the Mennonite community, under thirty years of age, less than a decade after his arrival in America.

A few years later, in April 1728, Hirschi is among the 207 German-speaking men who gathered at the home of Martin Mylin and signed (or made their marks on) a document in English, prepared by two justices, that would testify to their loyalty to the Crown and enable them legally to own land. This particular document was prepared to meet the objections to the usual loyalty oath; it recognized that these were men who "for Conscience' Sake [could] not swear at all" (Ruth, 2001, 222) But what these newcomers to America did not realize was that they had made an unqualified pledge of faithfulness to King George the Second.

By the 1750s, as war threatened a militia call-up, Mennonite leaders recognized their earlier error and petitioned the Pennsylvania Assembly to make clear that their loyalty to the king did not extend to "defending him with Sword in hand," though they were willing to obey laws and pay taxes. Six times the document uses the language of "Conscience"— its freedom, its dictates, its peace and goodness (MacMaster, 91-93). John Ruth assigns the authorship of this document to the fourth signatory, Bentz Hirschi (Ruth, 2001, 280).

Twenty years later, amid revolutionary fervor, Mennonites and German Baptists (Dunkers) joined in what Ruth calls "perhaps the most memorable statement made by the Lancaster Mennonites in their first two centuries" (Ruth, 2001, 325). Printed as a broadside for distribution in both German and English and attributed to Benjamin Hershey, the "Short and Sincere Declaration" clearly sets forth the claims of petitioners who "by the Doctrine of our Savior Jesus Christ, are persuaded in their Consciences to love their Enemies. . . " After recognizing that the founder of the Province, William Penn, granted "Liberty of Conscience to all its Inhabitants," the document comes to a climax: "we are not at Liberty in Conscience to take up Arms to conquer our Enemies, but rather to pray to God, who has Power in Heaven and on Earth, for US and THEM." The declaration uses "conscience" six times and names Jesus Christ five times, with several other references to Christ as Judge and Savior (MacMaster 266-267).

Reflecting on these documents and their author two and a half centuries later, one may well wonder, how did Hirschi get to be Hershey? Immigrating as a refugee from the Palatinate as a teenager, he learned English on the job. His literary sources were scanty—the Bible, *Martyrs Mirror*, the *Ausbund* hymnbook, perhaps also Menno's *Foundation Book,* and the much loved compilation of martyr epistles and devotional texts, *Golden Apples in Silver Bowls.* As he prospers on the land, he is soon called as a minister and community leader. Our sources tell of interaction with Moravian and German Reformed neighbors, as well as Quakers. In 1757 he joined with weighty Philadelphia Quaker Israel Pemberton to raise funds among the Lancaster Mennonites for needy Indians (MacMaster 145, 149). Richard MacMaster, authority on colonial religious history, has suggested that Hershey may have had a sympathetic neighbor at his elbow, enabling him to get his thoughts into decent English for the several important petitions.

However much he may have needed help to draft these documents, Hershey's work on behalf of his people, while framed in an idiom of humility and even submission, actually functions as a full-fledged, audacious statement of a comprehensive claim to liberty of conscience. Whether or not he was familiar with their work, he is standing in the company of William Penn, Roger Williams, and the radical Nonconformists of seventeenth century England. William Penn appears to be the most likely link from Enlightenment views of conscience and religion to the unlearned Mennonites of colonial Pennsylvania. Sitting in Newgate prison in 1670 as a despised Quaker, with plenty of time for contemplation, he produced his foundational tract, *The Great Case of Liberty of Conscience*. The religious liberty provisions found in colonial Pennsylvania were grounded in that work. His *Frame of Government* of 1682 and the Pennsylvania Charter of Privileges of 1701 demonstrate a philosophy of religious freedom ahead of its time.

The career of Thomas Jefferson (1743-1826), born into an aristocratic Virginian family and serving two terms as President of the United States, stands in marked contrast to the simple German immigrant Bentz Hirschi. The well-educated, intellectually curious Jefferson, apparently a shy person, spent much of his early life immersed in the books he gathered. After studying law and entering the Virginia House of Burgesses, influenced by the fiery Patrick Henry, Jefferson found himself in 1776 at the Second Continental Congress where he was called upon to draft the American Declaration of Independence.

Back in Virginia again as legislator and then governor, in 1779 he drafted "An Act for Establishing Religious Freedom" (it was not passed until 1786 when Jefferson himself was in France). The central contention of the document is that no one "shall be compelled to frequent or support any religious worship, place or ministry whatsoever, nor suffer on account of his religious opinions or belief; but that all men shall be free to profess . . . their opinions in matters of religion" (Blau 78). In the preamble, Jefferson set forth the reasoning to support these views: God has made man's mind free; religion should be propagated by reason, not coercion; forced support of religion, whether or not it is one's own, is sinful and tyrannical; opinions of men are not the concern of civil government; truth will prevail if left to herself.

One of Jefferson's most quotable statements on conscience and religion comes from his 1781 *Notes on Virginia*.

> But our rulers can have no authority over such natural rights, only as we have submitted to them. The rights of conscience we never submitted, we could not submit. We are answerable for them to our God. The legitimate powers of government extend to such acts only as are injurious to others. But it does me no injury for my neighbor to say there are twenty gods, or no God. It neither picks my pocket nor breaks my leg. (Blau 81)

These documents mark the culmination of a decades-long struggle in Virginia against the established church and in favor of "equal rights of conscience," a campaign carried forward by Jefferson, James Madison, and others. In the unfolding history of religious freedom in America, the Virginia debates function as prelude to the Bill of Rights and the famed First Amendment religious clause: "Congress shall make no law respecting an establishment of religion or prohibiting the free exercise thereof." It's worth noting that an earlier version of the proposed Amendment spoke of "the full and equal rights of conscience."

Reviewing the voluminous collection of documents from this period, the basic idea of "religion" emerges as a deeply personal phenomenon, equivalent to "conscience," apparently, as the terms are used almost interchangeably; "free exercise of religion" being equivalent to "equal rights of conscience." Respect for conscience in constitutional times could be rooted either in a theological conception of God as the author and ruler of conscience, or in a more humanistic Enlightenment concern for the integrity and autonomy of the individual, the possessor of certain "inalienable rights."

So how do Hirschi and Jefferson engage? As John Ruth would concur, Benjamin Hirschi and his brothers and sisters in the peace churches were not much interested in shaping the contours of a new political entity, the United States of America. Their motivation was to remain faithful to their tradition, which was in actuality much more than a tradition.

It was a distinctive called-out community seeking to live in faithful obedience to the Lord God.

Let's probe further the actual implications of Jefferson's eloquent and memorable language about freedom of conscience. When pushed to expose their practical meaning, these high-sounding affirmations of religion prove to be disconcertingly hollow. In actuality, for most of the next two centuries of the American experiment in freedom, the legally sanctioned "freedom of religion," remained limited to inward belief and its vocal expression. Claims to freedom for public actions in the name of religion, or of conscience, were regularly denied by laws and the courts until as recently as 1963.

The Mennonites and others who shared in the 1775 Declaration, however, were people of convictions that demanded action in the public square. Hirschi's document, although couched in language of submission and meekness, actually represents a bold claim to a freedom that exists beyond the jurisdiction of any worldly court or Congress. Jefferson the celebrated spokesperson for political independence is of course an actor on the same historical stage as the faithful separatist preacher, but in another sense they are not really on the same page. Richard MacMaster, writing on the experience of the peace churches during the American Revolution, highlighted their understanding of "discipleship as a separate and distinct way of life... Government officials found it hard to understand the sectarian position; when they spoke of religious liberty they meant by it the *freedom to worship* according to the dictates of conscience, never the *freedom to live* by conscience" (Macmaster 1, italics added).

CONSCIENCE AND WAR

No longer under the threat of actual martyrdom as in the Hans Landis case, "for conscience sake" has come to stand for the steadfast refusal of killing, warfare, and military service, rooted in historic nonresistant faith. Although widespread military conscription did not begin until the time of Napoleon, the nonresistant convictions of European Anabaptists formed a significant part of the motivation for emigration to the New World.

Thus, although the actual language of conscientious objection does not appear until the twentieth century, the idea is there from the beginning, often expressed by such terms as "defenseless" and "nonresistant." Significantly, in the colonial era, a number of states recognized "persons religiously scrupulous of bearing arms," creating exemptions for those opposed to militia service. Thus, the Pennsylvania Assembly in 1775, noting that "many of the good People of this Province are conscientiously scrupulous of bearing arms," urged others "to bear a tender and brotherly Regard toward this class of their Fellow subjects..." (MacMaster with Horst and Ulle 243, 257).

Undoubtedly the entire history of religious freedom in this area would have evolved much differently if the Second Amendment to the Constitution, designed to protect the right to bear arms, had been adopted as originally proposed by James Madison in 1789, including the proviso: "but no one religiously scrupulous of bearing arms shall be compelled to render military service." In the ensuing debate, the point was made that such objection might well be based on religious conviction, but could not be construed as a natural right. Although the House narrowly passed the Amendment, the Senate voted to strike the provision, the joint conference failed to restore it, and consequently the matter was left for Congress to decide by statute (MacMaster with Horst and Ulle 573-74).

It is surely one of the ironies of the American concept of religious freedom that this most crucial and long-standing area of conflict has never been guaranteed by the Bill of Rights. Conscientious objection in the United States, therefore, has for more than two centuries been subject to legislative decree rather than constitutional right. Consequently, the fate of conscientious objectors has zigzagged between persecution and grudging recognition, as we move across the decades from the colonial period, with differing legal status in several states, to the Civil War, where President Lincoln's generous instincts were countered by severe penalties in the Confederacy. Despite a paper provision acknowledging religious conviction in the World War One Draft Act, many peace church members were conscripted to face scorn and even brutality in army camps. This situation, quite unsatisfactory for both the war department and the objectors, led to intentional planning by both church and state for alternatives as World War II approached. Much has been written about these wartime experiences (see Hershberger, Keim and Stoltzfus, Sibley and Jacob, Wright); our purpose here is simply to recognize an unresolved issue in the unfolding history of competing loyalties for the allegiance of conscience.

To be sure, the grounds for conscientious objection under existing laws were broadened significantly by several Supreme Court pronouncements during the Vietnam War era. The highest court in the land, in two major decisions, agreed to stretch the language of religion in the Selective Service Act to include a variety of ethical and moral belief systems that could be understood as "parallel" to conventional concepts of religion. In effect, "conscientiousness" or sincerity has come to the fore as the measure for determining CO status. If this subjective test continues to be the rule, then the functional criterion for legitimate conscientious objection becomes readiness to suffer for one's beliefs. One has to ask if indeed this is the best that a secular society can do in a postmodern era that lacks standards for objective truth!

This very sketchy outline of the travails of conscientious objection in America implies an uncertain path into the twenty-first century. The treasured freedom, in actuality only an occasional privilege, remains equivocal and contested, still at the mercy of legislative whim. It is surely not far-fetched to suggest that in a time of severe national crisis, a frightened, angry, even vindictive Congress could abolish all the hard-won victories for the cause. And what might that mean for tomorrow's Mennonites?

Beyond Conscience

After reviewing some of the distance that "for conscience' sake" has taken us over some 20 centuries, it's time to stop and ask if this is really what we want to talk about. Does "conscience" actually convey the qualities of courage and obedience lifted up in our faith stories? Instead of "for conscience' sake," perhaps we should be saying something like "for Jesus' sake"!

Earlier I pointed out the problems with the conventional idea of conscience, its ambiguities, contradictions, and disputed meanings. Now I'm ready to set it aside; it's not an adequate vehicle for carrying the weight of Christian conviction embodied in the Anabaptist-Mennonite ideal of discipleship. We need to find better ways to express the steadfast commitment that inspired martyrs and war resisters to be faithful even unto death.

The basic issue is not a matter of following rules, but of relationships. The essential decision is not what to do or not do, but "whom will you serve?" It's a question of loyalty, of following Jesus—for Jesus' sake! To name Jesus is to answer the underlying question: By what authority can claims of conscience be confirmed?

John Ruth quotes from the 1940 booklet *The Christian Nonresistant Way of Life,* created by the Lancaster Conference leadership to give guidance to young men faced with conscription. Representing the "quiet spiritual consensus" from two centuries of Pennsylvania Mennonite history, the position advocated "was not pacifism . . . but following the Christ who laid down his life rather than defend it with the sword" (Ruth, 2001, 973-974). John goes on to tell stories of draftee experiences that both exemplify and expand this teaching.

Thus it is that we meet Clyde Mosemann, 20 years old, from the East Chestnut Street congregation in Lancaster, who was making excellent wages working in a local airplane propeller factory in 1940 (Ruth, 2001:974-975). We learn a bit more about Clyde's good life in the pre-war years, driving a new convertible, learning to fly in a local flying club, from the account in *Seeking Peace* (Peachey and Peachey, 1991, 198ff.). The crunch came when Mosemann discovered that the firm was about to begin a military contract; "his youthful teaching . . . now troubled his conscience" (Ruth, 2001, 975). After Pearl Harbor, with the United States now at war, Clyde and his friend Roy Bucher left their good employment and went to Florida, where they worked at low paying jobs and became involved with a Spanish-speaking mission church during winter 1941-42.

In the following spring, Clyde was refused the 4E conscientious objector classification by his draft board. He appealed this ruling several times and was finally ordered to appear in Federal Court in Philadelphia on June 17, 1942. As Clyde recalls, after some questioning of his beliefs and of church doctrine, the officer in charge "began a tirade of verbal abuse, accusing me of being a traitor to my country in time of need, and of being a coward" (Peachey and Peachey, 1991).

When I interviewed Clyde (now in his early eighties) in August 2002, he told me that he had prepared a lengthy written statement with numerous Scripture citations, but at that moment he looked out the window, saw the statue of William Penn atop City Hall, and instead of replying from his paper, he simply asked "Sir, was William Penn a coward and a traitor to his country?" The officer stuttered around a bit, admitted that Quakers were good people and that maybe Mennonites were okay too. A few weeks later Mosemann was reclassified as a conscientious objector.

Sixty years later, as Clyde recovered the memory of that defining moment, he described his experience in terms of Luke 12:11-12:"When they bring you before the synagogues, the rulers, and the authorities, do not worry about how you are to defend yourselves or what you are to say, for the Holy Spirit will teach you at that very hour what you ought to say."

Clyde Mosemann's story doesn't end there; in fact June 1942 is only a beginning. Following several years of Civilian Public Service, Clyde married Anna Burkhart and the couple moved to Goshen, Indiana, where Clyde attended college and seminary as Anna worked in a physician's office (Ruth, 2001, 1029). From Goshen, the Mosemanns entered into pastoral ministry and a few years later began more than a decade of missionary service in Uruguay and Argentina, fulfilling a sense of call to the Spanish-speaking world that began in Florida in 1941.

When in 2002 I asked Clyde "Why Goshen College?" (a long way from Lancaster both geographically and theologically in the 1940s), he laughed: "My brother had gone to Eastern Mennonite and came back wearing a plain coat; I wanted none of that!" He also mentioned his excommunication from Lancaster Conference because Anna was not a Mennonite Church member.

I'm captivated with Clyde Mosemann's story for two reasons. First is the surprising parallelism with my own biography; although I'm nearly a decade younger than Clyde, we share Lancaster County ancestry, youthful attraction to flying and fine cars, attendance at Goshen College, and missionary service in Latin America. But more important for the purposes of this essay, Clyde's pilgrimage pertinently demonstrates the shortcomings of the conventional idea of "conscience" as an explanation for life-shaping decisions. Mosemann told me that church teachings were quite important in his formation, but obviously he was not caught in unquestioning conformity. Although he took seriously the calling to nonresistance and Christian service, he rejected the given church regulations regarding marriage and plain clothing. Clyde's story represents a creative mixture of rebellion and loyalty—true to the deeper convictions of the church, annoyed by the petty stuff.

A few more sentences from John Ruth introduce another story that helps develop our thesis. In 1970, Duane Shank, eighteen-year-old draft resister and minister's son from the East Chestnut Street church, was taken by the FBI from the Eastern Mennonite College campus as a draft resister (Ruth, 2001, 1110). Sentenced to three years of community service on probation, Duane has continued on the path of activism against militarism and on behalf of peace and justice for three decades. Shank's experiences are detailed in *The Path of Most Resistance,* the narrative accounts of ten Mennonite young men who refused to cooperate with the Vietnam War draft. Although the voice of "conscience" does not show up as such in Duane's story, the authors of *Path* dedicate the book "To young people who struggle to follow conscience in times of military conscription" (Miller and Shenk 5). The language is commonplace, as we have observed, but my argument is that conscience is too limited a concept to explain the motivations of persons such as Duane.

In November 2002, I asked Duane to tell me more about the context for his 1970 decision. He noted many influences: parents and church, of course, but also teachers, books, Mennonite leaders, peers who both supported and questioned the direction he was moving. A few years ago he wrote: "I think the primary reason I resisted the draft 30 years ago was that the issue posed in stark terms the age-old question of where our ultimate loyalty lies? To God or to human rulers and systems? One cannot serve two masters. The fundamental faith declaration of Judaism and Christianity is the Sh'ma: 'The Lord is our God, The Lord is one, and you shall love the Lord your God with all your heart and with all your soul and with all your strength. . .' The false gods challenged in the Hebrew Scripture today go by the names of militarism, racism, and nationalism; but the challenge is the same. To what do we owe our ultimate, deepest loyalty? The answer is clear: There is one God, and to that God alone we give our heart, mind, soul, and strength" (Shank 2).

In my view, Shank has correctly emphasized loyalty as a fundamental quality of Christian faithfulness. Loyalty is relational, encompassing obedience to Christ in the context of church community. Of course, loyalty can be misguided, just as conscience may be, but the focus of loyalty can always be clearly identified. Loyalty has many dimensions: to family, to church, even to the best of the American ideal represented by Thomas Jefferson—but above all to God in Christ.

To be sure, we must also call attention to other qualities of Christian character—conviction, steadfastness, humility—all those expressions of belief and belonging that dominate the narratives from John Ruth.

Circling back now to an earlier encounter, we must ask: how can any of this help the fictional but exemplary Sam Moyer find his way, as he carries an heirloom family Bible into the intimidating realm of postmodernity?

Our primary discovery is that conscience alone does not make one a pacifist Christian—or, for that matter, any kind of Christian! At best, conscience is merely a tool for enabling moral judgment—the content of character comes from elsewhere. In John Ruth's narratives, we meet ordinary persons who demonstrate loyalty to ultimate causes and commitments, steadfastly holding to the path of duty under God. The faithfulness of those individual lives is nurtured and sustained by a thick stratum of community and tradition.

Thus our parting word to Sam Moyer, and anyone else listening: "Don't let your conscience be your guide; rather, ground yourself in loyalty to the community of faith—for Jesus' sake!"

Works Cited

Blau, Joseph L. 1964. *Cornerstones of Religious Freedom in America.* New York: Harper & Row.

Dunn, Mary Maples. 1967. *William Penn: Politics and Conscience.* Princeton, N.J.: Princeton University Press.

Hershberger, Guy F. 1951. *The Mennonite Church in the Second World War.* Scottdale, Pa.: Mennonite Publishing House.

Keim, Albert N., and Grant M. Stoltzfus. 1988. *The Politics of Conscience: The Historic Peace Churches and America at War, 1917-1955.* Scottdale, Pa.: Herald Press.

MacMaster, Richard K. 1976. *Christian Obedience in Revolutionary Times.* Akron, Pa.: Mennonite Central Committee.

———.with Samuel L. Horst and Robert F. Ulle. 1979. *Conscience in Crisis: Mennonites and Other Peace Churches in America, 1739-1789.* Scottdale, Pa.: Herald Press.

Miller, Melissa, and Phil M. Shenk. 1982. *The Path of Most Resistance.* Scottdale, Pa.: Herald Press.

Nelson, C. Ellis. 1978. *Don't Let Your Conscience Be Your Guide.* New York: Paulist Press.

Peachey, Titus, and Linda Gehman Peachey. 1991. *Seeking Peace.* Intercourse, Pa.: Good Books.

Pierce, C. A. 1955. *Conscience in the New Testament.* London: SCM Press LTD.

Preston, Ronald. 1986. "Conscience." In *The Westminster Dictionary of Christian Ethics,* ed. J. Childress and J. Macquarrie. Philadelphia: Westminster Press.

Ruth, John Landis. 1966. *Twilight Auction.* [Typescript in Goshen, Ind.: Mennonite Historical Library.]

———. 1976. *'Twas Seeding Time.* Scottdale, Pa.: Herald Press.

———. 1984. *Maintaining the Right Fellowship: A Narrative Account of the Oldest Mennonite Community in North America.* Scottdale, Pa.: Herald Press.

———. 1985. *A Quiet and Peaceable Life.* Intercourse, Pa.: Good Books.

———. 2001. *The Earth Is the Lord's: A Narrative History of the Lancaster Mennonite Conference.* Scottdale, Pa.: Herald Press.

Shank, Duane. 1999. "The Church and the Political Order." Unpublished manuscript in possession of the author.

Sibley, Mulford Q., and Philip E. Jacob. 1952. *Conscription of Conscience: The American State and the Conscientious Objector, 1940-1947.* Ithaca, New York: Cornell University Press.

Smith, Page. 1976. *Jefferson: A Revealing Biography.* New York: American Heritage Publishing.

Swartley, Willard M., and Cornelius J. Dyck, eds. 1987. *Annotated Bibliography of Mennonite Writings on War and Peace: 1930-1980.* Scottdale, Pa.: Herald Press.

Thomas, Norman. 1923. *The Conscientious Objector in America.* New York: B. W. Huebsch, Inc.

Wright, Edward Needles. 1931. *Conscientious Objectors in the Civil War.* Philadelphia: University of Pennsylvania Press.

Yoder, Sanford Calvin. 1940. *For Conscience Sake.* Goshen, Ind.: Mennonite Historical Society.

Chapter 16

An Instinct for Community

Reta Halteman Finger

My favorite neighbor lives directly across the street from me. Both college teachers, Ming and I share a mini-community by taking walks and attending plays and concerts together, and sharing a meal Saturday evenings, sometimes inviting other neighbors to eat with us. Though our political views are similar, Ming calls herself a Catholic by birth and an agnostic by persuasion, while I am a practicing Mennonite.

Since living in Virginia's Shenandoah Valley, Ming has been impressed by two things that characterize Mennonites here: one, there are many different kinds of them, and, two, they are more communally oriented than any other group she has known. Though she might approve of my potlucks and small-group meetings, she is astounded at the level of accountability demanded of Mennonites. One's personal lifestyle and ethics are one's own, she assumes; why should church-sponsored organizations care about the private lives of their members or employees?

If sharing community at some level for more than four hundred years continues to be instinctive for Mennonites—and for me as one of them—it is because of people like John Ruth. John has not only lived community among his own people for nearly all of his life, but has also helped us to see, through the artistry of historical storytelling, how very precious and unusual such shared life in one simple corner of the world can be.

As a young person living in Franconia, I was often impatient with my elders, seeing their lives as constricted, limited to daily concerns about the prices of milk or eggs, chicken diseases, "going to market," planting corn, crocheting, shelling lima beans, or canning peaches. I saw these stolid Pennsylvania Dutch people limited to gossiping about others in their congregation, or worrying about their children drifting away from the church, or how they would take care of the previous generation of Grammies and Grampops, or who could beat the neighbors planting peas in the spring or hanging out the wash on a Monday morning. I had a wider vision and higher ideals, I thought, than the earthbound roots from which I had sprung.

But John would sit with my parents, my Halteman grandfather, the Alderfers and the Landises and the Clemenses, hear their stories, take their pictures, learn their family trees. He was intrigued by my aunt's two-generation collection of family slides, and copied some for his own cache. He read through an attic stash of letters by and to me when I was a college student in the early 1960s. And in the process of researching such local color, John would weave together a dramatic account of Pennsylvania Dutch life in Montgomery County for the past three hundred years, or compile slides of daily activities along Route 113 since 1950.

Because of John's genuine interest in our people and his ability to tell their stories with earthiness and humor, he has given me a piece of my own history that I would never have put together on my own. Only a few years ago, while visiting my home church, John was telling me something about my Grampop Halteman I never knew. He ended with a reflection on the union of my temperamentally very different parents, something like: "Who could have guessed that a Guntz and a Halteman would together produce five such children!"

John Ruth's academic education and literary and historical talent never stood in the way of his relationships with the rest of us. We never saw him as Mr. Ruth, or Dr. Ruth, or Rev. Ruth, or even Pastor John, but simply as John. Part of his talent, I suppose, was perceiving and highlighting the abilities of these "ordinary people." We thought of him, perhaps unconsciously, simply as one of us, an equal who thought we were important enough to listen to and who actually delighted in telling *our* stories—stories which had never before sounded so clever, or profound, or funny.

I cannot say that it was because of John Ruth taking over our rowdy sixth-grade class at Franconia Mennonite School in mid-year that I eventually decided to seek a doctorate in New Testament. In 1952, neither of us could have imagined a female in that role. But many years later my Mennonite instincts pushed me toward a dissertation topic that could hardly have been more communal or Anabaptist. I decided to research the daily communal meals embedded in a community of shared possessions which, according to the Acts of the apostles, were enjoyed by the earliest Christians in Jerusalem. The rest of this essay will seek to share some of this hidden story of ordinary people living in intentional community. I hope to strengthen our biblical basis for the communal sharing so exemplified in the life of both John and Roma Ruth.

COMMUNING WITH WHOM?

As a young teenager, I remember our closed communion services as extremely solemn occasions. We observed this ordinance only once a year at Salford Mennonite Church, washing feet the Saturday before, and singing doleful songs about Jesus' suffering and death while people lined up to take one morsel of bread and one sip of (real!) wine. Having been warned on previous Sundays of the danger of "eating and drinking judgment against ourselves," we thus commemorated closed communion.

Today, with a more open communion and no dire warnings of judgment, we still limit ourselves to mere symbols of a meal and a mostly somber reflection on our vertical relationship with God. Though this ritual has a long tradition, I believe we have overlooked many of the multivalent meanings of the Lord's Supper both in our closed communion of the past and at our welcoming tables of the present. Is Eucharist more aptly (though unreflectively) celebrated in our Sunday potlucks? Or by inviting visitors or strangers to Sunday dinner? Or around refreshments served in "koinonia" groups? Or at the food pantries and soup kitchens opened for those in need of more nutrition? Did the ordinance truly become a sacrament the year our church gave us money and bags of groceries at Christmas because my father had severely broken his leg, had no insurance, and could not work for many months?

Outside of the actual Last Supper accounts in the Gospels, we have our clearest description of the meal ritual in 1 Corinthians 11:17-34, a text that accuses the Corinthians of abusing it. A daily common supper must lie behind this text, for, according to 11:21, it was meant to satisfy hunger. The problem was that those who came early—the wealthier Christians who did not have to work—ate the food before the poor manual laborers could get there after sundown. Thus Paul accuses them of not eating the *Lord's* Supper at all, but only their *own* suppers.

In fact, they are eating and drinking judgment on themselves by not "discerning the body" (1 Cor. 11:27-32). This phrase has a double meaning, for "the body" is not only the broken body of Jesus, but the entire body of believers. "This is the reason," says Paul, "that many of you are weak and ill and some have died" (v. 30). God is not magically striking down some people in judgment; this is what happens when poor people, living at subsistence level, do not get enough calories for their one regular meal of the day. Their immune systems weaken; they become ill; and some of them die. The only solution to truly celebrating the Lord's Supper is that "when you come together to eat, wait for one another" (v. 33).

This text and many others in early Christian literature clarify that for several hundred years the churches celebrated the Lord's Supper in the context of a whole meal, called the "agape meal" (i.e., Jude 12). This love feast was supposed to include everyone in the believing community, leveling the social gaps that existed in the culture around them. But as Christianity became linked with the Roman state in the fourth century, the ritual was reduced to mere symbols of nourishing food, and the theology of social equality and care of the poor were divorced from it. Lost forever, it seemed, was the powerful message of economic sharing that had enabled the early church to survive and flourish despite its impoverished origins.

First-Century Breadbreaking

Let us now move further back in time to the earliest beginnings of the Jesus movement in Palestine as we look for more evidence of daily meals eaten in community. Here we have only Luke's account in Acts, his second volume which parallels the story of the early church with the story of Jesus in his Gospel. After Jesus' resurrection, ascension, and ten days of prayer in the upper room, the day of Pentecost arrives, the Spirit falls on the 120 believers, and Peter preaches a mighty sermon. Three thousand people, some of them former enemies, repent and believe the good news. We can only imagine the amount of behind-the-scenes organizing that went on as the group of 120 tried to absorb hundreds more, but when the dust settles, we find this text:

They devoted themselves to the apostles' teaching and fellowship, to the breaking of bread and the prayers. Awe came upon everyone, because many wonders and signs were being done by the apostles. All who believed were together and had all things in common; they would sell their possessions and goods and distribute the proceeds to all, as any had need. *Day by day,* as they spent much time together in the temple, *they broke bread by households and ate their food with glad and generous hearts, praising God* and having the goodwill of all the people. And day by day the Lord added to their number those who were being saved. (Acts 2:42-47, emphasis added)

Luke was a skilled, artistic storyteller (not unlike John Ruth!) who liked to juxtapose individual dramatic stories between more generalized summaries like the above. In the next scene Peter and John heal a lame man who begs at the temple gate but is forbidden by Jewish law to go inside because of his disability (3:1-4:22). Made whole, he stuns the high priests by leaping and dancing within their sacred sanctuary (3:8-10). This nameless beggar represents the dregs of society, poorest of the poor. But now he belongs to the "in-group" and will be invited to the daily common meals, no longer as an expendable beggar but as a contributing member of the community.

"Meanwhile, back at the ranch" we find another summary of what's happening in the households (4:32-37). Daily common meals are not mentioned, but the community of goods is further emphasized, so that it becomes apparent that Luke sees this new movement as the fulfillment of the year of Jubilee described in Leviticus 25 and Deuteronomy 15, when land and wealth are redistributed so that none have need. Luke refers to Deuteronomy 15:4 when he says: "There was not a needy person among them" because of their radical sharing of goods.

Then follow both positive and negative examples of communal sharing by wealthier members of the community who actually own some real estate: Barnabas, the "son of encouragement" (4:36-37), who counteracts the Enron-style deception by Ananias and Sapphira (5:1-11). The Spirit has called this diversified community into being, and lying cannot be tolerated when shared possessions demand absolute trust in one another.

The narrative then zooms back to further conflict in the temple between the apostles and temple personnel (5:12-42) but returns again to household living (5:42-6:6) where continued growth has created a problem among the women:

> In those days, when the disciples were increasing in number, there was a grumbling of the Hellenists against the Hebrews because *their widows were being neglected in the daily (table) service* (Greek: *diakonia*). And calling to themselves the whole community of disciples, the twelve said, It is not pleasing to us to leave behind the word of God to serve tables. Examine therefore, brothers and sisters, men from among you who are well-spoken of and full of the Spirit and of wisdom, whom we will appoint for this need. And we will devote ourselves to prayers and to the service of the word." (Acts 6:1-4, author translation)

Though I will discuss these texts in more detail below, here we should remember that (1), the Jerusalem church practiced economic sharing so that no one was in need, and (2), the believers ate a common meal once a day in the households in which they lived, which included a bread-breaking ritual and spiritual celebration. But if you read Acts 6:1 in the NIV or the NRSV translations, you will be misled, for there the Greek word *diakonia* has been translated as "distribution." Rather than picturing a common table at which widows are for some reason being neglected, we now see poor old women alone in their huts missing out on the ancient equivalent of "meals on wheels." But in the context of meals, *diakonia* always means "serving at tables," so if we are to take seriously the common meals of Acts 2:46 and the fact that no one was in need (Acts 4:34), we cannot relegate these women to lonely, individual experiences of poverty. The mistake is reading our modern Western values of individualism and private property into the first century.

Social Location Determines Interpretation

Before I present evidence for the commonsense logic of a daily celebratory meal embedded in a community of goods in the Jerusalem community, we should note further bias in the interpretation of these texts. The idea of Christians sharing material possessions has not been well received in our Western religious tradition. Thus these texts have usually not been considered normative for church practice, nor have they been associated with our communion rituals. Note a few examples:

(1) Roman Catholicism did develop a communal lifestyle for some of its members, but only for a minority of Christians who remain celibate. Laity have not been encouraged to share property, assuming it would be destructive of family life (Hoffner 173).

(2) Reformers Martin Luther and John Calvin have been hugely influential in Protestant tradition. Yet their views about communal life were formed against the background of corruption in some Catholic monasteries and convents in the sixteenth century, as well as the communal emphases of the Anabaptists and the agitation of the peasants for more social justice. Luther's assumptions about a state church conflicted with his ideals of communal sharing, and he finally concluded that such community of goods as described in Acts 2, 4, and 6 must be entirely voluntary. He did not advocate it for the majority of lay Christians, and he urged the princes to violently stamp out the Peasants' Revolt ("The German Mass and Order of Service" and "Ordinance of a Common Chest [1523]).

John Calvin was even more negative. Luke was describing not a literal community of goods, he thought, but a spiritual unity. The rich believers' liberality was a result of this harmony, as they sold some of their goods to help the poor. Calvin was at pains to clarify this "on account of fanatical spirits who devise a *koinonia* of good whereby all civil order is overturned." Here he has the Anabaptists in mind because "they thought there was no church unless all men's goods were heaped up together and everyone took therefrom as they chose" (*Acts of the Apostles 1-13*, Calvin's Commentaries). Calvin was convinced economic equality would destroy civil order.

(3) Anabaptists in turn refuted the charges of the Lutheran and Reformed leaders. Those like Menno Simons insisted that, though they were committed to providing for the needs of the poor within their churches, they did not practice a literal community of goods because, Menno believed, that arrangement had been temporary (Friedmann, "Community of Goods," 659). Only the Hutterites did so at the time, and have perpetuated this lifestyle for over 450 years to this day (Friedman, "Hutterian Brethren," 854-857).

(4) As capitalist ideology and technology grew apace during the nineteenth century, some commentators so feared a breakdown of Western capitalism that they saw the early communalism of believers as unrealistic and short-lived. The conflict over the widows of Acts 6:1 showed

it was unworkable, and the famine described in Acts 11:28 was seen by some as the result of such an impractical experiment. The most egregious example I found was in the Acts volume of *The Expositor's Bible* published in 1903. Here, G. T. Stokes sees the community of goods as a downright evil, a bad mistake that should never have happened. The reason it is recorded in Acts is as "a significant warning for the mission field," to encourage missionary churches "to strive after a healthy independence amongst their members." The conflict concerning the widows "can be compared to the same evil spirit that bursts forth in almshouses, asylums, and workhouses, where charity cases are suspicious and quarrelsome despite receiving assistance" (Stokes 200).

(5) Throughout most of the twentieth century, the reaction against Soviet communism militated against Western Christians taking seriously any kind of actual community of goods and daily table fellowship as in the Acts account. One German scholar, Werner Elert, voiced the concerns of many when he insisted that a community of goods did not work then and would not work now because it suspended the natural order of economics (Elert 173ff).

(6) A more recent method of dismissing these texts is one generally held by scholars today, particularly redaction critics. Since Luke wrote a generation or two later, he did not know specifically what had happened in the early years of church growth and thus idealized its beginnings to inspire his own community. Luke used Greek utopian language like "friends have all things in common" to describe the first Christians, making it sound like a primeval "Golden Age." The well-known Lukan scholar Hans Conzelmann perhaps put it most bluntly: "We cannot speak of a failure of the experiment because it never happened in the first place" (Conzelmann 24).

Needed: A "Thick Description"

But New Testament scholarship has made some remarkable advances in the last two or three decades, among them a focus on social science criticism. In other words, the insights of archeology, social history, sociology, and anthropology are now being brought to bear on the biblical texts so that what has seemed obscure or counterintuitive can begin to make sense in an ancient agrarian, Mediterranean setting. One anthropologist, Clifford Geertz, says we must provide a "thick description" of a text or event or story which comes from another time or place to understand it.

In addition, the previous suspicion scholars from Christian traditions had toward their Jewish counterparts has been breaking down. Today New Testament scholarship can draw from centuries of Jewish reflection on the Hebrew Bible, the Mishnah, or the Talmuds.

What happens when we begin to apply such scientific insights to the Acts texts describing the early Jerusalem community of believers? It is true that Luke's description is about something out of the ordinary. Not everyone in first-century Palestine belonged to a large group practicing sharing of all their possessions and eating a daily common meal together. But how did this differ from what was normal in *their* culture *(not in ours)?* This is where we need a "thick description." So come with me back to the Mediterranean world at a time many centuries before our age. Forget about democracy and the "inalienable" rights of the individual to freedom and the pursuit of happiness. Totalitarianism reigns; the Romans rule the known world. Forget about the inherent, "self-evident" equality of all people; nothing in this world is more self-evident than that people are *not* created equal. Maybe five percent lived above subsistence level. A third of the Empire's population is enslaved, with no human or civil rights at all. Forget middle class life; it doesn't exist.

Forget capitalism, mass production of goods, mass transportation and communication; forget universal education. Forget social security or any social welfare for the poorest, outside of a few tithes and alms. Forget social mobility or social advancement; sons learn their father's trade, and most social mobility is downward, such as for second sons who do not inherit land and must fend for themselves. Forget gender equality; women are inherently inferior. Parents arrange daughters' marriages, though they cannot legally marry off a girl before she is twelve and a half.

Forget health care; it will be many centuries before doctors do more good than harm. The overall life expectancy is about twenty-nine. And with death so imminent, the health of the living is often quite poor. Forget childhood; by the age of six a child must work a full day. Forget growing old; half the children die before the age of ten, and only three percent of the population live to the age of sixty.

But do not forget taxes. They are very high. The Romans extort enough money from the Palestinian peasants to pay for their military occupation and for luxury goods for officials. Tithes are also burdensome, and most of these go to support the corrupt temple system and to feather the nests of powerful high priests and Sadducees who rule Judea under the Romans.

How can people survive under these conditions, you might wonder. The only way was to live in large, extended families, caring for each other, sharing possessions, demanding a high level of trust, never thinking of yourself as a rugged individualist—or even as a separate individual at all. Sociologists call these "kin-groups," whose shared economic life is called "generalized reciprocity." Many people in developing countries still survive only by this method of social security.

A kin-group may work together at one occupation, such as fishing or masonry, although most Palestinians worked the land, usually as sharecroppers. During the first century, peasant-owned land was continually lost to wealthy estates when drought or illness drove peasants into debt they could never repay. Pity the person who did not belong to a kin-group: the younger son going into a far country to earn a living, the orphan reduced to begging, the poor widow forced to sell her body to feed her children.

Creating a "Fictive Kin-Group"

How then could Jesus call people *out* of their families, away from their fishing nets and hoes, sometimes sounding dangerously anti-family, as when (in Luke 9:59-60) he tells a would-be disciple not to stay home and bury his father? How would people survive outside of their families and kin-groups?

But Jesus was reconstituting the family, creating a people not tied together by blood and kin but committed to himself and his vision of the in-breaking reign of God. This new kin-group was composed of male and female disciples who followed Jesus and those who provided hospitality along the way. No doubt many of them worked as day laborers when they could, women as well as men, contributing their wages to the common purse. And certainly they ate together each day. The gospels, especially Luke, are full of accounts of Jesus' meals with disciples, with Pharisees, with tax collectors and common people.

In a culture where getting enough calories to sustain life and health was a major concern, meals were celebratory and charged with deep symbolism. To honor Yahweh (or another god if you were a pagan), a bread-breaking ritual opened the meal. After the food came the ritual of the cup, again to honor the god, followed by drinking and conversation. People ate only within family groups or with their social peers, for to recline at a meal with someone implied you were socially equal with him (women did not always eat with men for this reason, or for the sake of propriety). That is why, for example, Zacchaeus the cheating, outcast tax collector nearly fell out of his tree when he heard Jesus invite himself to his house. And why this act of eating together across social lines brought him to repent of gouging his fellow citizens of their money. "Today salvation has come to this house," said Jesus, because of a common meal shared across social barriers.

This background helps us understand the sociological origins of the community of goods and communal meals in the ensuing Jerusalem community. First, the believers *had* to organize themselves into a new kind of kin-group to survive economically. The Galileans had left their region and livelihood; others joined from the Diaspora after their visit to the temple for Pentecost. Others were probably rejected from their extended families for following a crucified criminal. Jerusalem believers had to find spaces for these newcomers, and most of them would have to look for work in the area.

Because such kin-groups are not related biologically, sociologists call them "fictive kin-groups." They operate on the same principle as ordinary kin-groups. Tools and other household possessions are shared because it saves money. Kin-groups eat together by households, perhaps in the courtyard adjoining several houses or tenement buildings. Eating together builds community, besides being more efficient and economical. When one understands how ancient Mediterranean society operated, it is absurd to say that the Jerusalem community of goods failed because they were too idealistic and the money ran out. Belonging to a kin-group was the only way to survive! Further, the spiritual dimension of this shared meal, which included bread-breaking and joyfully praising God (Acts 2:46-7) served to weld the group together in their common anticipation of the in-breaking reign of God.

Besides continuing the pattern of Jesus' table fellowship and communal sharing, another factor no doubt contributed to the success of the Jerusalem community-of-goods. Down by the Dead Sea lived a celibate community of Jewish men called Essenes, who also lived in a community where possessions were shared and all meals were sacramental and eaten in common. The priestly Essenes had split off from the Sadducees as early as 150 BCE, denounced the temple system as corrupt, and set up alternate "pure" communities where they could perfectly keep the Law as a way to prepare for the coming of both a priestly and a kingly Messiah.

Smaller pockets of married Essenes were also scattered throughout Palestine. Both Philo (*Hypothetica* 11.1) and Josephus (*War* II.viii.3-4) set the full number at 4,000 and say they were well-regarded by the populace. In fact, not far from the traditional site of the Upper Room are the remains of the Essene Gate, with evidence that a community of Essenes were living in Jerusalem and quite possibly in the same quarter as the Jesus-believers (Riesner 209). Theologically, the Essenes differed from the Jesus-community in many ways, but their social practices must have provided a model for the new movement.

What About the Widows?

If this fictive kin-group with their communal meals was so successful, why do we hear about the complaints of the Hellenist widows in Acts 6:1? As noted above, some scholars have seen this as a sign that the community-of-goods was not ultimately workable. Later, redaction critics who see Luke as an editor shaping his material for the best effect, are skeptical about the historicity of this event. Ernst Haenchen, in his massive commentary on Acts (Westminster, 1971), suspects that the rift between the Hebrews (Aramaic-speaking Jews) and Hellenists (Greek-speaking Jews) was far wider than this text admits, and that Luke is using a small conflict to cover up a larger one. If it is only a matter of providing relief to a few widows, why not simply appoint a committee to take care of the problem? But again, if we use the insights of the social sciences, especially female-sensitive anthropology, this view can be challenged. The incident with the widows can be a window into the world of women hidden within a society constructed along patriarchal lines.

In the ancient Mediterranean world there was always a large gap between the roles of men and women, especially in the eastern part of the Roman Empire. Men were expected to operate in the public, political sphere; women labored in the private sphere of home life. Commensurate with their lower status, women were not mentioned in the literature of this culture unless (1) a woman was exceptional for some reason, or (2) only women were involved in a particular incident. Greek grammar contributed to this invisibility; all people-language was linguistically masculine unless only women were present. [One might write, for instance, about a meeting of women, one of whom brought a baby boy, and all the inflected endings of verbs, nouns, and adjectives would shift to masculine, implying to the reader that no women were present.]

Understanding how Greek literature functioned in a male-oriented culture rules out Haenchen's theory. Luke would hardly magnify a problem about women to the level at which the entire community had to be called together to solve it, had it not been a significant, community-wide issue. And since it pertained to serving at the common meal with its Lord's Supper celebration (rather than food distribution to individual widows), everybody *was* involved.

In all cultures I know of, past or present, women are mainly responsible for food preparation and serving, as well as home management. So what happens, then, if the Lord's Supper is continually reenacted in the private sphere of the household, in the context of a common meal? In his description of Jesus' last supper, Luke notes that Jesus had said that he was among them not as one who reclines at the table, but as one who serves (Luke 22:27)—essentially as one who does women's work. What kind of role reversals were going on during these revolutionary communal meals in Jerusalem? What kind of honor was given to the women's work of serving food? Who *really* served the eucharistic bread?

The problem described in Acts 6:1 has something to do with inequality regarding women, specifically, widows. Most commentators have seen these widows as the poorest, most vulnerable members of the community. However, the text says nothing about these widows being poor, and Acts 4:34 has already told us that there were no needy persons among this community. If common meals were eaten by households, these widows would have been there like everyone else. So how are they being overlooked or neglected while the meals are being served?

I suggest the possibility that these widows are the servers rather than the served. Is it possible that an informal group of widows—single women or older women less tied to domestic duties—were handling the food preparation and serving the meals? In a world where the only honor women received was for doing women's work well, it must have been a great honor to be in charge of the central communal event of the day. As the focus of worship shifted more and more from temple to household, the women's work would have gradually assumed higher status.

At the same time, the community was absorbing both native Hebrew, Aramaic-speaking Jews as well as Hellenist Jews from the Greek-speaking Diaspora. Many misunderstandings could have occurred because of language difficulties. Perhaps the Hebrew women serving at meals were actually the Galilean women who had traveled with Jesus and thus may have been accorded more honor than the Hellenist women. In light of the equality Jesus had exemplified, the Hellenists may have complained about not being treated on a par with the Galilean women.

But why then were seven *men* appointed to serve at tables? Again, we are dealing with a patriarchal society where men operate in the public sphere, so perhaps only men were named as overseers. The male apostles seem to have had some previous table serving duties, since they say they can't keep up with serving tables anymore (6:2). So Hellenist men may have been appointed to take their place—a good political move—to make sure no more conflicts arose. On the other hand, the community may have taken Jesus' words seriously when he said that he, a male and their leader, was among them as one who served, and they should do likewise. Perhaps these men really did help with the meals.

In any case, some of them seemed to forsake their role in the private sphere rather quickly, since we find two of them, Stephen and Philip, preaching and traveling to new mission fields (Acts 7-8). Women, no doubt, were holding the community together at home, presiding over the Lord's Supper each evening.

Conclusion

By using texts about meals in 1 Corinthians 11 and Acts 2 and 6, we are afforded a window into the communal meal practices, sharing of possessions, and other boundary-breaking behavior of the early Christians. Multiple meanings surround the Lord's Supper. The bread and wine may have symbolized the broken body of Christ and his risen presence in their midst, but according to Paul, it was not truly the *Lord's* Supper unless everyone from any social status ate it together, signifying equal inclusion. Bread and wine eaten in the context of a full meal also symbolize care of the poor, for when all eat together, there are no needy.

The poor are not "the other," to whom those with full stomachs give handouts. The agape meal also reminded the believers that women's work lay at the heart of their most sacred ritual, and that Jesus came in the female role of the food server, not in the role of the one sitting at the table.

Today we cannot fully escape our technological, capitalist, materialist culture. We can never go back to agrarian kin-groups using generalized reciprocity to subsist. The Montgomery County of simple rural Mennonites of my past has now exploded with housing developments to become one of the richest counties in the state of Pennsylvania. But I would like to see us use our Anabaptist instincts for community to wrestle with the multiple communal meanings of the Lord's Supper in our own culture and time. What pattern today would be as practical and justice-oriented as the "fictive kin-groups" of the early church? Is there some way to bring together the Eucharist of the sanctuary with the potluck in the church basement and the Wednesday evening soup kitchen or food pantry?

Many of our communal traditions derive from our Anabaptist ancestors taking seriously the communal sharing of the early Jerusalem church. Both John and Roma Ruth have led the way in showing us the value and strength of community life through their lived examples, their storytelling, and their art. May it inspire the rest of us to carry on!

Works Cited

Conzelmann, Hans. 1963. *Acts of the Apostles*. Minneapolis: Fortress Press.

Elert, Werner. 1961. *Das christliche Ethos*. Tübingen: Furche.

Friedman, Robert. 1955. "Community of Goods." In *Mennonite Encyclopedia*, vol. 1. Scottdale, Pa.: Herald Press, 658-62.

———. 1956. "Hutterian Brethren." In *Mennonite Encyclopedia*, vol 2, 854-65.

Hoffner, J. 1968. *Christliche Gesellschaft*. Kevelaer: Butson und Bercker.

Riesner, Rainier. 1992. "The Essene Quarter of Jerusalem." In *Jesus and the Dead Sea Scrolls*, ed. James Charlesworth. New York: Doubleday.

Stokes, G. T. 1903. *The Expositor's Bible*. New York: A. C. Armstrong & Son.

Chapter 17

Genius and the Verbal Dance: A Conversation with John Ruth About Language, Writing, and Community

Julia Kasdorf

During the early 1990s, I was busy with academic and artistic work that addressed the crisis of my becoming a Mennonite author, a story I have told too many times elsewhere. One troublesome touchstone in that work was John Ruth—a man who seemed to wear his authority as easily as he had once worn a plain suit. The problem was his little book, *Mennonite Identity and Literary Art* (Herald Press, 1978) and his infuriating denials of individual power that seemed evident enough to me, given his ordination-for-life by lot at the age of twenty, his Harvard Ph.D., and his many books and films.

I wondered whether those denials were somehow related to one of the difficult paradoxes of Mennonite culture—that we value community so much that it is difficult to know what to do with exceptional individuals when they emerge. Consequently they are both esteemed and regarded with distrust or even disdain. At the same time, there seems to be an unspoken rule that some may speak and some may listen, a rule which may be essential to maintaining certain patterns of order in the community, but which ultimately undermines the communitarian ethic. John Ruth became associated with these frustrations. Or, I should say that I'd begun a quarrel in my head with a figure named "John Ruth" who likely had very little to do with the real man called by that name. That much I realized, and I decided I needed to get over "John Ruth," so I proposed that we have a conversation.

This is that conversation, somewhat edited, tape recorded in the living room of the Ruth ancestral farmhouse on the Branch of the Perkiomen on January 21, 1995. In part, the occasion for the conversation was Ruth's project of creative nonfiction about his local community. On the tape, Roma, John's wife, is present only in the sounds of tea and supper being served, but eventually she joined the conversation, too.

Current Literary Projects

Julia: First I'd like you to talk a little about your current literary projects.

John: Well, it's one project. I find in my records that I was thinking about writing a quote "novel" for the last twenty or twenty-five years, and instead I've got assignments back-to-back-to-back: I wrote two conference histories; I wrote a book about Conrad Grebel. I wrote a book about the town of Souderton. There's only one book I've ever written that wasn't an assignment, that was the book about the Revolutionary War [*'Twas Seeding Time*], and I get more response to that than anything else.

But I always wanted to write something where the language itself would be of some quality. And so that I would bless the subject matter with some sensitive language. I just wanted to do that because language itself has interested me, then, second, one only has one's own story to tell. Some people can go—James Michener for instance, now I don't consider that literature—he just goes and does research and writes about something. I've done projects like that, too, but to me that's journalism.

Then there's this other utterance that you make . . . that you give utterance to. In other words, I have to be theological: "eternity intersects time." There's one place that it does—in your life, or your people, or your community, or something, and one can bear witness to this, one can give utterance to that. For better or for worse, like I say in one of my—here, here. . . . I've expressed it in so many words somewhere . . . [reads from the unpublished manuscript of his current project]:

The mill overlooked by the Alderfer farm was the oldest of eight on the northeast Branch of the Perkiomen. Since, though it had been Lower Salford's very first industrial site—nothing happened there for two and a half centuries—its story will be the more intriguing one to tell.

That's my challenge—to tell the story that won't get told. And to fly in the face of "Why should you bother?" Why should I tell that story? The only reason I'm telling that story is because eternity intersected with time. I don't mean to sound pious about it. And if you want to tell someone else's story . . . If you want to project yourself into the macro-culture and tell the story that will entertain [you can do that] . . . Sure you want to entertain . . . But no, you just want to give voice.

Julia: To?

John: The hearts that beat there.

Julia: So, you believe that you're telling the story of this community, which is really the genetic material that made you, too. So is it your story? Or is it the story that belongs to the group?

John: I think it belongs to the group. Insofar that I would try to make it my story, I'd better not try to imitate Rousseau and "unpack the secrets of my heart" unless my own heart carries more than its own idiom. If it does, if it's resonant, then it doesn't matter if I try to make it individualistic. That's the point: it has to resonate. If I'm talking about the group, it has to have a personality. If I'm talking about myself, it can't just be a reference to an atomistic existence. That won't be interesting.

Julia: So it's a self in relation to . . . history, to community?

John: Yes. What is a self? Who knows? And the minute you try to abstract it out of the communal matrix, it isn't anything.

Julia: So, do you think there's a relationship between your choice to write nonfiction and your discomfort with the original self, the genius voice? You're diminishing the power of that individual voice.

John: Well, maybe so. And maybe I should try to do the other thing. But the other thing would be as you've used the term *Romantic*. The Romantic is fine except when you push it to its extreme, then you get Ahab . . . you push Ahab and you get Robbespierre, or you get Manfred, or you get Mephistophiles, or you get Faust or something. And then it gets past where it starts to get interesting, as far as I'm concerned. To know the Mennonite experience is to have ecstasies in relationship. Not just the towering sense of individual autonomy.

Julia: Although in our culture—the larger, contemporary American culture, I mean—somebody writing a book about aesthetics probably wouldn't start with the idea of history. They might start with the idea of originality.

John: Originality? What is that?

Julia: I think it's understood as invention.

John: Is invention finding something that's already there? A possibility that already exists? A new factor that had never been brought into this particular combination before? I'm not against that. But I resist the notion that something hasn't ever existed in some form before. But that's just a stance, a suspicion of mine. It's wonderful to have that suspicion allayed, when you actually think "Hey, this is something new." I remember as a young fellow, the sensation of discovering something like that, reading something new in a book. I just had to pace around the room.

Except when [later] I see my son discovering it, then again I have that sense. Because at one time, all that opened up for me: the aurora of the future, the rosy dawn of possibility.

There are joys of aging as well as joys of becoming. Real joys. And, there are lessenings of the burdens. [When you are young] you think you have to invent the new way. You think you owe it to yourself and your potentialities to do it. And somehow there's a chemical that comes in eventually and says, "You haven't done it. But the world's great. It's immense. It's gorgeous. And you'll never exhaust it. Never, never. You're only on the cusp of the very beginning."

Julia: So, our culture's obsession with the new and the original. . . .

John: My goodness, where profundity is experienced is in the dialogue with what has gone before . . . just to see and bring in new relationships, that sort of stance. T. S. Eliot, "Tradition and the Individual Talent"—that still has a lot of power for me. You read your culture's monuments, and where you come along in the continuum you rearrange an item or two, and as you wiggle the whole thing, your slight change is what is novel, the new relationship that just wasn't there before. With the computer, we'll be able to recall data of any amount, and who knows what that will do to aesthetics.

Awe is awe. There will still be awe. We can rest assured of that. When a new angle shines a brilliant, penetrating light through something that we thought was deep, and it turns out to be shallow, well, Okay, we'll be glad for that. And the awe will be on the other side of that.

But as far as the individual. When I was young, I conceived of what I'm doing now in terms of, "I've never yet said the truth of my heart. I have something special." Looking back, I smile like an old person now: I've got something special? I don't have that burden now. But the beauty of youth is that aching urge to do it. That's built into us. It's wonderful, and in a way you never get rid of that entirely. But you may be confused if you think that you can only give utterance where utterance has stalled or failed. You have to realize that if you really do know something nobody else knows, then you ought to bless the world with it.

Julia: You've said utterance, you said voice, you talked about dialogue, and being in dialogue with the past. And the one thing in that book [*Mennonite Identity and Literary Art*] that was interesting to me is this phrase: "the process of the literary imagination in dialogue with the group consciousness." So whether you're in dialogue with the past or with the group where it is now—there's a sense of the group as a vague mass of information—but what of the individual, speaking? Can you talk about that?

John: Well that individual is like a prism that refracts the light, breaks it down into its component colors. That's just an analogy, but if you hang a prism there, ordinary light will turn into a rainbow on the wall. The beauty was all in there, but somebody had to refract it. And another analogy: it's a dance, life is a dance. You're always somewhere different on the floor. You're never in precisely the same relationship to the group, but the happiness lies in, for me—see, that's almost Anabaptist—to think of humans as one's fellow beings. We all see the same moon. We all reflect the same sun. We all feel our individuality, but we only learn to give language to it in relationship. None of us invent our own language. I don't know what thinking would be without language. Language is a communal phenomenon. Even when we talk, it's a verbal dance.

To me, the sensation of being taken up into the group, where my individual voice is heard and responded to, then into a whole interweaving—first a polyphony, then later a whole symphony, then later a whole unimaginable weaving of dialogue—that's the ecstasy of life, to be taken up into that. And the agony is the urge for it that is unfulfilled.

Julia: The urge to take part in a conversation.

John: There's a German word that talks about it—*Schar*—it means crowd, group, gathering, troop, band. [Pause, holds hand over his eyes, weeping.] I'm surprised that I'm emotional about it. It just sums it up.

The sound of it. It must be what I'm about. This *Schar*, this crowd, takes me up into it.

All I can say is that's what captures me, the kernel ecstasy of poetry. The artist must find what is fit, what is worthy, what is appropriate, what lets the sound of that sensation come through. The members of the troop are all different, and they dance together . . . I don't have any words for that except that it's music.

Julia: Is it what happens when we sing? What we experience when we sing?

John: Sometimes. Sometimes. I can be singing in Salford Church. . . . I studied hymns, you know, I wrote a thesis on hymns, so I know what I sing. I know even where in Isaac Watt's career this one came, stuff like that; it's all very rich. (And now the only thing that kills it is this shallow stuff that never thrilled anyone to start with, really.) Yeah. [Singing hymns sometimes] I'll block up and I can't sing just when it gets good. And this will hit me whether I'm sitting behind the pulpit in front of everyone or whether I'm there by myself. You know what's emotional. It comes in inauspicious places.

Julia: Right. But I'm trying to understand something here, trying to understand the connection between all these metaphors. You talk about voice and about writing. The voice that sings in a congregation, the individual voice that blends—there's a different relationship there between the one voice and the many voices—that's different from the voice that is like a prism that is listening to all these voices in history and somehow through that light. . .

John: When you write with that consciousness, if all you have ever known or felt is there, then it will inflect the sentence. It will choose one word over another. It will recall a word. It will invent a word. Those neologisms and those distortions will all be respectful of the people and place . . . only a person with deep respect will have that power . . . you can't get deep meaning out of a shell. Or just off the top of your head.

That is the frightening thing about my own life. I'm not sure I did wrong. Maybe I was right.

Only One Book

Julia: I wondered about that when you said that there was only one book, one big project that was yours, that all the other stuff was written in response to assignments for others. I just wondered what it feels like to be, in a sense, at the service of the community. I don't know who these assignments came from, I'm assuming....

John: One came from one conference, one came from another... the books, the movies... I never did one just for myself.

Julia: And it's all from the Mennonite world?

John: No, not all, though often related to it. But that I don't mind. But I never gave my angle on it exactly.

Julia: What would that mean for you?

John: It would mean a meditative voice rather than a badgering one, and it would express a view that would only be taken by someone who wasn't hectored by time or by the propelling of economic concerns. It would say, "Now this is worthy to just think about in itself." It would take unusual angles, and one of those unusual angles would be—and this is paradoxical—one by which you would give the benefit of the doubt to unprepossessing appearances. Where you say, "But there is, underneath, depth there; there is personality there; there is sensitivity there, and I'm going to be especially sensitive when overtly—like I said there, since 'nothing happened here, it may be the more intriguing story to tell.'" That's when my antennae go up. I won't let that pass.

Julia: So it's something about vision, something about what you are able to see and then express.

John: Well, all I know is that [we are] surrounded by beauty, and there is beauty in this world. There is crassness and there are all the bad things. But I feel all of that, and I remember coming over the hill by Salford with a teacher while in fourth grade.... We came over the hill in that '32 Ford, and all of a sudden there was this ochre sunset, absolutely clear like you get in the winter... and then the telephone poles like crosses. And we had to register it, it was just too outstanding. All of a sudden it was there. And she was a teacher who was sentimental and sensitive enough to realize we both had something... had experienced it together, and we didn't need a lot of verbal recognition, but we recognized it and we both had to say something, and we probably said something stupid like, "That's beautiful."

But why was that? She and I were neighbors, we didn't even know each other. She lived in a house next to ours. I didn't know her except that she was a teacher. God gives you... creation gives you something that vibrates, if it gets its chance to vibrate. And what really sets me off is for people to be able to grow up and go their way and really pay their respects to that. This, this, this has been here. There have been hearts, as I put it, there have been hearts here. A heart has been here.

I know from my encounters with my grandparents, and I look back, and I bask in that. I could *be*. I could *feel value*. How could it be? How had they accepted this misguided, unenlightened, ascetic life and yet still given me a place of warmth within it? But it happened. And I have to bear witness to it. I can't run somewhere else and bear witness to someone else's life. I have to bear witness to it, and if nothing else then, to an ecstasy of boredom if that's what it was. But it wasn't that. I must bear witness, to give utterance to it. You know, you don't even have to be religious to feel that way. And I've lived here, and I've sensed that and seen it.

You know, when you preach, you're well acquainted with this perhaps. There's a certain electricity in the air when your verbal formula or your cadence, or whatever, has let lose a certain feeling. It's in the air. So you know it happens even with dumb people, it happens with misguided people. A power has taken hold, and I've had to be humble . . . I've had to be . . . to be loyal, I've had to be willing to have done it in the context of a people who can't really appreciate it that much and who, if it goes over their heads, will just as soon criticize as not. But when you go to the college campuses, you always get some people there, but back home, well . . . I'm just trying to respond to what you've said.

Julia: Yeah. Do you think there's a connection between . . . well, first of all, I don't know the details of your life. How long were you preaching? Or how does that relate to your university work?

John: Well, I was preaching before I was teaching. I had to . . . at age 20 I had gone to college for one year. I hadn't acquired any kind of intellectual background. But I remember in high school, I was charmed by Shakespeare's language, and some poetry . . . [recites some lines] that was pretty basic, but I thought something's happening here with language Something's happening to my consciousness. . . . Something's happening. We were sitting in this mission hall, austere but all of a sudden you sing, "Each angel sweeps his lyre / And claps his wings of fire. . . . " All of a sudden, hey, wait a minute, there's something there!

So then when I taught, I asked myself real basic questions: "Why is language the way it is? What explains the phenomenon of language?" I have a list of questions somewhere, I wish I could remember them now.

So, they let me teach [at Eastern] a survey of American lit and a couple of seminars on ideas. That was fine except when the question came from several church leaders, "Do you want to do something with your own heritage? Do you want to write about it and think about it?" I said "Yes."

That was my second ordination. But instead, because I was a little too cooperative, I kept writing these conference assignments and the like. I feel providentially spared, because if I have a few good years left, I will tell this story. And I think that every thing that I've written so far will not be as important as what I'm now writing. The crazy thing about life is that you cannot fool life. And one of the possibilities is that I may have blown my chance. But I don't think so.

Julia: You mean by taking on these assignments?

John: By not writing when I was young. But when I think of the dumb things that I would have written . . .

Julia: Exactly. But I wanted to know about the professional relationship between preaching and writing. Preaching is oral. You know when you're connecting. You can see it in people's faces; it's more like a conversation. But writing, you're alone, you work for years on a book that goes out, and people read it far from you, alone. How do you see the relationship between preaching and writing—you see what I'm getting at?—and the notion of conversation in all of this?

John: I think there's an implied conversation always. Always, you're always talking to somebody. Sometimes I wonder if the audience is of any size, but there will always be people, and you're getting people who are really literate now in Mennonite circles. They're my primary audience, then anybody else. I have fun reading my stuff around here [near home]. I get very good response, but I don't know if it will carry over. There comes a time when you have to write to the audience you wish you had.

Julia: Have you ever felt that your voice in this conversation has been censored? Or that you've censored yourself?

John: I've censored myself. Yes.

Julia: Because you know who the listener is?

John: I don't get any pleasure in proving that I don't care what you think. I get a lot of pleasure in having people jolted but not attacked. I remember talking to a guy, a professor, about what to do with freshman, and I expressed some compassion for the students, how much they can take, and he said, "It's so much fun" [to shock them].

Well, like my aunt said, "I'm over that." The fun is how you can genuinely give them a sense of much more space, of ever opening up—that's what's fun. And being able to take readers who feel that their past is stale, and to walk them room through echoing room, and look at the pictures on the walls. I like that, and it can be done. You do that somewhat in your poetry. There's something to talk about, something to feel here. In the energies, in the strangenesses, in the familiarity that is only on the surface, that's exotic as anything underneath—that's the poetry.

See I have the problem of struggling with the greater language. Your language is your assurance. Your word is accurate.

Julia: I just write a simpler English.

John: I write a stodgier English, and if I could get some of that quality out, then there's something there.

Julia: Your writing is more erudite.

John: Well, that's not in right now. So, the thing is to give utterance, to say here, in this dance, there was a knowledge of or experience of joy. Or of anguish. Where it was precluded or occluded, but the sum is our ecstasy and agony. Wow. And who would have been able to inhibit it? It only made the water run faster or harder closer to the source . . . but then there must also be a chance for the mind to explore. If it only deadens it, if it is just sedated, that's not really it. We see it brutalized more, but you see that everywhere, not just among Mennonites.

I've seen people's faces relax as I communicate with them, where I'd blend the grace of sensitive language to something that is frozen in them, and they're afraid that that's all there is [brutality in the past]. If you let it flow, and give it language, then they feel that there was power there, and there was meaning there. And of course, there was happiness there, or the anguish itself had a bigger meaning. When you do that, you can see gratitude on the faces. . . .

The artist doesn't simply do a dance to show off. The artist lends a power to those who have it not, but who can recognize it. That's the crazy thing—some can recognize it instantly, when it's there . . . or they can find it when you didn't think they could. That's one of the great rewards.

Some Very Simple Questions

Julia: I want to ask some very simple, specific questions about that book *Mennonite Identity and Literary Art.* . . .

John: May I give you a preamble? Jim Juhnke made me write that book.

Julia: Okay. You didn't want to do it? It was another assignment?

John: I'm no theoretician. I just had to spin off what was on my mind then.

Julia: But, John, it's useful. It's powerful. I'm still talking about it all these years later.

John: I spun that off. Don't tell anybody this, but he came to my house, and he had to have titles, so I sat down and in almost less time than it takes to tell you, I wrote, what is it—four titles? Then I went out there [to Kansas] and gave the four lectures, and I came home and brushed them up. They're about my prejudices.

Julia: When you were working on it, who was your audience?

John: Frankly—and you'll laugh at this—I wanted to give hope to a Mennonite audience. That's all. Don't think that you're stuck with something. Don't think that you have to escape who you are to be. Expose it. Give it depth of language. If it's nothing but staleness, Okay, but expose it, dismiss it, then move on. But where are you going to stand?

And, furthermore, there's one place there where I say, "Has our ethos ever been given good language?" If it's incapable of receiving good language, then it is phony. But I'm not sure of that, not with the emotions I've had in the experience of it. I've had as powerful emotions in that as I have in reading anything . . . I was raised here where I had the double experience of knowing how arbitrary everything was, and yet it woke intimations of . . . [chuckles]—this is going on sentimentality—intimations of immortality.

I was in church, listening to the droning of the preacher, and saw this gorgeous green maple leafage, and it was lovely out there in the light, the color, brilliant, organic. And here I was sitting, listening to this unaesthetic drone. And yet I would feel a melancholy beauty in it. And I thought, something more than I know is going on or we wouldn't sit and listen to this! They wouldn't do it. Nobody says we have to, and I knew plenty of people who said, "The heck with that" and got out. But I didn't want to, and I'd think, "Why is that?" And then when I came to the age of youth, I would connect beauty with say, some girl, and that surprised me, too. I'd thought of this in fourth grade already, and I linked the two together. There was an inexpressible, unexpressed range of beauty out there, and I was seeing some of it. Like that guy said in his poem, there was a local Mennonite who wrote this poem about 1835, and I translated it. He wrote it in German [mumbles the lines in German]:

> When I have met a lovely child
> on whom God hath with beauty smiled
> the thought will ever come to me:
> the God who from nothing at all
> so many beauteous things may call
> oh how much greater must He be.

It's only the little bit that you see, and all you have to do is extrapolate. I always have that sense on hand, but maybe I'm forgetting and being guardedly optimistic.

Julia: I think, that in a sense, you and I have a notion that writing is remembering. What I'm wondering is whether there isn't somehow that we (I mean Swiss Mennonites) aren't constituted in a way that understands writing as a communal activity. This idea of relationship and the way you're writing, I wonder if it isn't somehow connected to that sense of community.

John: Absolutely. Absolutely. . . . But we don't want shallow insights about community, pro or con. You could say lots of shallow things about community now. You could be scared of it. But if it doesn't grip one, like Jonathan Edwards said, "The things of God are so great that there is no fitness in our speech about them, unless there is also greatness." We're talking about something so profound here, not something that truncates or diminishes. To the extent that it diminishes richness of language or of insight, then judge it.

Call it what it is. Say "that's not it." And it has not yet borne much fruit. Yet you yourself show that it's possible. I try to say that somewhere: why hasn't the Swiss Mennonite mentality done anything? There's a weakness in it. We've yielded to jargon. There's a weakness in it. We've said a lot of in-house talk that doesn't get past the intramural. We've had coarse, but not . . . well, some coarseness is good, but crude . . . There's an elegance of communal mentality, too. I used the word dance, because it's a patterned movement.

Julia: And the pattern is a conversation?

John: It is a conversation.

Julia: It's not just a problem with the community, it's also education. There hasn't been enough reading.

John: Right. There must be a dialogue with great exemplars. Literature doesn't arise out of just being in your own head. And you could also say that about music or painting.

Julia: And even if I claim my poems are extensions of the oral tradition, they aren't just that.

John: And if they were worthy extensions, they would be good. But that's the nice thing about your poetry, it's not ostentatious. Well, no—it's plain like a quilt, and some of those quilts can be pretty surprising. Like a sampler can be surprising. "Plain" wouldn't do it justice.

Julia: Let's go back to writing from "the covenant community"—the center of the community—well, I wonder if you can really see the community if you're in the center of it.

John: That's a unique perspective, and you're saying you can't have perspective there?

Julia: I wonder.

John: You can look out from it. And you can see things you might not see from another point.

Julia: But how can you know? You, for example, you didn't stay here. You didn't get ordained and stay here. You went away and then came back. And I'm wondering. . . .

John: No. I would quite agree with you. Staying there with no movement and without considering alternatives and without actually experiencing them . . . that's not a preparation for looking out from the center . . . to just stay in one place without moving around, that's not a dance. You can't triangulate anything. You have to have your *wanderjahr*, you have to go around and study with various masters. See what is behind art, what is true, what is the fact, what is the secret of the phenomenon of our people.

If what you are experiencing is only one more example—and it is—only one more example of human possibility, that's one thing. But I can't help having a slight messianic complex. The Jews sure have it. The Jews are telling the world—and they love to believe that they have it—any Jew will tell you, unless they are secularized, "God appeared here on Sinai, thus and so, thus and so, the whole world will come to Zion." And there's an analogy—it's silly if you take it too far—but, do you have something to say from who you are or don't you?

And for me, in a Christian sense, not just in a sectarian sense, you will always have something to say because your situation will always be different, and you speak to your own times. Sometimes you'll have to put up or shut up. You probably will hide that as an artist, so that the superficial seeker won't stumble all over it and fail to recognize any of it. It will probably be implicit in your work: your kernel idea, and one can always deduce it from the whole profile of one's work, if they never state it in a formula—and they won't state it. Let the church people do that . . .

Every artist is different. For me, I'm trying to bear witness to something which is that I'm interested or heard the call . . . of a collection of human beings, a class, a race, a family where you are just by fate . . . we are a family. You talk about "Mennoniting" your way, and all that stuff that gets shallow. It's our background . . . it can be expressed cosmologically, historically, theologically, but on every level that's what it's all about. . . . [Recites a poem by John Milton, "At a Solemn Musick":]

> . . . With those just spirits that wear victorious palms,
> Hymns devout and holy psalms
> Singing everlastingly,
> As once we did, till disproportioned sin
> Jarred against nature's chime, and with harsh din
> Broke the fair musick that all creatures made
> To their great Lord, whose love their motion swayed
> In perfect diapason, whilst they stood
> In first obedience, and their state of good.
> Oh may we soon again renew that song
> And keep in tune with Heav'n. . . .

You see, he's evoking a mythical past that may have never literally have been. Then, something "jarred against nature's chime," something jarred—leaving behind a longing, and I know it sounds puny to say that I long for it, too. But there is that inbred longing in me to recover that dance, that concert. At least we say imaginatively that it was "once" so, and the longing is to recover it. To evoke it, to recognize, to give utterance to that longing. And you might say, "That happens only in the imagination," but that's a big "only." First comes the imagination, and arguably just a dream. And yes, it's a dream. It's a dream.

If I would have to be forced to reduce what I'm saying to a formula, it would be this: It's about the coming together of something that isn't working, but that is meant to work, either by push or by pull. Which means that either it is meant to come together or is evolving toward it. And you have a chance, at some level or other, to feel that happening.

If a person evokes the joy of life itself, the joy of beauty, the joy of love or whatever, that's part of that manifold, trilling voice, too. Some voices stand out. Some voices don't say anything. But to a person like yourself to whom language presents itself, and you realize its possibilities, the fact that you can imagine it means that you've got to say it. And your metaphor may not be the dance, and it probably won't be.

Julia: I want to believe this idea that writing is conversational, and I do believe it at one level. On another level, publishing is very much an individual act. Putting your name on a book, even if that book contains information of the whole community, an individual authored that and put it out in the world, and the individual is responsible for that.

John: But when you're younger—and I think this is necessary—there is this essential anxiety that your individual, essential existence needs to be answered to. That's natural and good, but somehow, as you keep growing, the chemistry shifts to "If I could just be part of the choir."

A Matter of Authority

Julia: I also see you as someone to whom authority has been given. You couldn't do that, John. You couldn't dissolve into the group.

Roma: You'll never be just a part of the choir.

Julia: People give you authority.

John: Well, maybe, maybe. But it's in the nature of anyone who speaks. If you speak and your voice represents what they recognize as real, then sure, they automatically afford some respect. If you misrepresent reality, then you either fool them or you lose them.

Julia: In other words, if you just speak the truth. . . .

John: I'm not sure what point you're making there.

Julia: I'm not making a point. I'm just worrying through this idea out loud. . . because it's also my problem, because I find now that people also grant me this authority, and I don't know what to do with it.

John: It's irrelevant to you.

Julia: Yeah, and it's uncomfortable, and it's not something I want necessarily . . . so that even though I like to talk about this work being a conversation and somehow being a community project. . . .

John: You'd like to think it's just you.

Julia: No. It's just that I know it isn't seen as a community project, because. . . .

John: They would like to incorporate you, to confiscate you. They would like to absorb you.

Julia: No. I'm talking about something different.

Roma: She's had to go out on her own to do this.

John: Yes, but when she writes "Mennonites," it's "Oh, yes, let's put it in *Gospel Herald* [a denominational Mennonite magazine]."

Julia: I think on one hand, I'm granted authority as "that's our writer," but people don't see that I did this, but I did it out of our culture, and maybe they could do it, too.

John: Which isn't right. Which isn't true.

Julia: But maybe it is true. I think Mennonites are willing to grant authority very easily to the Amway seller, to the preacher, to anyone who comes along and speaks with authority. People will give up authority—and so that's an individualizing and isolating process for the author, [taking them] out of the community. You know the names of all these powerful preachers through the years, they've had a lot of authority; people have granted them authority.

So, even though we have this belief in community, we also have this singling out of individuals and focusing on them. There's something complicated about that.

John: Do you think Mennonites do that more than other people?

Julia: I think Mennonites—and now I'm thinking of those in traditional communities without a lot of education—I think with education comes a sense of discernment and you don't grant authority as easily.

Roma: Sure, sure.

Julia: But you're somebody who has been seen and recognized and granted authority in the pulpit and also of the pen, so even if you want to think of your project as something that comes out of the community, it's not seen that way.

John: Well, what do they think it is?

Julia: It's the work of a genius.

Roma: You. Yeah. They say, "I'd never be able to attain it."

John: Well, if that's the way they look at it, there's nothing that can be done about it. I'm not sure what the effect of that is.

Roma: She's just stating something, I'm not sure she wants you to do something about it.

John: What's the significance of it as far as what I do—as far as what you or I do?

Roma: Because you're saying it comes out of the community and she is saying that it's not a community project.

John: I agree that it's not a community project. And the word *genius* simply means that you have the whole genus in yourself: the general in the individual. That's what a genius is. If you as an individual bring the general into focus by the curvature of a particular lens you then become the lens that focuses meaning. Then that meaning is focused back into the group.

Postscript

After the interview, John planned to drop me at a bus stop a few towns north, but as things go sometimes, we got to talking and lost the way, and I ended up spending the night and taking a morning bus back to New York City. When we pulled into the lane that evening, Roma was not surprised to see me in the car, and they both were as gracious in their hospitality as John had been in the interview.

Now, as I listen to the conversation, I revisit John and Roma with gratitude for their generosity to a young writer seeking her way. And I find my heart full of thanksgiving for John's unique perspective and language—and for his work, which has cleared a path and taken certain turn
 s that I will never need to take.

Chapter 18

To Make One Story Out of Many: The Local and the Global in Church History

John A. Lapp

Part of the historian's work is to make one story out of many stories.
—*John L. Ruth,* The Riddle of Things Past, *1998, 5*

The only reason I'm telling that story is because eternity intersected with time.
—*John L. Ruth to Julia Kasdorf,* The Measure of My Days, *2004, 275*

Mature reflection teaches us that there is a spirituality of history.
—*John L. Ruth, "Muddy Creek Farm Library Dedication," 2002, 6*

John Ruth is rightly admired for what he once called "stories that become luminous" (Ruth, 1978:12). His histories of eastern Pennsylvania Mennonite history demonstrate both mastery of sources and imaginative reconstruction of spiritual memories into a resonating story.

Readers quickly discover, however, that Ruth also weaves local stories on a large canvas. Not only does he carefully explain the European origins of the communities he describes, he also follows the wanderings of these people individually and collectively throughout North America and beyond. Whether local or global, John's histories demonstrate his passionate insight that "the intensest specificity fosters the truest generality" (Ruth, 1978, 7).

This linking of the local and global is a significant dimension of *The Earth Is the Lord's: A Narrative History of the Lancaster Mennonite Conference.* In the first paragraph of the preface Ruth says he will describe "a fellowship that by migration and mission, has sent out spiritual spores around the globe" (Ruth, 2001, 34). This big story ends with a reflection on how "the family conversation was being enriched with earnest African-American and Hispanic voices—indeed, with a global variety of accents" (Ruth, 2001, 1132).

The globalizing of Lancaster Conference Mennonites is of relatively recent vintage. The first missionaries left in the 1890s; the first overseas programmatic effort of Eastern Mennonite Missions began in 1933. While he devotes more than fifty pages to the mission story, the passion for missions permeates all dimensions of Lancaster Mennonite history since the 1930s.

Ruth is one of the few Mennonite historians to observe how mission becomes a two-way street. Missionaries may be sent but they also send back letters and reports. Authentic missionaries take up residence. In doing so they adopt new lifestyles and test alternative religious practices. Missionaries are frequently influenced by the spiritual passions of other missions. Lancaster Mennonites, like all churches, discovered they could not bear witness without being witnessed to.

The "unusual spiritual excitement" of the East Africa Revival in the 1940s not only changed the patterns of mission and church there but also "helped to spiritualize (and relativize) the forms of obedience" (p. 1007) in the sending conference. This movement in Tanzania along with the gifted and articulate church emerging in Ethiopia were major forces in changing Lancaster religious practices as well as creating a fresh consciousness that the Christian narrative will always include diversity and plurality.

In autumn 2002 I enjoyed the opportunity of joining John Ruth and Beth Graybill in teaching a course on Eastern Pennsylvania Mennonites. Burrowing deeper into the experience of this Mennonite heartland became a stimulating counterpoint to my ongoing task as coordinator of the Global Mennonite History Project sponsored by Mennonite World Conference. What follows reports and reflects on what John Ruth once said is "part of the historian's work—to make one story out of many stories."

A Global Church

In 1994 the Mennonite World Conference (MWC) reported that for the first time in Mennonite and Brethren in Christ history more Mennonites lived in the global South (Africa, Asia, Latin America) than in North America and Europe. By 2003 just as the fourteenth Assembly of Mennonite World Conference was scheduled to meet in Bulawayo, Zimbabwe, they reported that slightly more of us are living in Africa alone (451,959) than in North America (451,180).

Mennonites are not exceptional in this accounting. Already in the 1970s astute observers were predicting that by the first decade of the twenty-first century more Christians would be living in the South than in the North. Now the estimated Christian population in the South is more than 55 percent of the total world Christian population—about 1.1 billion out of a total Christian population of two billion. This is a striking contrast to the year 1900 when over 90 percent of all Christians (98 percent of all Mennonites) were in Europe and the Americas. Penn State historian Philip Jenkins calls this twentieth century development "The Christian Revolution." There can be no doubt, he says, "that the emerging Christian world will be anchored in the southern continents" (Jenkins 14).

John Ruth noted that already in the 1960s there were more Mennonite members of Lancaster Conference initiated churches in Tanzania than in Pennsylvania. Now Mennonite heartlands as densely situated as eastern Pennsylvania, central Ohio, northern Indiana, southern Manitoba, or central Kansas, exist in northwest Tanzania, southwest Zimbabwe, south-central Congo, central (Java) Indonesia, (Andra Pradesh) India and the Paraguay Chaco. Today nearly twice as many Mennonites live in the Congo as in Canada.

Simply following the numbers in Wilbert Shenk's words requires "a massive redefinition of Mennonite identity" (Shenk 6). No longer can Mennonite be understood as German or Dutch, Swiss or Russian, American or Canadian. No longer can Mennonites be identified with one racial characteristic or several Germanic dialects. In the era of global culture it could well be that the most authentic global institution is the global church. Shenk entitled his article, "A Global Church Requires a Global History" (Shenk 3).

The implications are revolutionary. Already in 1972 C. J. Dyck, then Executive Secretary of the MWC noted that Mennonites in the

South had difficulty relating to the Reformation origins of this tradition. Yet Mennonites in Central America uninspired by the boundary markers of North American missionaries are inspired when they learn that Anabaptism was a sixteenth-century social reality that dealt with contemporary economic and political strains and stresses. This was a history with which they could identify.

Perhaps the most perplexing agenda for a global church is how to create mechanisms for belonging and accountability in a spiritual family that literally reaches around the globe. Eastern Mennonite Missions learned quickly that maturing churches want relationships with church bodies rather than mission agencies. Lancaster Conference wisely decided to involve its Bishop Board in an internationalizing process. The Mennonite World Conference at the same time was being urged by the new majority churches to take a leadership role in coordinating Mennonite activity around the world. Well-established independent northern bodies have not easily learned that in the church where burdens are to be shared, this includes governance of the church on all continents to and from all continents.

The Dutch Mennonite Mission Board (ADS Zendung) recently announced that fifteen of their young people would join twenty Tanzanian Mennonite young people to spend three weeks in a work camp in summer 2003 where they would study the Scriptures together and build a library for the Kisare Nursing School. Their goal would be "fellowship, communion, interdependence, solidarity, mutual accountability, and mutual encouragement to live and act more faithfully." The project entitled "Strangers No More" (Eph. 2:19) emphasized their "experience of the church as a worldwide body" (MWC News Service, June 2003).

This event illustrates the new ecclesiology in the process of formation. New alliances emerge and fresh relationships are formed. Older forms of leadership from western churches now require a close listening to peoples who were unrepresented on the world stage. Former ecclesiastical prerogatives are superceded; clerical leadership is sometimes displaced by professional experience. One notable part of this new epoch is the injection of more youthful experimental congregations relating to older more formal congregations. In many cases the median age of the members of numerous southern congregations is in the twenties whereas the median age in many northern congregations is in the fifties. One only needs to listen to the music to catch a certain discontinuity.

John Ruth, writing the history of one Pennsylvania conference, ended up recording a worldwide story. The most dramatic developments occurred in Africa at the end of 1933. When Orie Miller and Elam Stauffer briefly considered establishing the missions in southern Sudan they could not have known that the then unevangelized Dinka people would in sixty years be almost solidly Christian—Anglican and Roman Catholic. When the Tanzania church was established in 1934 there were less than 25 million Christians in Africa, almost all in Egypt, Ethiopia, and South Africa. By 2003 there were 360 million. In a number of African states Christianity is the numerically dominant faith. The Mennonite and Brethren in Christ population of 450,000 in Africa is a substantial contribution to this Christian revolution.

A Global History

John Ruth once noted that "memory is the stuff of identity." Such an identity requires a "meaningful past mediated via story... The cluster of stories by which a living tradition is carried leads individuals to a sense of who they are" (Ruth, 1978, 9-10).

Soon after the aforementioned announcement by MWC in 1994, a group of historians from all continents gathered at Associated Mennonite Biblical Seminary in Elkhart to explore what our task might be in this new historical situation. This group while "celebrating these developments" confessed that we must find new ways to understand and interpret the historical processes by which we have reached this stage" (Shenk 128).

The findings of that consultation noted that for a global history "a reorientation is required if we are to capture the full meaning of human experience, especially the church." Such a re-orientation will recognize that although we are "members of a body which encircles the globe" we continue to be embedded in "the partiality of parochial perspectives" (Shenk 129). The consultation sensed handicaps in not knowing non-European languages and that there were few written records of the newer now majority churches. A daunting challenge to historians taught that without documents, there could be no history.

Prof. James Juhnke of Bethel (Kan.) College caught the spirit of the meeting when he declared, "The time has come for the creation of a new world Mennonite history" (Shenk 19). The findings report rather brashly urged that a "comprehensive account of the Mennonite and Brethren in Christ experience as a global community should be published by 2005" (Shenk 132). They recommended that Mennonite World Conference be asked to sponsor such a project.

At the thirteenth MWC Assembly held in Calcutta in January 1997 the General Council authorized the project and I was invited to be organizer and fund raiser. With the assistance of an Organizing Committee representing all continents and the major Mennonite groups the project was further conceptualized and the first writer was named in 1999.

Bedru Hussein, MWC Vice President for Africa summarized the vision in a thoughtful paragraph:

> The Global Mennonite History Project is rooted in a call from the churches of the South to be recognized as full-fledged actors in the Anabaptist-Mennonite story—and to be able to tell the story from their own perspective. The goal is not primarily academic, but rather to provide materials for identity formation and leadership training in churches around the world.

At the first meeting of the writers the purpose of the Global Mennonite History was defined as telling the "story of Mennonite and Brethren in Christ churches, as well as their regional and global relationships, with the goal of nurturing a sense of belonging together, promoting mutual understanding and stimulating the renewal and extension of Anabaptist Christianity worldwide."

As the project developed we determined that such a pioneering effort could not attempt to be comprehensive. Rather the first task was to encourage people who had not told their stories before to have the opportunity to do so. When it became clear that there were few professionally trained historians in Africa and Asia, we decided to seek out responsible church member writers who could develop appropriate research skills. Above all this required attention to oral history skills respecting the deep cultural divide between societies built on documents and those who major in oral communication.

At one time the project planners envisioned a single volume history. Then they determined to have one volume written for each continent. While at first thought the focus was on Africa, Asia and Latin America, the committee and writers felt a global history also required volumes on

Europe and North America as well. Between 2003 and 2007 we expect to publish a five-volume Global Mennonite History.

Even though there was a paucity of trained historians in the southern churches, long ago we learned that everyone is a historian. Everyone has some sense of the past however limited and everyone who has secondary and professional education has read history. Every village storyteller preserves an inherited memory. One early discovery was that not only North American and European historians needed to be reoriented. The writers had to be constantly reminded that this new history required a perspective deeply rooted locally and continentally rather than an imitation of Euro-American norms. There was and is a constant temptation to rely on mission resources rather than developing the story from an African, Asian, or Latin perspective.

Jaime Prieto, professor of church history and cultural studies at the Latin American Biblical University in San Jose, Costa Rica, is among the best trained of our writers. He interviewed over 300 individuals as a basis for writing the Latin America Mennonite story. While his volume on Latin America will not be the first published, he has helped to conceptualize the entire task.

The individual volumes will include a basic narrative of the churches on each continent, the general historical context in which these churches have lived and worked, and maps of geographic locations. They will generously incorporate visual historical background material, and the various ethnicities involved in the story, men and women as coparticipants. Primary documentation will be gathered and listed to supplement the text: hymns, writings, poetry, excerpts from sermons, and an analytical conclusion. Each volume is expected to highlight stories that demonstrate the life and character of these churches. (From a memo: John A. Lapp to Writers, Jan. 19, 2002).

Probably no volume will include all these elements. Writers are urged to tell the story first of all for the people of their own continent. Second, each writer is encouraged to tell the story in such a way as to inform and arouse interest of readers on other continents. It was instructive to hear the Indonesian writer explain what he wanted the Japanese to know about his church, and the Congolese writer to mention what Paraguayan members ought to know about the Congo church. Third, writers are expected to describe their histories in a way intrinsic to the story of the global Christian church.

The complexity of the continental stories required a group effort. Only Latin America had a single writer; with multiple authors there is an inevitable unevenness. Not all the stories are the same. But careful readers will learn much about the church in Tanzania from the Zambia story and vice versa; both church and society have similarities as well as differences. The Africa volume was released at the Mennonite World Conference Assembly in Bulawayo, Zimbabwe, in August 2003. As befits a global history, this volume was printed both in Bulawayo and in Kitchener, Ontario. There will be translations into Spanish and French.

Creating this global history is based on the notion that a meaningful and relevant worldwide church will evidence a sense of shared community. Charles Villa-Vicencio, a South African scholar, suggests that sharing memories is what reconciliation in a Pauline sense is all about. Previously distant or hostile people become friends developing a common identity.

> It involves sharing our recollections of the past. It involves telling our stories to one another and listening intently to the stories we are told—which involves reaching beyond the words and the "facts" to what lies behind the words. . . It is a process that involves more than empathy. It involves hermeneutical relocation whereby we see, hear and understand in a different way. The exercise involves more than the surrender of our own perception of truth. It involves . . . a fusion of horizons. (Villz-Vicencio 34)

That is the high goal of the global Mennonite history. Now that we have in hand the first product, I admit to having recurring doubts about the effectiveness of one volume, even five, to achieve such a goal. At the very least this will be for many readers the beginning of seeing the Christian story from another's point of view. These volumes will also demonstrate in the words of Dana L. Robert that, "the strength of world Christianity lies in its creative interweaving of the warp of a world religion with the woof of its local contexts." (Robert 56)

Many questions remain. Will this endeavor be truly global? What is Mennonite or Brethren in Christ about this story? Will it meet the exacting demands of historical scholarship? Is it possible to create one story of a people who live in more than sixty countries and speak at least that many languages? Can there be one story for a people some of whom have carried a denominational label for nearly five centuries and others who don't use this rubric at all in churches less than fifty years old?

These questions are, of course, not a new reality for the church or for historians of the church. Ever since the first Pentecost, Christian disciples have frequently "heard each other speaking in the native language of each... about God's deeds of power," asking "What does this mean?" (Acts 2:6-12). Now at another fresh moment in the church's pilgrimage our task is both ecclesial and historical "to make one story out of many stories."

Now that the first volume of this global history is available, we realize that one book can only tell a small part of the Mennonite experience in Africa. There is so much we do not know. There is much more research that needs to be done.

This has been an enormous learning process for all involved. Careful listening requires patience and a readiness to learn from below as well as from above. Self-confident northerners are not famous for these traits. Powerless southerners are not sure that questioning the dominant, given narrative has sufficient rewards to even bother. And if some are troubled by competing narratives in Europe and North America, how will we deal with the diversities of Africa, let alone Asia or Latin America?

Much must be unlearned as new learnings bubble up. There have been many moments of fresh insight. For instance, Pakisa Tshimika, a Congolese-American member of the organizing committee asked insightfully, "Why are people in the South so eager to become Mennonites when Mennonites in the North are so often apologetic about their tradition?" I. P. Asheervadam, the writer of the India story, is a Dalit, at the bottom of Indian society. He thanks God for the missionaries' commitment to bringing "gospel equality," a liberating reality for millions of Indians. Barbara Nkala, one of the Zimbabwe writers, insists that Christianity in Africa respect traditional religion which prepared fertile ground for the explosive growth of the Christian movement.

The process of taking seriously younger churches is itself important. Everyone, every congregation, every conference has a story if we have patience to uncover it and listen to its rhythms. Just as authentic mission injects new ways of understanding church and church life, this project is bringing new obligations in its wake.

When the Asian and African writers visited the Netherlands and the United States they spent days exploring historical libraries in Amsterdam, Fresno, Goshen, Grantham, and Newton. They discovered museum collections of artifacts collected in China, Congo, Zimbabwe, Indonesia, India, and Paraguay. They asked questions how these items found their way to these locations. They wondered who owned the reports of missionaries and administrators. Should not these be held by the people whose lives and churches were being described?

The Congolese writer Erik Kumedisa was so moved by what he saw that he wrote a proposal for a "Congo Mennonite History Museum." He observed that in Europe and America "history remains alive among the churches and they are proud of their heritage... In the Congo there are no similar structures which can help the churches to be more aware of their history." He proposed "an archival and information center" with an active program of "historical research." He asked for funding a conference in the Congo to "build interest" for such an ongoing project (unpublished manuscript, March 2002). At another time he inquired about the possibility of getting copies of all the missionary papers and mission board records of the several groups at work in this country.

When the global history project was conceived it was anticipated that this project would be completed after the publication of the five volumes. Several of these historian-churchmen writers have challenged this. They propose a continuing network of church historians for mutual learning and encouragement. This network might provide the means for digging deeper into the Mennonite and Brethren in Christ story in each country, continent, then continuing relationships.

John Ruth again provides some clues for accomplishing the task. As an avid collector of sources—literary and oral as well as material—he would empathize with the interests of Kumedisa. Even after years of research and 1,132 pages of text, he says there is much more to report about Lancaster Mennonite history. As a historian he appreciates diversity while being suspicious of superficial unity. He is respectful of dissenters who either challenge or seek to preserve the reigning narrative. He recognizes that incarnational faith-truth in human form must define realities in ways that accept difference while embodying a new social reality, the reconciled and reconciling people.

John understands that the most potent vehicle for uniting diverse experience is to create and communicate a meaningful story—"information connected by narrative which has a focus and carries a theme" (Ruth, 1978, 9). Remembered stories accumulate into an enormous treasure. Mennonite history, John suggests, can be exactly that, dramatic stories which contain "meanings that impinge forcibly on our present consciousness" (Ruth, 1978, 18). Local stories and global stories become singular through their "participation in the overarching story of God's redemptive act of incarnation" (Ruth, 1978, 19).

THE SPIRITUALITY OF HISTORY

Perhaps the most important task of the Christian church in the twenty-first century is to work out an ecclesiology that will incorporate churches from every continent and hundreds of ethnicities in a uniting community. Jesus in his farewell prayer for his disciples, the first functioning church, was that "they may all be one" (John 17:20).

While this vision for the entire worldwide Christian movement will only be completed in the *eschaton*, this vision so intrinsic to denominational missions, requires deliberate pursuit. For people known as Mennonite and Brethren in Christ (other denominational families as well) a worldwide functioning communion requires new kinds of organization, new attitudes for respectful and nurturing relationships. Such a global communion also requires new narratives that include the near and far, the powerful and the powerless, representing diverse languages, cultures, economic status, and political opportunity. I believe the task of constructing such a narrative is as essential and as complex as the new order of inter-church relationships.

One of the striking words that John Ruth uses with considerable frequency is the word "spiritual." In 1978 he referred to the Franconia Mennonite Conference as "my own spiritual and geographic home" (Ruth, 1978, 7). In 1990 while describing "America's Anabaptists: Who They Are" (*Christianity Today*) he suggested that the sense of togetherness and community Anabaptist people have long held to is "a kind of spiritual DNA." In both his major histories he describes "a spiritual family" from whom he elicits a "spiritual memory." In *The Earth Is the Lord's* this word is used several hundred times. He also uses the word "spirituality" identified as Anabaptist or practical or obedience (Ruth, 1990, 25).

In November 2002 John made the dedicatory remarks for the new building of the Muddy Creek Farm Library. Here he noted Old Order Mennonite "spirituality" within the larger "spiritual family." Then he introduced the phrase, "the spirituality of history." He noted that for years Franconia Mennonites had little awareness of "how knowledge of an earlier age can relate to a later one" (unpublished manuscript 4). He noted that most people and most Christians "live with a bargain basement memory of the past" or operate "on our own version of what constitutes the record of God's doings with our people" (unpublished manuscript, 4). As in much of his writing, John references a number of Scriptures that illustrate his argument (1 Cor. 10:11).

As I reflect on the imposing tasks of our time—constructing a world-wide ecclesiastical framework with a supporting narrative, John Ruth's highlighting of the spiritual dimension of all reality, of all inspired history, of all church life surely provides a vital key to integrating a living tradition with a new world reality.

So far as I could discover, John nowhere tells us precisely how he defines "spiritual" or "spirituality." But he provides many clues. To be spiritual is to breathe godliness. It means being related to Christ and the body of Christ. Spirituality is practical and practiced, the result of memory and obedience. To be spiritual reflects commitment, an identity embodied in a loving, self-giving character. Spirituality requires attention and nurture or it can become "stale" and "uninteresting." To be spiritual is more than an inner feeling or individual excitement. Spirituality is rooted, disciplined, and formative. It is evangelical and reconciling. To be spiritual is to belong to a people with a long remembered past and a far-reaching present.

When John describes the Anabaptist and Mennonite insight it represents a spirituality:

> For centuries Mennonites claimed the gospel of Christ as a power that reconciled them, not only as individuals to their God, but also as social creatures to their fellow human beings. They learned this not from philosophy but from the New Testament... Where Christ's cross was thus accepted as the key to life's meaning a new order emerged. This was the Anabaptist confession, the open secret of their witness, their evidence that God was at work in the world. (Ruth, 1984, 538)

Since the book of Acts, church history has had a local and global dimension. The multitude of stories have become one. The local incorporates the global; the global incorporates the local. Creating, preserving, telling this story is a spiritual process "because eternity intersected with time."

Works Cited

Irvin, Dale T. 1998. *Christian Histories, Christian Traditioning: Rendering Accounts.* Maryknoll, N.Y.: Orbis Books.

Jenkins, Philip. 2002. *The Next Christendom: The Coming of Global Christianity.* New York, Oxford University Press.

Robert, Dana L. 2000, April. "Shifting Southward: Global Christianity Since 1945." *International Bulletin of Missionary Research.*

Ruth, John L. 1978. *Mennonite Identity and Literary Art.* Scottdale, Pa.: Herald Press.

———. 1984. *Maintaining the Right Fellowship: A Narrative Account of Life in the Oldest Mennonite Community in North America.* Scottdale, Pa.: Herald Press.

———. 1990, Oct. 22. "America's Anabaptists: Who They Are." *Christianity Today.*

———. 2001. *The Earth Is The Lord's: A Narrative History of the Lancaster Mennonite Conference.* Scottdale, Pa. :Herald Press.

———. 1998, Jan. "The Riddle of Things Past: A Meditation." Goshen, Ind.: *Mennonite Historical Bulletin.*

———. 2002, Nov. 9. "Muddy Creek Farm Library Dedication." Unpublished mss.

Shenk, Wilbert. 1997, Winter/Spring. "A Global Church Requires a Global Identity," *Conrad Grebel Review* 15.2

Villa-Vicencio, Charles. 1997. "Telling One Another Stories: Toward a Theology of Reconciliation." In *The Reconciliation of Peoples: A Challenge to the Churches*, ed. Gregory Baum and Harold Wells. Maryknoll, N.Y.: Orbis Books.

The Contributors

Ervin Beck, Professor Emeritus of English at Goshen College, has taught and done research and publication in English literature, international literature, folklore and Mennonite literature. He is the author of *MennoFolk: Mennonite and Amish Folk Traditions* (Herald Press, 2004) and was chair and co-chair, respectively, of the Mennonite/s Writing in the U.S. (1977) and Mennonite/s Writing: An International Conference (2002) held at Goshen College. On his website he maintains extensive bibliographies of U.S. Mennonite Literature, Canadian Mennonite Literature and Mennonite Folklore and Folk Arts. He was chair of the Mennonite-Amish Museum Committee at Goshen College and served as copy editor for The *Mennonite Quarterly Review* 1968-2003. Children and grandchildren of John and Roma Ruth have studied English and folklore with him at Goshen College.

John Richard Burkholder, Professor Emeritus of Religion at Goshen College, has also taught at Associated Mennonite Biblical Seminary and at schools in Costa Rica and South Africa. He has published in the fields of theology and social ethics, with special attention to peace and conflict studies. He holds a Ph.D. in Religion and Society from Harvard University and was ordained to ministry in the Mennonite Church in 1954.

Tony Campolo is Professor Emeritus of Sociology at Eastern University. For ten years he served on the faculty of the University of Pennsylvania. He did his undergraduate education at Eastern University and holds a Ph.D. degree from temple University. He is a frequent guest on television shows ranging from "Larry King Live" to "Politically Incorrect" and has been co-host of "Hashing It Out," on the Odyssey Television Network. Campolo is author of twenty-nine books, most recently *Which Jesus?* As the founder of the Evangelical Association for the Promotion of Education, he has organized schools and universities in various Third World countries as well as creating a variety of ministries for "at-risk" children in urban neighborhoods across North America. He is married to the former Peggy Davidson, has two children and four grandchildren..

Reta Halteman Finger teaches at Messiah College as Assistant Professor of New Testament. She edited *Daughters of Sarah* magazine for seventeen years, co-edited *The Wisdom of Daughters: Two Decades of the Voice of Christian Feminism* (Innisfree Press, 2001), and authored *Paul and the Roman House Churches* (Herald Press, 1993). John Ruth was a neighbor, family friend, her sixth grade teacher, and pastor of her home church for many years.

Jan Gleysteen grew up in Amsterdam, Holland, where he took his training in illustration and design at the Municipal School for Applied Arts and the Royal Academy. In the early 1950s, he spent much time crisscrossing Europe by bike. He moved to the United States in 1953 to study at Goshen College and work at Mennonite Publishing House, where he served for over three decades as artist, writer, editor, and lecturer, primarily in Anabaptist-Mennonite historiography. In 1969 John L. Ruth and Gleysteen embarked on a series of research trips to document European Mennonite history. This first excursion resulted in the *Martyrs Mirror Oratorio*, the film *The Quiet in the Land,* and *Conrad Grebel, Son of Zurich*, all by John Ruth. In 1970 Gleysteen first took a group of friends on a three-week bus tour of Europe to visit the places he knew so well. This was the beginning of TourMagination, a tour company which specializes in travel with an emphasis on Anabaptist-Mennonite life and thought. Now retired in Goshen, Indiana, Jan continues to speak and lead tours. He and his wife, Barbara, are members of the College Mennonite Church in Goshen, Indiana.

Leonard Gross grew up in the Doylestown (Pa.) Mennonite Church and graduated from Goshen College in 1953. He served under the Mennonite Central Committee in Germany, working with North German Mennonite youth, 1954-1957. After completing seminary at Goshen Biblical Seminary, he taught at Bethany Christian High School, 1959-1964. In 1968 he received the Ph.D. degree from the University of Basel, Switzerland and accepted an invitation to teach history at

Western Michigan University. He was Executive Secretary of the Historical Committee of the Mennonite Church and editor of the *Mennonite Historical Bulletin* 1970-1990 while also teaching part-time at Associated Mennonite Biblical Seminary, and at Goshen College. He continues in research, writing, and translation work in Anabaptist-Mennonite studies, and currently serves as secretary of the Mennonite Historical Society and as conference historian of the Indiana-Michigan Mennonite Conference. He is author of many articles and books, including *The Golden Years of the Hutterites* (Herald Press, 1980, rev. 1998).

Jeff Gundy has taught writing and literature at Bluffton College since 1984. A graduate of Goshen College and Indiana University, he also taught at Hesston College. He has published three books of poems and two prose books, including *Rhapsody with Dark Matter* (poems, Bottom Dog Press, 2000) and *Scattering Point: The World in a Mennonite Eye* (nonfiction, SUNY Press, 2003). He and his wife Marlyce have three sons.

Ann Hostetler is Associate Professor of English at Goshen College, where she teaches literature and creative writing. She is the author of *Empty Room with Light: Poems* (DreamSeeker Books of Pandora Press U.S., 2002) and the editor of *A Cappella: Mennonite Voices in Poetry* (University of Iowa Press, 2003). Her scholarship on American literature has appeared in *PMLA, ESQ: A Journal of the American Renaissance*, and *The Mennonite Quarterly Review*. Her poems have appeared in many journals including *The American Scholar, Cream City Review, Mid-America Poetry Review, Mothering*, and *The Mennonite*.

Julia Kasdorf is the author of two collections of poetry, a book of essays, *The Body and the Book: Writing from a Mennonite Life*, and a biography, *Fixing Tradition: Joseph W. Yoder, Amish American* (Pandora Press U.S., 2002). She directs the graduate creative writing program at Penn State University and lives in Bellefonte, Pennsylvania, with her husband the artist David Kasdorf and their daughter Amelia Clare.

John A. Lapp is Executive Secretary Emeritus of Mennonite Central Committee and currently coordinator of the Global Mennonite History Project for Mennonite World Conference. Lapp is a native of Montgomery County, Pennsylvania, and a graduate of Eastern Mennonite College, Case Western Reserve University, and University of Pennsylvania. He taught at Eastern Mennonite College, Goshen College, Associated Mennonite Biblical Seminary, Elizabethtown College, and Bishop's College in Calcutta, India. He was dean and provost of Goshen College 1972-1984. Lapp has authored many articles as well as several books including *Mennonite Church in India 1898-1962* (1972) *The View From East Jerusalem* (1980). He is the husband of M. Alice Weber. They have three children and five grandchildren.

Eloise Hiebert Meneses is Associate Professor of Cultural Anthropology at Eastern University. Her interests include ethnicity, global economics, and history of India. She lives with her husband Michael, and children, Holly and Andrew, in Lansdale Pennsylvania, and attends Wellspring Church of Skippack (Pa.).

Elmer S. Miller grew up in the Elizabethtown, Pennsylvania area and graduated from Eastern Mennonite College (1954) and Seminary (1956). From 1956 to 1963 he and his wife, Lois, served with the Eastern Mennonite Board of Missions under assignment to the Argentine Toba people. In 1967, he received a Ph.D. in anthropology from the University of Pittsburgh. From 1966-1996 Elmer was a faculty member and administrator at Temple University. He has written books and articles on the Argentine Toba and missions, most recently *Nurturing Doubt: From Mennonite Missionary to Christian Anthropologist* (University of Illinois Press, 1995) and *Peoples of the Gran Chaco* (Bergin & Garvey, ed., 1999).

Elizabeth Morgan is a professor of English at Eastern University. She receive her B.A. from Eastern College, M.A. from University of North Carolina, and Ph.D. from Drew University. She has written on the creative process and global poverty and edited a collection of refugee stories. She has produced films for public television on the revolution in El Salvador and on issues resulting from the 1995 Fourth World Conference on Women in Beijing. Her recent book, *Aeroplane Mirrors: Personal and Political Reflexivity in Post-Colonial Women's Novels*, was published by Heinemann as part of the *Studies in African Literature* series.

Composer, conductor, and teacher **Alice Parker** was born in Boston, Massachusetts in 1925. She began composing as a young child, graduated from Smith College and from the Juilliard School where she studied choral conducting with Robert Shaw, with whom she collaboratively produced choral arrangements of folksongs, hymns, and spirituals known worldwide. Parker worked extensively with Mennonites during the 1960s, composing several compositions for them including the opera, *Martyr's Mirror*. Other Mennonite-inspired works are the opera *Singers Glen* and the cantatas *Christopher Dock, Melodious Accord, Sacred Symphonies, Sermon from the Mountain: Martin Luther King* and *That Sturdy Vine: Mennonite Singing*. A book about congregational hymn-singing entitled *Melodious Accord: Good Singing in Church*, was published by Liturgy Training Publications in Chicago, as were four videos produced by John Ruth. Parker continues to perform and teach through her organization, Melodious Accord, and works with composers and conductors at her home in western Massachusetts through the Fellowship Program. She also travels widely, giving performances of her works and workshops on her methods.

John D. Rempel received a B.A. in history at Conrad Grebel College, University of Waterloo in 1966. And later his M.Div. from Associated Mennonite Biblical Seminary, Elkhart Indiana. In 1971 He studied under the World Council of Churches at the Free University of West Berlin and the Protestant Seminary of East Berlin. For sixteen years he was chaplain and lecturer at Conrad Grebel College, University of Waterloo and during that period earned his Th.D. from the Toronto School of Theology. In 1989 Rempel became minister of the Manhattan Mennonite Fellowship in New York City, a position he held for ten years. During that time he taught theology at two local seminaries and started the Mennonite Central Committee Office at the United Nations, a position he assumed full time in 2000. In 2003 he joined the faculty of Associated Mennonite Biblical Seminary. Reemple's many writing include *Planning Worship*, a guide to accompany the *Hymnal: A Worship Book* (Herald Press, 1992) on whose development committee he served, and T*he Lord's Supper in Anabaptism* (Herald Press, 1993). He edited the *Mennonite Minister's Manual* of 1998 (Herald Press).

Ervin R. Stutzman is Academic Dean and Associate Professor of Church Ministries at Eastern Mennonite Seminary. He also serves as the Moderator for Mennonite Church United States, a recently merged denomination comprising the former General Conference Mennonite Church and the Mennonite Church. Before coming to Eastern Mennonite Seminary, he served the Mennonite Church in the roles of pastor, district overseer and conference moderator. He received his Ph.D. from Temple University and holds masters degrees from the University of Cincinnati and Eastern Mennonite Seminary. His bachelor's degree was granted by Cincinnati Bible College.

The Editors

Joseph S. Miller has served as a pastor in the Mennonite Church USA, including at Waterford Mennonite Church in Goshen, Indiana. He is currently living and working in Lancaster County, Pennsylvania. From 1978 to 1985, he was Administrator of the Mennonite Heritage Center in Harleysville, Pennsylvania, which operates a historical library and archives and a museum. In 1985 he accepted an assignment with Mennonite Central Committee to serve with that relief and service organization in Budapest, Hungary. While living in Budapest he experienced first hand the final years of communist rule in Hungary and Eastern Europe. His work in Hungary involved numerous projects with the Hungarian Baptist Church. At the same time he was a student at the Baptista Téológiai Szeminárium.

Since returning to North America, Miller has served as a pastor at Bethel Mennonite Church, Lancaster, Pennsylvania and at Waterford Mennonite Church, Goshen, Indiana. He is currently the Lead Pastor at Mellinger Mennonite Church, Lancaster, Pennsylvania and is a candidate in the doctor of ministry program at Grace Theological Seminary, Winona Lake, Indiana. He and his wife, Julie Zimmerman, have one son, Reuben, who has served as co-editor of this volume.

Miller received his undergraduate degree in history at Bethel College, North Newton, Kansas. At Villanova University, he received a masters degree in Religious Studies.

Reuben Z. Miller is living near Heidelberg, Germany, serving in a voluntary service assignment with the German Mennonite Peace Committee. His responsibilities include the day-to-day operations of the Military Counseling Network. Prior to moving to Heidelberg, he had lived in the Shenandoah Valley of Virginia since graduating from Eastern Mennonite University in 2000. His studies in the field of history afforded him the opportunity to do extensive research on EMU's second president, A. D. Wenger, as his senior thesis. Miller was a regular contributor to student publications including *The Weather Vane* and *The Shenandoah* and was editor-in-chief of the latter in 1999-2000. Miller volunteered in the postwar relief effort of International Mennonite Organization in Bosnia and Herzegovina in 1996 and 1997. He plays guitar, banjo and mandolin in a local old-time and bluegrass band called "Rural Sprawl."

www.ingramcontent.com/pod-product-compliance
Ingram Content Group UK Ltd.
Pitfield, Milton Keynes, MK11 3LW, UK
UKHW041432180426
11947UKWH00007B/393